Careers In Public Accounting

A Comprehensive Comparison of the Big Eight Firms

Carli, this comparison could not have been completed without your support, patience, and counsel. Thank you.

Colby, thanks for understanding why Dad could not play.

Careers In Public Accounting

A Comprehensive Comparison of the Big Eight Firms

James C. Emerson

The Big Eight Review, Inc.

Redmond, Washington

The Big Eight Review, Inc.

In May, 1983, The Big Eight Review, Inc. began publishing a monthly newsletter summarizing events affecting the world's largest accounting firms. The newsletter also includes special reports on subjects of current interest each month, as well as an Annual Report in July of each year. To meet the growing need among accounting graduates for information about the firms the company also publishes a book, "Careers In Public Accounting - A Comprehensive Comparison of the Big Eight Firms," and an audio cassette program, "Successful Interviewing With The Big Eight Firms."

The editor of The Big Eight Review and author of "Careers In Public Accounting" and "Successful Interviewing" is James C. Emerson. Prior to creating his newsletter, Mr. Emerson was with the accounting firm of Ernst & Whinney, in both their Chicago and Seattle offices, for almost ten years. In addition to his publishing business, Mr. Emerson has an active consultation practice in Seattle.

Copyright

Library of Congress Catalog Card : 87-71857

ISBN 0-943945-00-3

Contents

Introduction

Introduction

Several months ago I returned from lunch to find a phone message on my desk, "Desperate college student needs to talk to you immediately." I promptly returned the call to learn this accounting graduate student had recently received approval from her professor to prepare a thesis on the subject, "The Marketing Strategies of The Big Eight International Accounting Firms." Knowing she had just been given approval for an impossible assignment, I asked how she was doing on collecting data. She said her initial search for data was shocking. "How could these firms be so large and so powerful without even a thread of available information regarding their vital statistics, geographic strengths, industry specialties or business strategies?", she asked, "Certainly you can help me."

After explaining that the firms are privately owned partnerships and sensitive about disclosing information regarding their people, clients, and operations, let alone business strategies, I suggested she have her professor call me and I would gladly explain the thesis would be difficult, if not impossible, to complete. My offer was obviously the best news this young lady had heard in weeks.

Our Objective

After receiving two or three variations of this request per week from students, university placement directors and many other interested parties over the last few years, we felt the time had come to begin accumulating comparative information on the world's largest public accounting firms. We also believed that our constant involvement with information regarding the Big Eight firms as we prepare our monthly newsletter, The Big Eight Review, made us the perfect candidate to analyze the information gathered. To the best of our knowledge this comprehensive comparison of the Big Eight firms is the first ever completed.

We have organized this guide from the career perspective for two reasons. First, more than half of the requests we receive for information are from university placement personnel or students attempting to differentiate among firms for career purposes. And second, university career planning and placement offices in major universities across the country have been strong supporters of our monthly newsletter since our inception in 1983. Preparing this guide with them in mind is one way we have to say thank you.

The Big Eight Firms

Though it may seem we are getting off to a confusing start, the following nine organizations make up the Big Eight International Public Accounting Firms:

> **Arthur Andersen & Co.**
> **Arthur Young & Co.**
> **Coopers & Lybrand**
> **Deloitte Haskins & Sells**
> **Ernst & Whinney**
> **KMG Main Hurdman**
> **Peat, Marwick, Mitchell & Co.**
> **Price Waterhouse**
> **Touche Ross & Co.**

The reason for nine is really quite simple. The eight largest firms based on domestic (US) revenues only are all the firms listed above excluding KMG Main Hurdman. The eight largest firms based on worldwide revenues are all the firms listed above excluding Touche Ross or Deloitte Haskins & Sells. To solve this problem the business community has been given the opportunity to accept the terminology known to very, very few as The Big Nine or just include nine firms in The Big Eight. Due to the worldwide acceptance for the words Big Eight the business community has continued to use this phrase to mean the ultimate in quality, independent, and reliable financial information, financial consultation, and tax advice. As the Big Eight now includes KMG Main Hurdman our analysis naturally includes information regarding this firm.

For those curious about why we have analyzed only the Big Eight firms, we have included a section in the appendices titled "The US Top Twenty" which explains our reasons.

Peat Marwick Mitchell and KMG Main Hurdman Merger

The Wall Street Journal announced on September 3, 1986 that Peat Marwick Mitchell and KMG Main Hurdman would merge their worldwide operations to become the largest public accounting firm. As of this printing the firms had agreed in principle to a merger, but the final approvals and details had not been completed. The manner in which information is presented in this comparison should enable readers to assess the effect of this merger on the firms and marketplace. While we could have combined figures and provided estimates for the new organization it was our opinion that it would have been premature. Merger discussions which have reached this point in the past have not all been consummated.

As will also be clear from information in this guide, KMG has many US offices in cities where Peat Marwick is not located. Due to these differences in the nature and locations of the firms' US practices, it would also be premature to assume that the combined US operation will be a simple addition of offices, people, clients, etc.

Sources of Information Regarding the Firms

We have already indicated to you that publicly available information regarding the firms is scarce, however, there are organizations which in one way or another cover news regarding the Big Eight. While the periodic publications or services of these organizations do not attempt to gather, compile or analyze comparative information in the same way we wish to with this publication, they do provide pieces to the puzzle we have attempted to complete. You will find reference to the following organizations in our guide as we give credit for certain information. We also list these organizations with some detail on their publications and/or services as this answers the very common question we receive as to which organizations and people are knowledgeable regarding the Big Eight firms and the public accounting profession in general. While this list is brief, to the best of our knowledge it is complete.

The Big Eight Review, Inc., 2824 Sahalee Drive East, Redmond WA 98053, 206-747-5294, publishes a monthly newsletter, summarizing news affecting the Big Eight firms, and this career guide. Newsletter is $145 per year.

Career guide is $310 with special discounts for newsletter subscribers, universities and public libraries. Executive publisher is James C. Emerson.

The Data Financial Press, Inc., P.O. Box 801, Menlo Park CA 94026, 415-321-4553, publishes a directory of publicly traded companies and the accounting firms who audit them, updated semi- annually, $70 per update. Editor is Spencer P. Harris. The data regarding client companies and auditors included in this comparison has been provided by Data Financial Press. A special thank you to Spencer Harris for his assistance, interest and counsel.

Professional Publications, Inc., 3690 North Peachtree Road - Suite 200, Atlanta GA 30341, 404-455-7600, publishes six accounting profession newsletters, $96 to $159 per year. Executive publisher is Robert A. Palmer.

Lafferty Publications, Inc., 2 Pear Tree Court, London England EC1R0DS, 01-251-5545, publishes monthly newsletter focusing on international public accounting events, $756 per year. Executive publisher is Michael Lafferty.

National Association of Accountants, 10 Paragon Drive, P.O. Box 433, Montvale NJ 07645, 201-573-9000, organization of accountants in industry, public accounting, government and teaching interested in the management uses of accounting. Performs research, maintains library and publishes monthly magazine, Management Accounting. Alfred King, managing director of professional services.

Services Rating Organization, Inc., 631 East Big Beaver, Troy MI 48083, 313-528-3333, performs market research studies for public accounting firms, law firms and commercial banks in major US and Canadian cities. Prices based on extent of study and location. Brian Raftery is consultant for the public accounting industry.

American Institute of Certified Public Accountants, Inc., 1211 Avenue of the Americas, New York NY 10036, 212-575-6200, publishes professional journal, maintains extensive

library of current materials relating to the public accounting profession. Under direction of Auditing Standards Board establishes generally accepted auditing standards. Services and publications available in some cases to membership only. Philip B. Chenok, President and J. Michael Cook, Chairman.

Each state also has a CPA society to organize local practitioners and sponsor continuing professional development courses. As a source of information about the profession and/or Big Eight firms the societies will vary greatly. Contact the American Institute in New York for the address and phone number of your state's CPA society.

Confirmation of Information In This Guide

To ensure accuracy we requested that the firms correct and or confirm certain information in this comparison. Corrections received have been incorporated. All information in this guide should, however, be considered an estimate of the publisher, The Big Eight Review, Inc.

Readers of this comparison should recognize that regardless of the care we used in making assumptions and developing estimates, certain variances from actual figures must exist. We do, however, believe our consistent application of methods to develop estimates makes all information contained herein particularly meaningful and unique for comparative purposes.

Organization of this Guide

As previously mentioned, the catalyst for preparing this comparison of firms was to provide a needed source of information and analysis for accounting graduates faced with the decision of selecting a Big Eight firm for a career in public accounting. The choice of an accounting firm for a career is a very personal decision and we in no way can make that selection for any graduate. It is simply our desire to assist in the career planning process by providing critical information and analysis which, prior to this guide, was not available.

Regardless of your reason for desiring information about the world's largest and most powerful accounting firms, we hope this guide is in some way helpful and able to answer your questions. If you have any comments or questions please feel free to call or write.

Profiles of the Firms

Profiles of the Firms

In this "Profiles of the Firms" section it is our simple objective to summarize information. The comments we include can be referenced to subsequent sections of this comparison for support. In the past, many observers have concluded that the only way to differentiate among firms is to develop rather soft generalizations. We believe these profiles and the information which follows demonstrates that meaningful, useful and interesting comparisons can be made based on specific data and analysis.

To assist you in understanding our terminology in these profiles, please note that we analyzed industry specialization and expertise by establishing the following 11 segments:

> Services
> Financial Institutions, Securities Brokerage
>   and Insurance
> Retail Trade
> Wholesale Trade
> Utilities
> Communications
> Transportation
> Manufacturing
> Construction
> Mining
> Agriculture

For purposes of our geographic comments we regionalized the states into the following 9 areas:

> Northeast - RI, MA, VT, NH and ME
> Greater New York - NY, NJ, PA, and CT
> Mid-Atlantic - DC, DE, MD, WV, VA, NC and SC
> Southeast - FL, GA, AL, MS and TN
> Central - OH, IN, MI and KY
> Midwest - IL, KS, NB, WI, MN, IA, ND, SD and MO
> Southwest - TX, CO, OK, NM, AR and LA
> Western - CA, HI, AZ, UT and NV
> Northwest - WA, OR, ID, MT, WY and AK

We are pleased to present our constructive profile of each firm based on their revenues, industry specialties, geographic strengths, estimated partner compensation, marketing expertise, visibility success, and professional liability challenges.

Arthur Andersen

Arthur Andersen leads the Big Eight in domestic and worldwide revenues with its US portion of $1.182 billion securing a dominant market share position for the firm. Viewed separately, the firm's Management Information Consulting division is also the world's largest of its kind, surpassing such consulting giants as McKinsey, Booz Allen and Towers Perrin.

Arthur Andersen emerges as the leader, or is among the leaders, of every industry segment we analyzed. In terms of specialization, the firm's practice is extremely broad-based. In the regulated industries such as utilities and communications, it is exceptionally strong, with clients such as Pacific Gas and Electric (CA), Waste Management (IL), Georgia Power (GA), GTE (CT) and Illinois Bell Telephone (IL). No other Big Eight firm in America is a leader in service to all industry segments.

Geographically, Arthur Andersen is absolutely dominant in the vicinity of its midwest home base of Chicago, and has very large practices in the southeast, southwest and western United States. With the exception of some markets along the east coast, Andersen is a leader in all regions of the country.

In terms of market share leadership, city by city, the firm is a major factor in 43 of the 59 major US cities we reviewed. No competing firm achieves this level of market penetration. Andersen has fewer offices (a total of 69) than any of its competitors, and, with an average of 200 professionals in each office, nearly double the average office size. The organization's largest office is in Chicago, where local office and world headquarters professional staff exceed 2000.

On the average, each Arthur Andersen partner is responsible for overseeing over $1 million in professional fees to clients annually. This revenue per partner leads the Big Eight firms and is a principal factor in our estimate that Andersen partners are among the most highly compensated Big Eight professionals.

" 'Mirrors of Excellence,' a study of corporate management practices, called the firm of Arthur Andersen a model of organizational excellence."

As an organization, Arthur Andersen was one of the first firms to emphasize marketing of its professional services. This emphasis appears to be a vital part of the firm's consistently strong growth in revenues.

The firm has had its share of professional liability problems over the last few years with several challenges currently in process.

Recent events involving Arthur Andersen include:

September, 1986 - KMG rejected Arthur Andersen, Ernst & Whinney and Deloitte Haskins & Sells' offers to merge in favor of Peat Marwick Mitchell.

February, 1986 - The firm issued a comprehensive report on accounting practices used by the Federal government. The study called for the Government to adopt an accrual basis of accounting.

February, 1986 - "Mirrors of Excellence," a study of corporate management practices, called the firm of Arthur Andersen a model of organizational excellence.

January, 1986 - The firm issued 1985 Annual Report to its people, disclosing record revenues and growth. The report stressed team work and "culture" at the firm.

September, 1985 - Arthur Andersen completes a merger with Pacific Basin based SGV Accounting Group. This combination represented an important strategic step for the firm, with significant growth expected in this part of the world.

Arthur Young

Arthur Young's worldwide revenues of $1.160 billion are extremely well-balanced between the United States ($545 million) and other parts of the world ($615 million). As the international economy becomes less and less centered around the United States, this firm's exceptionally strong operations outside the US will increase in strategic importance.

Arthur Young is a leader in service to the construction industry, with that segment's two largest companies, McDermott Int'l (LA) and Flour Corp. (CA), as clients. The firm is among the leaders in service to the extractive industries as well as the transportation segment, serving such giants as American Airlines (TX), Pan Am (NY) and PSA (CA). In addition to these specialties, this firm has considerable clientele in the service, wholesale and retail trade, and manufacturing segments. Other companies such as Mobil Corp. (NY), Pepsico Inc. (NY), McDonalds Corp. (IL), Lockheed Corp. (CA), American Express (NY) are also part of the firm's impressive list of major clients.

Geographically, Arthur Young is most influential in greater New York and the southwest and western regions of the US. In the San Francisco Bay area the firm performs exceptionally well, with significant practices serving high-technology companies such as Apple Computer, Spectra-Physics and Winn Enterprises.

We estimate that partner compensation at Arthur Young is within the mid-range for Big Eight firms.

While Arthur Young did not demonstrate an emphasis on the expansion of its practice quite as early as some of its competitors, recent performance would indicate that the firm is quickly making such a move. In Public Accounting Report's tally of net public client gains, Arthur Young was first during this past year. In terms of visibility, Arthur Young has enjoyed extraordinary success, including a highly appealing ad campaign, a bestselling tax guide, and the recent

"In terms of visibility, Arthur Young has enjoyed extraordinary success, including a highly appealing ad campaign, a bestselling tax guide, and..."

"The 1985 Arthur Young Tax Guide...replaced J. K. Lasser as the nation's favorite personal tax reference."

release of the Arthur Young Guide to Financing Growth and The Arthur Young Preretirement Planning Book.

With the minor exception of problems involving one bank (JMB) in England, this firm has an impressive record in the professional liability area. As a result many industry experts estimate that it has the lowest professional liability premiums in the profession.

Recent events involving Arthur Young include:

June, 1986 - Arthur Young ranked first in the Big Eight Review's annual poll of firms which received the most media attention.

January, 1986 - Arthur Young ranked first in Public Accounting Report's summary of net public client gains for the past year.

January, 1986 - The firm unveils a new computer audit risk analysis system, hailed by the media as having the potential to significantly reduce client audit fees.

January, 1986 - The 1985 Arthur Young Tax Guide ranked #1 on the New York Times bestseller list and replaced J. K. Lasser as the nation's favorite personal tax reference.

October, 1985 - William L. Gladstone, 54, succeeded William S. Kanaga as chairman of the firm.

Coopers & Lybrand

"American Telephone & Telegraph is one of forty-six major US communications companies which employs the expertise of Coopers & Lybrand."

"No other firm dominates the eastern US as does Coopers & Lybrand."

"Among the largest Big Eight firms, Coopers & Lybrand has demonstrated by far the cleanest professional liability record."

Coopers & Lybrand's estimated worldwide revenues of $1.375 billion places the firm among industry leaders based on professional fees. While the firm has not confirmed its revenues, experts have approximated the US portion to be $779 million, again giving Coopers a strong market position.

American Telephone & Telegraph is one of forty-six major US communications companies which employs the expertise of Coopers & Lybrand. The firm dominates service to this segment. C&L is also a leader in service to the utility, insurance, manufacturing, extractive and agricultural specialties. In the service segment, clientele include such companies as Dunn & Bradstreet, Humana, and Ramada Inns.

No other firm dominates the eastern US as does Coopers & Lybrand. It is a market share leader in many eastern seaboard cities, such as Boston, Hartford, Jacksonville, Miami, New York City, Stamford and West Palm Beach. Coopers & Lybrand is also a major factor in the central and northwestern US. In the central region, service to the automotive industry, including Ford Motor Co., gives Coopers significant penetration in the Michigan and Ohio markets.

A strong ratio of staff members to partners makes compensation at Coopers above the average for Big Eight firms.

The firm's growth in revenues over the past eight years has placed it among the leaders. In 1978, Fortune magazine referred to Coopers & Lybrand as the most aggressive organization in terms of marketing its services. Though firm's momentum has recently slowed, Coopers remains a marketing leader.

Among the largest Big Eight firms, Coopers & Lybrand has demonstrated by far the cleanest professional liability record. There were no significant settlements, and the suits in process do not appear to pose any major problems.

12

"Auditing Standards Board chairman Jerry Sullivan of Coopers & Lybrand ..... will guide the ASB as it tackles significant issues involving the role of the accountant in our society."

Recent events involving Coopers & Lybrand include:

June, 1986 - Coopers resigned from the $1 million audit of USF & G. Differences in opinion over accounting for investment gains was an apparent factor.

February, 1986 - Coopers & Lybrand employee benefits expert Harold Dankner, cited in the February, 1986 Big Eight Review newsletter as the most recognized Big Eight expert by the media for this specialty. Firm has leading actuarial, benefits and compensation consulting practice.

January, 1986 - Auditing Standards Board Chairman Jerry Sullivan of Coopers & Lybrand announced that his committee would consider whether auditors should analyze and disclose business risks in their report to shareholders. Mr. Sullivan will guide the ASB as it tackles significant issues involving the role of the accountant in society.

Deloitte Haskins & Sells

1986 revenues for Deloitte Haskins & Sells worldwide are estimated to exceed $1 billion. In a study by Public Accounting Report, the firm was acknowledged as having one of the fastest growing US practices since 1982. Deloitte revenues are approximately half within and half outside the US.

The firm has long been known as the auditor's auditor, and excels in service to several industry segments. Its strength in manufacturing reaches far beyond General Motors Corporation to include such leading corporations as Rockwell Int'l, Honeywell, Proctor & Gamble and Monsanto. Construction, transportation, utilities, wholesale trade and the insurance and securities portion of the financial services segment represent additional areas of emphasis for Deloitte.

Geographically, the firm is strongest in greater New York, the southeast and the west. In the southeast, Deloitte is a market share leader in Fort Lauderdale, Miami and West Palm Beach while the western cities of San Diego, Honolulu, and Tucson also provide vital markets. San Francisco clients such as Kaiser Aluminum & Chemical, McKesson Corp., and United Artists Communications provide a base to make this firm very competitive in the Bay Area.

Although average partner compensation at Deloitte Haskins & Sells falls in the mid-range when compared with other Big Eight firms, under the leadership of managing partner J. Michael Cook, a new performance-based partner compensation plan has been adopted. As a result, in 1986, new partners at Deloitte were among the most highly compensated first-year partners.

Deloitte has not traditionally been an aggressive marketeer, yet it has recently demonstrated an intention to emphasize expansion. For the current year the firm is showing great success on Public Accounting Report's tally of client gains.

14

"Deloitte Haskins & Sells can boast a virtually impeccable professional liability record."

Deloitte Haskins & Sells can boast a virtually impeccable professional liability record. We are not aware of any significant suits in process.

Recent events involving Deloitte Haskins & Sells include:

September, 1986 - KMG rejected Arthur Andersen, Ernst & Whinney and Deloitte Haskins & Sells merger offers in favor of Peat, Marwick, Mitchell & Co.

March, 1986 - Firm formed "Capital Connection," a computerized network of capital sources, to assist growing companies with financing.

December, 1985 - Partners David Thompson and Albert Pastino issued paper on the role large corporations can play in financing and support for emerging businesses.

June, 1985 - J. Michael Cook, 42, elected chairman of the firm. Mr. Cook became chairman of AICPA in 1986.

Ernst & Whinney

"...this firm's recent merger with Thorne Riddell has made E & W number one in Canada and adds significantly to its $376 million in revenues outside the US."

"With its roots and US headquarters in Cleveland, E & W is a significant factor in the manufacturing segment, having more than 385 major public clients."

"In the central region alone, (Ernst & Whinney) it has nearly 50% more professional staff and major clients than its nearest competitor."

With $809 million in domestic revenues, Ernst & Whinney is one of the nation's dominant accounting firms. In addition, this firm's recent merger with Thorne Riddell has made E & W number one in Canada and adds significantly to its $376 million in revenues outside the US.

Bank America, First Interstate Bank, Lincoln National Insurance Corp., and Transamerica are a few examples of the 270 major financial institutions which rely on Ernst & Whinney's financial service industry expertise. With its roots and US headquarters in Cleveland, E & W is a significant factor in the manufacturing segment, having more than 385 major public clients. The firm is also a leader in the service, wholesale trade and transportation segments.

In the mid-atlantic, central, midwest, and southwest regions, this firm is among the leaders in terms of market share. In the central region alone, it has nearly 50% more professional staff and major clients than its nearest competitor. Cleveland, Dayton, Indianapolis, Louisville, and Toledo represent exceptionally strong markets for Ernst & Whinney. The firm has demonstrated its broad US client base by enjoying market leader status in nearly half the major cities we analyzed.

Ernst & Whinney partners are among the most highly compensated Big Eight professionals.

E & W has been a leader in practice development and is currently the fastest growing Big Eight firm worldwide. Fortune magazine's 1978 analysis of Ernst & Whinney as "sleepy" and "not on the competitive edge" is simply no longer appropriate. Under the leadership of Ray Groves, the firm's worldwide revenues have grown from $385 million in 1978 to $1.185 billion in 1985.

The significant number of financial institutions served by Ernst & Whinney has led to its involvement in recent professional liability suits. Several remain outstanding.

"E & W has been a leader in practice development and is currently the fastest growing Big Eight firm worldwide."

Recent events involving Ernst & Whinney include:

September, 1986 - KMG rejected merger offers by Arthur Andersen, Ernst & Whinney and Deloitte Haskins & Sells in favor of Peat Marwick & Mitchell.

August, 1986 - Thorne Riddell broke its affiliate relationship with KMG to join Ernst & Whinney. The combined firm became the largest in Canada.

January, 1986 - As support for tax reform was losing momentum, David Berenson, National Director of Tax Policy and Practice for E & W, predicted in an interview with Forbes Magazine that major tax reform would pass.

KMG (Klynveld Main Goerdeler)

"In Europe, this firm is a dominant factor, serving such giants as Daimler-Benz, KLM and Philips NV..."

"This firm's national office claims as a partner perhaps the most well-known US tax expert, Sidney Kess."

"Peat Marwick and KMG agreed in principle to merge their worldwide operations. The combined organization would eclipse Arthur Andersen as the largest accounting firm in the US and worldwide with $2.6 billion in total revenues."

With international revenues approaching $1 billion, European based KMG received nearly 75% of its professional fees from clients outside the United States. In Europe, this firm is a dominant factor, serving such giants as Daimler-Benz AG, KLM and Philips NV of the Netherlands.

In the United States, KMG practices under the name KMG Main Hurdman. While the US arm does not dominate service to the large public clients in our analysis, the firm has considerable clientele in the manufacturing area. Union Carbide (CT), Pfizer (NY), Avon (NY), and Diebold (OH) are all clients of KMG.

Geographically the firm is most powerful in the greater New York and western areas of the US. Of the major cities, we estimate that the firm enjoys its greatest market penetration in San Francisco and Sacramento. The relatively recent merger with J. Forbes, a California based firm, certainly contributed to this position.

While we estimate that partner compensation at KMG Main Hurdman is lower than the Big Eight average, the partnership promotion would typically come slightly sooner.

This firm's national office claims as a partner perhaps the most well-known US tax expert, Sidney Kess.

In terms of professional liability problems, KMG has remained extremely clean. No major difficulties are in process.

Recent events involving KMG include:

September, 1986 - Peat Marwick and KMG agreed in principle to merge their worldwide operations. The combined organization would eclipse Arthur Andersen as the largest accounting firm in the US and worldwide with $2.6 billion in total revenues.

August, 1986 - Thorne Riddell broke affiliate relationship with KMG to join Ernst & Whinney.

April, 1986 - Former KMG affiliate in Japan, Tohmatsu Awoki, joined Touche Ross.

September, 1985 - James Hendrix was named managing partner of KMG, US operations.

September, 1985 - Peat and KMG called off preliminary merger discussions.

Peat Marwick Mitchell & Co.

"Nearly 400 financial institutions with over $1 trillion in assets are clients of Peat Marwick."

"For a true sense of the caliber of these organizations, consider that Citibank with 81,000 employees, Aetna Life & Casualty with 41,000 employees, and Manufacturers Hanover with 32,000 employees belong to this elite group."

"With the minor exception of service to the communications sector, Peat Marwick has significant practices in every industry segment we analyzed."

"In a city by city comparison, the firm's market share strength in the US is nearly identical to competitor Arthur Andersen."

"...very aggressive while maintaining professionalism."

Worldwide revenues for Peat Marwick Mitchell & Co. approximate $1.5 billion, with over $1 billion from domestic operations. Due to consistent and substantial annual revenue growth, Peat Marwick has maintained a leadership position among the Big Eight firms in terms of professional fees.

Nearly 400 financial institutions with over $1 trillion in assets are clients of Peat Marwick. For a true sense of the caliber of these organizations, consider that Citibank with 81,000 employees, Aetna Life & Casualty with 41,000 employees, and Manufacturers Hanover with 32,000 employees belong to this elite group. In other industry specialties such as services, retail and wholesale trade, transportation, manufacturing, construction and mining, this firm has had similar success. With the minor exception of service to the communications sector, Peat Marwick has significant practices in every industry segment we analyzed.

In the US, PMM is exceptionally strong in literally all geographical areas, and is considered a leader in the northeast, greater New York, and the mid-atlantic region. In a city by city comparison, the firm's market share strength in the US is nearly identical to competitor Arthur Andersen.

We estimate that compensation for Peat Marwick partners is above the mid-range for the Big Eight firms.

Peat has been consistently aggressive in marketing its services. In 1978, Fortune magazine described the firm as very aggressive while maintaining professionalism and continually looking to expand its scope of services. Those adjectives remain appropriate today. PMM has also been a leader in media visibility, and over the past three years Peat partners have more frequently been quoted as experts than specialists from any other firm. Compensation expert Peter Chingos, national tax partners Peter Elinsky, Gerald Portney and Robert Brown, and New York City tax partner Robert

"...over the past three years Peat partners have more frequently been quoted as experts than specialists from any other firm."

Willens are examples of Peat specialists who are held in the highest regard by financial editors throughout the country.

The firm has had its share of liability problems, with Penn Square Bank continuing as a concern.

Recent events involving Peat Marwick include:

September, 1986 - Peat Marwick and KMG agree in principle to merge worldwide operations. The combined organization would eclipse Arthur Andersen as the largest accounting firm in the US and worldwide with $2.6 billion in total revenues.

June, 1986 - Peat Marwick retained Beatrice Companies (IL) audit while ownership and management of company changed.

April, 1986 - Peat Marwick bought a four building office complex in Montvale, NJ, and plans to move its administrative, communications, and computer facilities from New York City.

September, 1985 - Peat and KMG called off preliminary merger discussions.

Price Waterhouse

"Price Waterhouse has maintained a well proportioned practice with an enviable level of fees internationally."

"While major clients continue to include IBM and numerous other corporate legends, the broad range of industry specialties of Price Waterhouse is equally impressive."

"Price Waterhouse partners lead the Big Eight firms in initial and average compensation."

"...Leon Nad, vice chairman-tax consulting (for PW), has been the most quoted accountant in America since the Big Eight Review began measuring visibility in 1983."

Domestic operations of this firm approach $650 million, while revenues from outside the US parallel this level at nearly $600 million. Price Waterhouse has maintained a well-proportioned practice with an enviable level of fees internationally.

Clients such as Walt Disney Co. and MCA Inc. are two entertainment giants in the service segment which depend on Price Waterhouse. The firm is also a leader in service to such major money center banks as Chase Manhattan with $87 billion in assets and insurance companies such as CIGNA with $16 billion in income. But the industry specialties of Price Waterhouse are not limited to these. Indeed, this firm is a leader in retailing, serving clients such as F. W. Woolworth, Lucky Stores and Carter Hawley, as well as the transportation, manufacturing, construction and extractive industries. While major clients continue to include IBM and numerous other corporate legends the broad range of industry specialties of Price Waterhouse is equally impressive.

With the headquarters for many major US corporations in New York City and Los Angeles, Price Waterhouse is geographically most influential in the northeast, greater New York and the west. City by city, PW is highly competitive in markets on both coasts, including such major areas as Hartford, Los Angeles, Anchorage, New York City, Orlando, Sacramento, San Diego, Stamford, Tampa and Washington, DC.

Price Waterhouse partners lead the Big Eight firms in initial and average partner compensation. The average partner is responsible for nearly $1 million in annual billings and continuously supervises more than twelve professional staff members.

For years the name Price Waterhouse has been one of the most recognized names in the field of accounting and firm partners are often sought by the media for their expertise and opinions. For example, Leon Nad, vice chairman-tax consulting,

"The firm has done an excellent job of protecting its highly regarded reputation during a very difficult period for the profession in general."

has been the most quoted accountant in America since the Big Eight Review began measuring visibility in 1983. Other firm experts, including managing partner Joseph Connor, have become valuable resources for financial editors in helping to explain complex accounting and tax matters.

Price Waterhouse has encountered only negligible professional liability difficulties, and, based on our analysis, has no matters of significance currently outstanding. The firm has done an excellent job of protecting its highly regarded reputation during a very difficult period for the profession in general.

Recent events involving Price Waterhouse include:

July, 1986 - Thomas Raleigh, 59, succeeded John Zick as co- chairman of operations and firm deputy managing partner.

June, 1986 - Firm chairman Joseph Conner recommended expanding the audit role to include reviewing the management discussion and analysis section of annual reports.

April, 1986 - Former IRS commissioner Roscoe Egger, 65, returned to Price Waterhouse as special tax consultant.

December, 1985 - Price Waterhouse issued a white paper entitled, "Challenge and Opportunity for the Accounting Profession: Strengthening the Public's Confidence," in response to the profession's growing confidence and liability crises.

Touche Ross

"Since 1982 this firm has achieved a 47% growth in US fees, outpacing all other Big Eight firms."

"No other Big Eight firm approaches the penetration Touche Ross has in the retail segment."

"...Touche Ross is a market leader in fifteen major US cities..."

"The Big Eight Review's list of the 25 most quoted accountants in America for 1986 included more Touche Ross partners than any other firm."

Touche Ross' international professional fees, totaling nearly $1 billion, are evenly distributed between the United States and other countries. Since 1982 this firm has achieved a 47% growth in US fees, outpacing all other Big Eight firms.

From the standpoint of industry specialization, Touche is strongest in the wholesale and retail segments. For instance, the nation's largest retailer, Sears Roebuck (IL), is a Touche Ross client as well as such other giants as Federated Department Stores (OH), Associated Dry Goods (NY), Allied Stores (NY), Southland (TX) and Macy (NY). No other Big Eight firm approaches the penetration Touche Ross has in the retail segment. It also enjoys vigorous practices in the service and manufacturing areas, where clients include such household names as Chrysler (MI), Boeing (WA), RCA (NY), Pillsbury (MN), and Litton Industries (CA).

While Touche Ross is a market leader in fifteen major US cities, its strongest regions are greater New York and the central and northwestern US.

By our estimates, partner compensation here is slightly less than the average for Big Eight partners. By contrast, however, the partnership level is achieved, on the average, approximately 1-2 years earlier than in other firms.

The Big Eight Review's list of the 25 most quoted accountants in America for 1986 included more Touche Ross partners than any other firm. The firm and its partners have significantly increased their visibility with the media over the past few years.

Touche has made few professional liability settlements, and, by our analysis, has only minor situations outstanding.

Recent events involving Touche Ross include:

April, 1986 - Former KMG affiliate in Japan, Tohmatsu Awoki, joined this firm. The combined entity became a leader in the Japanese market.

September, 1985 - Edward Kangas, 41, was named new chief executive of Touche Ross & Co.

July, 1986 - Robert Rennie, currently chairman of Touche Ross Canada, was elected chairman of the Board of Governors of Touche Ross International.

Vital Statistics

Vital Statistics

The major firms have all become somewhat more open regarding their vital statistics in the last ten years, however, it remains very difficult to find this information in one place and organized in a comparative manner. The primary purpose of our vital statistics section is to present information from a wide variety of sources in a useful, organized manner. As this information relates to the career planning process we thought you may find the following considerations to be particularly meaningful.

International and Domestic Summary

While size is only one factor in determining strength and appeal it obviously will be important to many of you. Note in particular the size of the firm's operations outside the US. As the world economy becomes less and less centered around the United States, penetration into the international markets is increasingly important for the Big Eight firms.

Industry Strengths

Industry specialization is absolutely critical to the current practice of public accounting. Maintaining and/or obtaining clientele is often very dependant on specialized firm industry expertise. To meet this challenge the firms have all organized their practices into industry groups. The industries identified by each firm tend to be slightly different, however, we selected ten specialties for purposes of this analysis based on the four digit SIC code system. While some firms have as many as twenty- five industry groups, we felt including more than ten in our analysis would tend to make it more clerical than useful. In each specialty we have identified the firms which have been most successful serving these groups based on the number and size of their public clients. For each segment we also list several companies and their accountants to give you a further sense of the types of organizations included in each specialty. This information should not only give you an overview of the firm practices by industry, but may help identify firms which are strong serving industries of interest to you.

Major Domestic Offices

The firms all have a different philosophy in terms of establishing and maintaining offices. For instance Arthur Andersen has the fewest offices and they all tend to be rather large with a full complement of audit, tax and MCS specialists. Peat Marwick on the other hand has considerably more offices with fewer professionals, on the average, in each. They believe being closer to their clients is important in providing quality service. We have estimated the number of professional staff at fifteen of the firms' larger offices as well as provided the total number of US offices and average office size. If the office you are considering differs greatly from the firm's average you may want to inquire as to how this variance could affect your career. The firms discuss environment, advancement, compensation, client diversity, training, etc. in terms of their average size offices. Being in a much larger or much smaller office could change many of the career norms. (Please keep in mind we have aggregated physical locations for this analysis only when the offices are physically in the exact same city. For instance some of the firms

have more than one office in Chicago. Our professional staff estimates for Chicago have been aggregated to include all Chicago proper locations. They do not include, however, professional staff at any of the Chicago suburban locations like Oakbrook or Schaumburg as these are outside of Chicago proper. Please also note that national and regional professional staff physically located at a particular office have been included in our figures. This makes a difference in cities such as New York, Washington DC, Atlanta, Chicago, Dallas, Denver, Los Angeles and San Francisco. Each firm may compile and disclose professional staff information in slightly different ways. We believe our method is not only logical, but more importantly it is consistent to make comparisons meaningful.)

Personnel, Offices and Public Clients By Region

As many of you are aware, all the Big Eight firms, for operational purposes, are organized into regions. Each firm defines these regions in a varying manner, however, we have defined nine regions for purposes of gathering and analyzing data for you. Regional definitions are attached. To give you additional perspective on the geographic differences among firms we have provided number of offices, number of public clients, and number of personnel for each firm by region. While your career decision involves selecting a particular office of a firm you must recognize you are also selecting a geographic region. The strength of firms vary among their geographic regions. You should be aware of these differences. It is quite unusual to be in the same office for one's entire career, however, it is very typical to remain in the same region for your career. The data we have provided in this section and the more detailed regional information included in a separate chapter should help you make this important regional analysis.

Market Share Leadership

While international, national and regional strengths may be significant long term considerations, it is understandable why information regarding the local office and marketplace is initially important to you. We have identified the firms which are the market share leaders in 59 major cities of the country. The specific basis for this analysis is explained in greater detail immediately prior to the results. Please keep in mind that by providing information on firm leadership by city we are by no means implying a judgement or making a career evaluation for you. When you, however, make the evaluation we thought this analysis of local leadership would be helpful. It happens to also answer a common question we receive. As career professionals will counsel, the firm selection process is far more dynamic and complex than merely identifying local market leadership. For instance, an office with new local leadership might be poised to increase their practice and market share. This environment, in your analysis, could be more exciting, more challenging and offer more opportunity for you.

In summary this vital statistics section has been provided to give you a broad perspective of the firms, their offices, their clients, and their geographic differences. Understanding how the firms compare on these bases should provide you with a sound foundation to consider the more detail information in subsequent sections.

International and Domestic Summary

International and Domestic Summary

	AA	AY	CL	DHS	EW	KMG	PMM	PW	TR
Worldwide Revenue $	1,574	1,160	1,375	953	1,185	975	1,445	1,234	973
Worlwide Revenue Ranking	1	6	3	9	5	7	2	4	8
US Revenue $	1,182	545	779	528	809	234	1,004	645	513
US Revenue Ranking	1	6	4	7	3	9	2	5	8
Revenue Outside US $	392	615	596	425	376	741	441	589	460
Revenue Outside US Ranking	8	2	3	7	9	1	6	4	5
Number of US Partners	1,167	750	987	762	1,089	529	1,356	662	857
Number of US Prof. Staff	14,337	6,397	9,530	6,892	9,435	3,000	10,732	7,990	6,132
Partner/Prof. Staff Ratio	12.2	8.5	9.7	9.0	8.7	5.7	7.9	12.1	7.2
Partner/Prof. Staff Ranking	1	6	3	4	5	9	7	2	9
Number of US Offices	69	94	96	106	119	86	113	96	87

(revenues in millions)

(The Statistical information above is based on 1985 results. These figures are from either the November, 1985 issue of International Accounting Bulletin/Lafferty Publications, or the March, 1986 issue of Public Accounting Report/Professional Publications.)

Industry Strengths

Industry Strengths - Services

Industry Segment: Hotel, Advertising, Data Processing, Motion Picture, Recreation, Health Care, Etc. Services

Four Digit SIC Codes Included: 7000 to 9999

Total Public Companies In This Segment: 782

Leading Firms Serving This Segment
  (Client assets and sales in millions):

Firm	# of Clients	Client Assets	Client Sales
Arthur Andersen	126	$ 38,382	$ 24,624
Ernst & Whinney	97	12,461	9,306
Peat Marwick	112	12,617	8,695
Price Waterhouse	84	10,869	10,176

Analysis: The above firms lead this category, however, all nine firms have considerable practices serving clients in the service industry. For instance Arthur Young serves Beverly Enterprises in CA, Coopers & Lybrand serves Dunn & Bradstreet in NY, Main Hurdman serves Dravo in PA, Deloitte serves United Artists in CA, and Touche Ross serves ADP in NJ.

Major Companies In This Segment:

Auditor	#Emp	Company Name	Sales	ST	City
AA	137000	MARRIOTT CORP	4242	MD	BETHESTA
AA	112000	ARA SERVICES INC.	2652	PA	PHILADELPHIA
AY	105000	BEVERLY ENTERPRISES	1691	CA	PASADENA
EW	62000	HOSPITAL CORP. OF AMERICA	4152	TN	NASHVILLE
MH	62000	NATIONAL MEDICAL ENTERPRISES INC	2530	CA	LOS ANGELES
CL	56000	DUN & BRADSTREET CORP.	2772	NY	NEW YORK
AA	50000	HOLIDAY CORP.	1804	TN	MEMPHIS
CL	43000	HUMANA INC	2280	KY	LOUISVILLE
AA	42000	AMERICAN MEDICAL INTERNATIONAL	2256	CA	BEVERLY HILLS
AA	34000	HILTON HOTELS CORP	684	CA	BEVERLY HILLS
PW	29000	DISNEY (WALT) CO.	2015	CA	BURBANK
PMM	26000	AMERICAN BUILDING MAINTENANCE	424	CA	SAN FRANCISCO
PMM	25000	RYDER SYSTEM INC	2905	FL	MIAMI
AA	19000	WACKENHUT CORP	279	FL	CORAL GABLES
AA	18000	MANOR CARE INC	454	MD	SILVER SPRING
TR	18000	AUTOMATIC DATA PROCESSING INC.	1030	NJ	ROSELAND
PW	17000	MCA INC	2099	CA	UNIVERSAL CITY
CL	15000	STONE & WEBSTER INC.	321	NY	NEW YORK
CL	14000	FOSTER WHEELER CORP	1228	NJ	LIVINGSTON
DHS	14000	FPL GROUP INC.	4349	FL	JUNO BEACH
TR	14000	COMPUTER SCIENCES CORP	723	CA	EL SEGUNDO
MH	13000	DRAVO CORP	893	PA	PITTSBURGH
AA	13000	FOTOMAT CORP	236	CT	WILTON
CL	13000	RAMADA INNS INC	583	AZ	PHOENIX
PW	12200	INTERPUBLIC GROUP OF COMPANIES	691	NY	NEW YORK
TR	11100	CARE ENTERPRISES	239	CA	Laguna Hills

Major Companies - Continued:

Auditor	#Emp	Company Name	Sales	ST	City
PMM	11000	KINDER CARE LEARNING CENTERS INC	192	AL	MONTGOMERY
AA	11000	EQUIFAX INC	564	GA	ATLANTA
AA	11000	CAESARS WORLD INC	661	CA	LOS ANGELES
EW	10000	SELIGMAN & LATZ INC	342	NY	NEW YORK
AA	9000	ROLLINS INC	281	GA	ATLANTA
AA	9000	INTERNATIONAL SERVICE SYSTEM INC.	137	NY	NEW YORK
PW	8800	OGILVY GROUP INC.	490	NY	NEW YORK
EW	8700	REPUBLIC HEALTH CORPORATION	540	TX	DALLAS
EW	8000	VOLT INFORMATION SCIENCES INC	410	NY	NEW YORK
AA	8000	MGM GRAND HOTELS INC	353	NV	LAS VEGAS
AA	7400	SERVICEMASTER INDUSTRIES INC	1005	IL	DOWNERS GROVE
PMM	7400	WEBB (DEL E.) CORP.	271	AZ	PHOENIX
PW	7200	RESORTS INTERNATIONAL INC	426	FL	NORTH MIAMI
PMM	7000	TWENTIETH CENTURY-FOX FILM CORP	783	CA	LOS ANGELES
AA	6800	UNIVERSAL HEALTH SERVICES INC	506	PA	KING OF PRUSSIA
DHS	6800	UNITED ARTISTS COMMUNICATIONS	408	CA	SAN FRANCISCO
AA	6600	CENCOR INC	56	MO	KANSAS CITY
AA	6300	LA PETITE ACADEMY	83	MO	KANSAS CITY

Industry Strengths - Financial Institutions, Securities Brokerage and Insurance

Industry Segment: Commercial Banks, Savings and Loans, Life and Casualty Insurance, Security Brokers and Real Estate Brokers and Developers

Four Digit SIC Codes Included: 6000 to 6799

Total Public Companies In This Segment: 1,639

Leading Firms Serving This Segment
(Client assets and sales in millions):

Firm	# of Clients	Client Assets	Client Sales
Peat Marwick	391	$ 1,179,684	$ 162,709
Ernst & Whinney	270	722,818	100,227
Price Waterhouse	120	674,042	87,601
Arthur Andersen	228	330,163	54,178

Analysis: If insurance were broken out separately, certainly Coopers & Lybrand and Deloitte Haskins & Sells would have been included. Had securities brokerage been separately shown certainly Deloitte Haskins & Sells would again been listed. It becomes quite clear why Peat Marwick and Ernst & Whinney have borne the brunt of all the recent problems in the banking industry. Both firms have significant practices in this area.

Major Companies In This Segment:

Auditor	#Emp	Company Name	Sales	ST	City
EW	83000	BANKAMERICA CORP	13880	CA	SAN FRANCISCO
PMM	81000	CITICORP	22504	NY	NEW YORK
DHS	79000	TRANSWORLD CORP.	2152	NY	NEW YORK
AY	76000	SPERRY CORP.	5687	NY	NEW YORK
AY	68000	AMERICAN EXPRESS CO.	11850	NY	NEW YORK
PMM	63000	CITY INVESTING CO. LIQ. TRUST	169	NY	NEW YORK
TR	61000	PRUDENTIAL INS. CO. OF AMERICA	14332	NJ	NEWARK
PW	49000	CIGNA CORP.	16197	PA	PHILADELPHIA
PW	45000	CHASE MANHATTAN CORP	9733	NY	NEW YORK
DHS	44000	MERRILL LYNCH & CO INC	7117	NY	New York
AA	43000	HOUSEHOLD INTERNATIONAL INC	8686	IL	PROSPECT HEIGHTS
PMM	41000	AETNA LIFE & CASUALTY CO	18612	CT	HARTFORD
DHS	38000	METROPOLITAN LIFE INSURANCE	7316	NY	NEW YORK
EW	34000	FIRST INTERSTATE BANCORP.	5235	CA	LOS ANGELES
PMM	32000	MANUFACTURERS HANOVER CORP	8385	NY	NEW YORK
PMM	31000	SECURITY PACIFIC CORP	5537	CA	LOS ANGELES
CL	31000	TRAVELERS CORP	14594	CT	HARTFORD
EW	31000	TRANSAMERICA FINANCIAL CORP	390	CA	LOS ANGELES
AA	30000	NORTHWEST INDUSTRIES INC	1432	IL	CHICAGO
DHS	30000	EQUITABLE LIFE ASSURANCE	2595	NY	NEW YORK
CL	25000	AMERICAN INTERNATIONAL GROUP	5782	NY	NEW YORK
AA	22000	USG CORPORATION	2526	IL	CHICAGO

Major Companies – Continued:

Auditor	#Emp	Company Name	Sales	ST	City
AA	22000	CONSOLIDATED FREIGHTWAYS INC.	1882	CA	PALO ALTO
TR	22000	LOEWS CORP	6700	NY	NEW YORK
CL	22000	RELIABLE LIFE INSURANCE COMPANY	84	MO	WEBSTER GROVES
PW	20000	CHEMICAL NEW YORK CORP	5651	NY	NEW YORK
CL	20000	BANK OF BOSTON CORP	3436	MA	BOSTON
CL	20000	STATE FARM MUTUAL AUTO INS.	6684	IL	BLOOMINGTON
EW	19000	HANCOCK (JOHN) MUTUAL LIFE INSUR.	2351	MA	BOSTON
PW	19000	NEW YORK LIFE INSURANCE	3830	NY	NEW YORK
AA	18000	MARSH & MCLENNAN COMPANIES INC	1368	NY	NEW YORK
AA	17000	HUTTON (E.F.) GROUP INC	3139	NY	NEW YORK
DHS	17000	ALEXANDER & ALEXANDER SERVICES	914	NY	NEW YORK
PMM	17000	CONTINENTAL CORP	5092	NY	NEW YORK
PMM	16000	NORWEST CORP.	2546	MN	MINNEAPOLIS
AA	16000	SUNTRUST BANKS INC.	1819	FL	ORLANDO
PMM	16000	MELLON BANK CORP.	3222	PA	PITTSBURGH
AY	16000	PAINE WEBBER GROUP INC.	1885	NY	NEW YORK
EW	16000	TRANSAMERICA CORP	5590	CA	SAN FRANCISCO
PMM	15000	WELLS FARGO & CO	3362	CA	SAN FRANCISCO
EW	15000	AMERICAN GENERAL CORP	5677	TX	HOUSTON
PMM	15000	KEMPER CORP	2882	IL	LONG GROVE
AA	14000	FIRST CHICAGO CORP	4370	IL	CHICAGO
CL	14000	FARMERS GROUP INC	993	CA	LOS ANGELES

Industry Strengths - Retail Trade

Industry Segment: Retail Trade

Four Digit SIC Codes Included: 5200 to 5999

Total Public Companies In This Segment: 416

Leading Firms Serving This Segment
   (Client assets and sales in millions):

Firm	# of Clients	Client Assets	Client Sales
Touche Ross	74	$ 94,587	$ 103,686
Peat Marwick	71	30,696	74,952
Price Waterhouse	48	22,421	56,754
Arthur Andersen	61	17,345	32,087

Analysis: Touche Ross is the clear leader in the retail segment. Arthur Young should no doubt also be mentioned as their clients include McDonalds in Chicago and Wal-Mart in Arkansas.

Major Companies In This Segment:

Auditor	#Emp	Company Name	Sales	ST	City
TR	466000	SEARS ROEBUCK & CO	40715	IL	CHICAGO
PW	310000	K MART CORP.	22420	MI	TROY
PMM	179000	PENNEY (J.C.) COMPANY INC	13747	NY	NEW YORK
PMM	167000	SAFEWAY STORES INC	19651	CA	OAKLAND
CL	165000	KROGER CO	17124	OH	CINCINNATI
AY	145000	MC DONALD'S CORP.	3695	IL	OAK BROOK
EW	128000	DAYTON-HUDSON CORP	8793	MN	MINNEAPOLIS
TR	128000	FEDERATED DEPARTMENT STORES INC	9978	OH	CINCINNATI
EW	122000	AMERICAN STORES CO	13890	UT	SALT LAKE CITY
PW	118000	WOOLWORTH (F W) CO	5958	NY	NEW YORK
AY	93000	WAL-MART STORES INC.	8581	AR	BENTONVILLE
AA	77000	MAY DEPARTMENT STORES CO	5080	MO	ST LOUIS
PMM	76000	MELVILLE CORP	4775	NY	HARRISON
PMM	72000	WINN DIXIE STORES INC	7774	FL	JACKSONVILLE
PW	68000	LUCKY STORES INC	9382	CA	DUBLIN
PW	65000	SAGA CORP	1340	CA	MENLO PARK
DHS	65000	GREAT ATLANTIC & PACIFIC TEA CO	6615	NJ	MONTVALE
TR	64000	ASSOCIATED DRY GOODS CORP	4385	NY	NEW YORK
TR	64000	ALLIED STORES CORP	4135	NY	NEW YORK
TR	63000	SOUTHLAND CORP	12719	TX	DALLAS
DHS	57000	RAPID AMERICAN CORP	2183	NY	NEW YORK
PW	56000	CARTER HAWLEY HALE STORES INC	3978	CA	LOS ANGELES
TR	55000	MACY (R.H.) & CO. INC.	4368	NY	NEW YORK
CL	53000	ZAYRE CORP	4036	MA	FRAMINGHAM
AA	50000	WICKES COMPANIES INC.	4362	CA	SANTA MONICA

Major Companies - Continued:

Auditor	#Emp	Company Name	Sales	ST	City
TR	49000	SUPERMARKETS GENERAL CORP	5123	NJ	WOODBRIDGE
CL	47000	WENDYS INTERNATIONAL INC	1100	OH	DUBLIN
PMM	44000	STOP & SHOP COMPANIES INC	3689	MA	BOSTON
PMM	40000	PUBLIX SUPER MARKETS INC.	3446	FL	LAKELAND
TR	36000	ALBERTSONS INC	5060	ID	BOISE
PW	35000	TANDY CORP	2841	TX	FORT WORTH
AA	32000	WALGREEN CO	3162	IL	DEERFIELD
DHS	32000	MC CRORY CORP.	1038	NY	NEW YORK
PMM	31000	ECKERD (JACK) CORP	2966	FL	LARGO
PW	31000	GRAND UNION CO	2529	NJ	ELMWOOD PARK
PMM	25000	REVCO (D.S.) INC.	2396	OH	TWINSBURY
AA	25000	CARSON PIRIE SCOTT & CO	1302	IL	CHICAGO
TR	24000	SERVICE MERCHANDISE COMPANY INC	2526	TN	NASHVILLE
AA	23300	SCOTTYS INC	453	FL	WINTER HAVEN
CL	23000	VICORP RESTAURANTS INC	384	CO	DENVER
CL	23000	SAMBOS RESTAURANTS INC	293	CA	CARPINTERRIA
AA	22000	MERCANTILE STORES CO INC	1880	DE	WILMINGTON
EW	21000	SHONEYS INC	547	TN	NASHVILLE
PW	21000	CAVENHAM (USA) INC	2529	CT	NORTH DARIEN

Industry Strengths - Wholesale Trade

Industry Segment: Wholesale Trade

Four Digit SIC Codes Included: 5000 to 5199

Total Public Companies In This Segment: 294

Leading Firms Serving This Segment
(Client assets and sales in millions):

Firm	# of Clients	Client Assets	Client Sales
Arthur Andersen	61	$ 92,950	$ 39,345
Touche Ross	38	5,910	24,194
Peat Marwick	43	6,482	16,191
Ernst & Whinney	35	3,786	11,628
Deloitte Haskins	18	4,711	12,933

Analysis: While all the firms have clientele in this segment, the above firms tend to have a slightly greater share, particularly Arthur Andersen and Touche Ross. It is also interesting that Arthur Young has two of the largest clients in this segment in Universal Leaf Tabacco in Richmond and Advanced Medical Concepts in San Ramon (CA).

Major Companies In This Segment:

Auditor	#Emp	Company Name	Sales	ST	City
TR	25000	SUPER VALU STORES INC	6588	MN	EDEN PRAIRE
AA	17000	DWG CORP	1046	FL	Miami Beach
TR	15000	FLEMING COMPANIES INC	7095	OK	OKLAHOMA CITY
AY	14000	UNIVERSAL LEAF TOBACCO CO INC	1070	VA	RICHMOND
PMM	14000	PITTSTON CO	1251	CT	GREENWICH
AY	14000	ADVANCED MEDICAL CONCEPTS	624	CA	SAN RAMON
EW	13000	GENUINE PARTS CO	2279	GA	ATLANTA
DHS	12000	MC KESSON CORP.	6285	CA	SAN FRANCISCO
DHS	12000	LOWE'S COMPANIES INC.	2073	NC	NORTH WILKESBORO
AA	11000	CSS INDUSTRIES INC.	1	PA	PHILADELPHIA
PMM	9300	WETTERAU INC	3081	MO	HAZELWOOD
TR	8700	SYSCO CORP	2628	TX	HOUSTON
PMM	8000	FARMLAND INDUSTRIES INC	4371	MO	KANSAS CITY
EW	8000	MALONE & HYDE INC	2601	TN	MEMPHIS
PMM	7200	SAXON INDUSTRIES INC	378	NY	NEW YORK
PMM	7000	NASH FINCH CO	1327	MN	ST LOUIS PARK
AA	6300	SALOMON INC.	27896	NY	NEW YORK
MH	6000	NCH CORP.	375	TX	IRVING
PMM	5000	PACIFIC GAMBLE ROBINSON CO	783	WA	KIRKLAND
AA	4800	GRAYBAR ELECTRIC CO. INC.	1490	NY	NEW YORK
TR	4700	FARM HOUSE FOODS CORP	1119	WI	MILWAUKEE
EW	4600	PRICE CO.	1871	CA	SAN DIEGO

Major Companies - Continued:

Auditor	#Emp	Company Name	Sales	ST	City
EW	4400	DIBRELL BROTHERS INC	382	VA	DANVILLE
PW	4300	CFS CONTINENTAL INC.	1377	IL	CHICAGO
PW	4100	NIKE INC.	946	OR	BEAVERTON
AY	4000	KAY CORP	645	VA	ALEXANDRIA
TR	3500	ASSOCIATED MILK PRODUCERS	2465	TX	SAN ANTONIO
AA	3500	RYKOFF-SEXTON INC.	853	CA	LOS ANGELES
PW	3500	WILSON SPORTING GOODS CO.	248	IL	RIVER GROVE
PMM	3400	PREMIER INDUSTRIAL CORP	434	OH	CLEVELAND
EW	3400	LD BRINKMAN CORP	255	TX	KERRVILLE
DHS	3300	BEARINGS INC	496	OH	CLEVELAND
AA	3200	UNIVAR CORP	952	WA	SEATTLE
TR	3100	GODFREY CO.	534	WI	WAUKESHA
DHS	3100	BERGEN BRUNSWIG CORP	2435	CA	Orange
AY	2600	STEEGO CORP.	203	FL	WEST PALM BEACH
CL	2500	HEALTHCO INTERNATIONAL INC.	307	MA	BOSTON
CL	2500	ANIXTER BROS INC	651	IL	SKOKIE
TR	2400	DIANA CORP.	887	IL	LANSING
EW	2400	STEWART & STEVENSON SERVICES INC	257	TX	HOUSTON
CL	2100	SOUTHERN STATES COOPERATIVE INC	677	VA	RICHMOND
PW	2100	OMNICARE INC.	193	OH	CINCINNATI
AA	2100	UNITED STATIONERS INC	546	IL	DES PLAINES
PMM	2100	ACE HARDWARE CORP	1009	IL	OAK BROOK

Industry Strengths - Electric, Gas and Sanitary Services

Industry Segment: Electric, Gas and Sanitary Services (utilities)

Four Digit SIC Codes Included: 4900 to 4999

Total Public Companies In This Segment: 325

Leading Firms Serving This Segment
    (Client assets and sales in millions):

Firm	# of Clients	Client Assets	Client Sales
Arthur Andersen	112	$ 217,833	$ 118,603
Deloitte Haskins	63	177,614	80,989
Coopers & Lybrand	42	75,514	30,428

Analysis: Three firms very clearly dominate services to this industry segment. With the exception of Price Waterhouse and Peat Marwick who serve a much smaller number of companies in this group, the remaining firms have very, very limited utility practices.

Major Companies In This Segment:

Auditor	#Emp	Company Name	Sales	ST	City
AA	31000	SOUTHERN CO	6814	GA	ATLANTA
AA	29000	PACIFIC GAS & ELECTRIC CO	8431	CA	SAN FRANCISCO
DHS	23400	AMERICAN ELECTRIC POWER CO INC	4848	OH	COLUMBUS
PW	22000	CONSOLIDATED EDISON CO OF N.Y.	5498	NY	NEW YORK
AA	20000	WASTE MANAGEMENT INC	1625	IL	OAK BROOK
DHS	20000	DUKE POWER CO	2899	NC	CHARLOTTE
DHS	19000	ENSERCH CORP	3391	TX	DALLAS
AA	19000	COMMONWEALTH EDISON CO	4964	IL	CHICAGO
AA	17000	BROWNING-FERRIS INDUSTRIES INC	1145	TX	HOUSTON
DHS	17000	TEXAS UTILITIES CO	4170	TX	DALLAS
AA	17000	SOUTHERN CALIFORNIA EDISON CO	5169	CA	ROSEMEAD
TR	16000	COASTAL CORP	7254	TX	HOUSTON
AA	15000	GEORGIA POWER CO	3444	GA	ATLANTA
DHS	14000	PUBLIC SERVICE ELECTRIC & GAS CO	4409	NJ	NEWARK
PMM	14000	TEXAS EASTERN CORP	5457	TX	HOUSTON
DHS	14000	MIDDLE SOUTH UTILITIES INC	3238	LA	NEW ORLEANS
CL	14000	GENERAL PUBLIC UTILITIES	2870	NJ	PARSIPPANY
DHS	13000	PACIFIC LIGHTING CORP	5083	CA	LOS ANGELES
DHS	13000	PACIFIC LIGHTING CORP.	5083	CA	LOS ANGELES
CL	13000	DOMINION RESOURCES INC. (VA)	2712	VA	RICHMOND
CL	12000	VIRGINIA ELECTRIC & POWER CO	2612	VA	RICHMOND
DHS	12000	HOUSTON LIGHTING & POWER CO.	3533	TX	HOUSTON
AA	12000	COLUMBIA GAS SYSTEM INC	4053	DE	WILMINGTON
DHS	12000	HOUSTON INDUSTRIES INC	4062	TX	HOUSTON
AA	11000	CONSUMERS POWER CO	3298	MI	JACKSON
CL	11000	PHILADELPHIA ELECTRIC CO.	3014	PA	PHILADELPHIA
AA	11000	INTERNORTH	10727	NE	OMAHA

Major Companies - Continued:

Auditor	#Emp	Company Name	Sales	ST	City
PW	11000	DETROIT EDISON CO	2788	MI	DETROIT
PW	11000	NIAGARA MOHAWK POWER CORP	2695	NY	SYRACUSE
DHS	10000	PACIFICORP	1983	OR	PORTLAND
AA	9900	ALABAMA POWER CO	2414	AL	BIRMINGHAM
DHS	9694	SOUTHERN CALIFORNIA GAS CO	4616	CA	LOS ANGELES
AA	9400	CENTRAL & SOUTH WEST CORP.	2711	TX	DALLAS
DHS	9300	CAROLINA POWER & LIGHT CO	1935	NC	RALEIGH
CL	9100	BALTIMORE GAS & ELECTRIC CO	1755	MD	BALTIMORE
AA	9100	NORTHEAST UTILITIES	2081	CT	HARTFORD
AA	8700	CONNECTICUT LIGHT & POWER CO.	1756	CT	HARTFORD
DHS	8400	PENNSYLVANIA POWER & LIGHT CO	1977	PA	ALLENTOWN
DHS	8300	AZP GROUP INC.	1175	AZ	PHOENIX
PW	7700	CONSOLIDATED NATURAL GAS CO	3282	PA	PITTSBURGH
AA	7500	OHIO EDISON CO	1755	OH	AKRON
DHS	7400	NORTHERN STATES POWER CO	1789	WI	EAU CLAIRE
PW	7300	UNION ELECTRIC CO	1592	MO	ST LOUIS
AY	7000	PUBLIC SERVICE CO. OF COLORADO	1747	CO	DENVER

Industry Strengths - Communications

Industry Segment: Communications

Four Digit SIC Codes Included: 4800 to 4899

Total Public Companies In This Segment: 172

Leading Firms Serving This Segment
(Client assets and sales in millions):

Firm	# of Clients	Client Assets	Client Sales
Coopers & Lybrand	46	$ 244,026	$ 130,259
Arthur Andersen	42	82,966	42,628

Analysis: With the very minor exception that Arthur Young serves Southwestern Bell Telephone in St. Louis, and Price Waterhouse serves Western Union and MCI, Coopers & Lybrand and Arthur Andersen completely dominate this industry.

Major Companies In This Segment:

Auditor	#Emp	Compnay Name	Sales	ST	City
CL	338000	AMERICAN TELEPHONE & TELEGRAPH	34910	NJ	BERKELEY HEIGHTS
AA	184000	GTE CORP.	15732	CT	STAMFORD
CL	94000	BELLSOUTH	10664	GA	ATLANTA
CL	92000	NYNEX CORP.	10314	NY	NEW YORK
CL	79000	BELL ATLANTIC CORP.	9084	PA	PHILADELPHIA
AA	76000	AMERICAN INFORMATION TECHNOLOGIES	9021	IL	CHICAGO
CL	74000	PACIFIC TELESIS	8499	CA	SAN FRANCISCO
AY	72000	SOUTHWESTERN BELL TELEPHONE CO.	7925	MO	ST LOUIS
CL	70000	U S WEST INC.	7813	CO	ENGLEWOOD
CL	55000	NEW YORK TELEPHONE CO.	7055	NY	NEW YORK
CL	53000	SOUTHERN BELL TEL. & TEL. CO.	5784	GA	ATLANTA
CL	38000	SOUTH CENTRAL BELL TELEPHONE	4014	AL	BIRMINGHAM
CL	33000	BELL TELPHONE CO OF PA	2444	PA	PHILADELPHIA
CL	32000	MOUNTAIN STATES TEL.& TEL.CO.	3477	CO	DENVER
CL	30000	MICHIGAN BELL TELEPHONE CO.	2153	MI	DETROIT
CL	29000	NEW ENGLAND TELEPHONE & TELEGRAPH	3086	MA	BOSTON
CL	28000	CBS INC.	4677	NY	NEW YORK
AY	27000	UNITED TELECOMMUNICATIONS INC	3198	MO	KANSAS CITY
AA	25000	GENERAL TELEPHONE CALIFORNIA	2444	CA	Thousand Oaks
AA	24000	ILLINOIS BELL TELEPHONE CO.	2688	IL	CHICAGO
AA	24000	PACIFIC NORTHWEST BELL TELEPHONE	1634	WA	SEATTLE
AA	22000	CONTINENTAL TELECOM	2557	GA	ATLANTA
CL	22000	NEW JERSEY BELL TELEPHONE CO.	2504	NJ	NEWARK
CL	17000	NORTHWESTERN BELL TELEPHONE CO.	2120	NE	OMAHA
CL	16000	CHESAPEAKE & POTOMAC TEL CO (MD)	1211	MD	BALTIMORE
CL	14900	OHIO BELL TELEPHONE CO	1670	OH	CLEVELAND
PW	14000	WESTERN UNION CORP	1134	NJ	UPPER SADDLE RIVE
CL	14000	SOUTHERN NEW ENGLAND TELEPHONE	1304	CT	NEW HAVEN

Major Companies – Continued:

Auditor	#Emp	Company Name	Sales	ST	City
PMM	13000	AMERICAN BROADCASTING COMPANIES	0	NY	NEW YORK
PW	12000	MCI COMMUNICATIONS CORP	2542	DC	WASHINGTON
AA	12000	CENTEL CORP.	1326	IL	CHICAGO
AA	12000	GENERAL TELEPHONE CO OF SOUTHWEST	1063	TX	SAN ANGELO
CL	12000	CHESAPEAKE & POTOMAC TEL CO (VA)	1260	VA	RICHMOND
AA	11000	GENERAL TELEPHONE CO. OF FLORIDA	863	FL	TAMPA
CL	10000	INDIANA BELL TELEPHONE CO. INC.	820	IN	INDIANAPOLIS
AY	8000	CAPITAL CITIES/ABC INC.	1021	NY	NEW YORK
CL	7000	WISCONSIN BELL INC.	898	WI	MILWAUKEE
AA	6700	GENERAL TELEPHONE NORTHWEST	604	WA	EVERETT
AA	5600	GENERAL TELEPHONE CO OF SOUTHEAST	425	NC	DURHAM
CL	5500	ALLTEL CORP.	672	OH	HUDSON
AA	5200	GENERAL TELEPHONE CO OF INDIANA	400	IN	FORT WAYNE
CL	5100	CINCINNATI BELL INC	467	OH	CINCINNATI
PMM	4800	TELE COMMUNICATIONS INC	577	CO	Denver
CL	4800	STORER COMMUNICATIONS INC.	537	FL	MIAMI

Industry Strengths - Transportation

Industry Segment: Transportation

Four Digit SIC Codes Included: 4,000 to 4,799

Total Public Companies In This Segment: 196

Leading Firms Serving This Segment
(Client assets and sales in millions):

Firm	# of Clients	Client Assets	Client Sales
Ernst & Whinney	31	$ 37,850	$ 25,548
Peat Marwick	43	29,579	18,468
Arthur Andersen	39	25,817	25,200
Price Waterhouse	14	22,884	16,151

Analysis: While the above four firms are accountants for approximately 70% of all the clients and assets in this segment Coopers & Lybrand, Deloitte Haskins & Sells and Arthur Young deserve mention. These firms serve some rather large clients. For example, Coopers is auditor for Burlington Northern in Seattle and Consolidated Rail Corp. in Philadelphia, Deloitte is auditor for Union Pacific Corp. and Trans World Airlines in New York and Leaseway Transportation in Ohio and Arthur Young serves American Airlines in Texas and Pan Am in New York.

Major Companies In This Segment:

Auditor	#Emp	Company Name	Sales	ST	City
TR	152000	UNITED PARCEL SERVICE	7687	CT	GREENWICH
AA	76000	UAL INC	6383	IL	ELK GROVE TOWNSHIP
PW	62000	SANTA FE SOUTHERN PACIFIC	6438	IL	CHICAGO
EW	52000	CSX CORP.	7320	VA	RICHMOND
AY	50000	AMR CORP	6131	TX	Dallas/FW. Airport
CL	47000	BURLINGTON NORTHERN INC	8651	WA	SEATTLE
DHS	44000	UNION PACIFIC CORP	7798	NY	NEW YORK
PW	40000	EASTERN AIR LINES INC	4815	NY	MIAMI
PMM	40000	NORFOLK SOUTHERN CORP.	3825	VA	Roanoke
AA	39000	DELTA AIR LINES INC	4684	GA	ATLANTA
CL	39000	CONSOLIDATED RAIL CORP.	3208	PA	PHILADELPHIA
DHS	29000	TRANS WORLD AIRLINES INC.	3725	NY	NEW YORK
EW	29000	CHESAPEAKE AND OHIO RAILWAY CO	2215	OH	CLEVELAND
PW	29000	ATCHISON TOPEKA & SANTA FE RR CO	2091	IL	CHICAGO
EW	28000	SEABOARD SYSTEM RAILROAD INC.	2860	FL	JACKSONVILLE
AA	27000	FEDERAL EXPRESS CORP. (THE)	2031	TN	MEMPHIS
AY	25000	PAN AM CORP.	3484	NY	NEW YORK
EW	21000	ROADWAY SERVICE INC.	1580	OH	AKRON
AA	21000	YELLOW FREIGHT SYSTEM INC	1530	KS	OVERLAND PARK
PMM	20000	PUROLATOR COURIER INC.	800	NJ	PISCATAWAY
DHS	19000	LEASEWAY TRANSPORTATION CORP	1430	OH	BEACHWOOD
PMM	17000	SOUTHERN RAILWAY CO.	1795	VA	NORFOLK
EW	16000	NWA INC.	2655	MN	ST PAUL

Major Companies - Continued:

Auditor	#Emp	Company Name	Sales	ST	City
EW	16000	PIEDMONT AVIATION INC	1527	NC	WINSTON-SALEM
PMM	14000	TEXAS AIR CORP.	1944	TX	HOUSTON
PMM	14000	USAIR GROUP INC.	1765	VA	ARLINGTON
AA	13000	CONTINENTAL AIRLINES CORP.	1185	TX	Houston
AA	13000	MINSTAR INC.	881	MN	MINNEAPOLIS
AA	11000	CHICAGO & NORTH WESTERN TRANS.	897	IL	CHICAGO
PMM	11000	ILLINOIS CENTRAL GULF RR CO.	1014	IL	CHICAGO
EW	11000	BALTIMORE & OHIO RAILROAD CO	1064	MD	Baltimore
PMM	10000	WESTERN AIR LINES INC.	1307	CA	LOS ANGELES
PMM	9400	OVERLAND EXPRESS INC	96	IN	INDIANAPOLIS
EW	8900	ARKANSAS BEST CORP	582	AR	FORT SMITH
EW	8700	SEA-LAND CORP.	1634	NJ	EDISON
AY	8600	OVERNITE TRANSPORTATION CO	470	VA	RICHMOND
AA	8200	CAROLINA FREIGHT CORP	523	NC	CHERRYVILLE
DHS	7600	SOO LINE CORP.	618	MN	MINNEAPOLIS
PMM	7500	PEOPLE EXPRESS AIRLINES INC.	978	NJ	NEWARK
PW	7400	EMERY AIR FREIGHT CORP	876	CT	WILTON
AY	6800	TIGER INTERNATIONAL INC.	1147	CA	LOS ANGELES
AA	6100	FLYING TIGER LINE INC	905	CA	LOS ANGELES
AA	5800	PRESTON CORP.	350	MD	PRESTON
DHS	5200	ST. LOUIS SOUTHWESTERN RAILWAY	436	CA	SAN FRANCISCO

Industry Strengths - Manufacturing

Industry Segment: All Types of Manufacturing

Four Digit SIC Codes Included: 2000 to 3999

Total Public Companies In This Segment: 2,701

Leading Firms Serving This Segment
    (Client assets and sales in millions):

Firm	# of Clients	Client Assets	Client Sales
Arthur Andersen	446	$ 228,665	$ 274,070
Arthur Young	276	128,840	165,643
Coopers & Lybrand	317	232,667	283,281
Deloitte Haskins	253	177,089	226,754
Ernst & Whinney	385	142,501	187,721
KMG Main Hurdman	119	28,609	30,856
Peat Marwick	308	169,649	201,299
Price Waterhouse	304	409,896	470,435
Touche Ross	293	157,989	107,723

Analysis: All the firms continue to base their practices serving the various types of manufacturing companies in our country. While there are differences in market share among firms it is certainly fair for any firm to say they have considerable practices and experience serving companies in this segment. As has often been mentioned Price Waterhouse continues to serve the major blue chip companies in this segment. Notice the sales volume of their clients. Arthur Andersen and Ernst & Whinney with their midwest headquarters have for some time dominated in terms of number of clients.

Major Companies In This Segment:

Auditor	#Emp	Company Name	Sales	ST	City
DHS	811000	GENERAL MOTORS CORP	96372	NY	NEW YORK
PW	406000	INTERNATIONAL BUSINESS MACHINES	50056	NY	ARMONK
CL	369000	FORD MOTOR CO	52774	MI	DEARBORN
CL	338000	AT & T TECHNOLOGIES INC.	34910	NJ	BERKELEY HEIGHTS
PMM	304000	GENERAL ELECTRIC CO	28285	CT	FAIRFIELD
AA	232000	ITT CORP.	12715	NY	NEW YORK
PW	185000	UNITED TECHNOLOGIES CORP	15749	CT	HARTFORD
AY	164000	MOBIL CORP.	55960	NY	NEW YORK
AY	150000	PEPSICO INC	8057	NY	PURCHASE
EW	148000	REYNOLDS (R.J.) INDUSTRIES INC.	16595	NC	WINSTON-SALEM
PW	146000	DU PONT (E.I.) DE NEMOURS & CO.	29483	DE	WILMINGTON

Major Companies - Continued:

Auditor	#Emp	Company Name	Sales	ST	City
PW	146000	EXXON CORP	91620	NY	NEW YORK
PW	134000	GOODYEAR TIRE & RUBBER CO	9585	OH	AKRON
PW	129000	EASTMAN KODAK CO	10631	NY	ROCHESTER
PW	126000	WESTINGHOUSE ELECTRIC CORP	10700	PA	PITTSBURGH
DHS	123000	ROCKWELL INTERNATIONAL CORP	11338	PA	PITTSBURGH
PW	117000	GRACE (W.R.) & CO.	7260	NY	NEW YORK
CL	114000	PHILIP MORRIS INC	15964	NY	NEW YORK
AA	111000	TENNECO INC.	15400	TX	HOUSTON
TR	108000	CHRYSLER CORPORATION	21256	MI	HIGHLAND PARK
AA	105000	INTERNATIONAL STANDARD ELECTRIC	4647	NY	NEW YORK
TR	104000	BOEING CO.	13636	WA	SEATTLE
AA	103000	GENERAL DYNAMICS CORP	8164	MO	ST LOUIS
PMM	102000	XEROX CORP	8948	CT	STAMFORD
EW	97000	MC DONNELL DOUGLAS CORP.	11478	MO	ST LOUIS
TR	97000	RCA CORP	8972	NY	NEW YORK
DHS	94000	HONEYWELL INC	6625	MN	MINNEAPOLIS
AA	93000	SARA LEE CORP.	8117	IL	CHICAGO
MH	91000	UNION CARBIDE CORP	9003	CT	DANBURY
PMM	90000	MOTOROLA INC	5443	IL	SCHAUMBURG
AY	88000	LOCKHEED CORP.	9535	CA	BURBANK
CL	87000	DIGITAL EQUIPMENT CORP	6686	MA	MAYNARD
PMM	86000	BORG WARNER CORP.	3330	IL	CHICAGO
TR	86000	PILLSBURY CO	4671	MN	MINNEAPOLIS
PMM	86000	BEATRICE FOODS CO.	12595	IL	CHICAGO
CL	85000	MINNESOTA MINING & MANUFACTURING	7846	MN	ST PAUL
PW	84000	HEWLETT PACKARD CO	6505	CA	PALO ALTO
PW	80000	UNITED STATES STEEL CORP	18429	PA	PITTSBURGH
AY	78000	TEXAS INSTRUMENTS INC	4925	TX	DALLAS
CL	77000	AMERICAN BRANDS INC	7308	NY	NEW YORK
CL	75000	JOHNSON & JOHNSON	6421	NJ	NEW BRUNSWICK
AA	73000	DART & KRAFT INC.	9942	IL	NORTHBROOK
CL	73000	RAYTHEON CO	6409	MA	LEXINGTON
PW	70000	RALSTON PURINA CO.	5864	MO	ST LOUIS

Industry Strengths - Construction

Industry Segment: Construction

Four Digit SIC Codes Included: 1500 to 1999

Total Public Companies In This Segment: 90

Leading Firms Serving This Segment
  (Client assets and sales in millions):

Firm	# of Clients	Client Assets	Client Sales
Arthur Andersen	17	$ 7,433	$ 4,323
Peat Marwick	13	6,163	2,824
Arthur Young	8	7,797	8,580
Price Waterhouse	11	2,988	1,115
Deloitte Haskins	10	1,924	1,752

Analysis: The construction segment is the smallest of all publicly held industries both in terms of companies, assets and sales volume. This is one segment where we suspect privately owned companies represent a larger portion of the total market. On the basis of our analysis of just public companies the above firms serve nearly 70% of the market.

Major Companies In This Segment:

Auditor	#Emp	Company Name	Sales	ST	City
AY	35000	MC DERMOTT INTL. INC.	3257	LA	NEW ORLEANS
AY	30000	FLUOR CORP	4168	CA	IRVINE
CL	22000	MORRISON KNUDSEN COMPANY INC	2122	ID	BOISE
DHS	12000	FISCHBACH CORP.	1039	NY	NEW YORK
PW	7000	STANDARD SHARES INC.	269	NY	NEW YORK
DHS	3900	BURNUP & SIMS INC	180	FL	FORT LAUDERDALE
PMM	3600	ROUSE CO	247	MD	COLUMBIA
AA	3600	US HOME CORP	922	TX	HOUSTON
TR	3300	COMSTOCK GROUP INC.	469	CT	DANBURY
PW	3200	KAUFMAN & BROAD INC	420	CA	LOS ANGELES
EW	2500	OPELIKA MANUFACTURING CORP	63	IL	CHICAGO
AA	2500	IREX CORP.	127	PA	LANCASTER
PMM	1800	RYAN HOMES INC	566	PA	PITTSBURGH
AY	1500	PULTE HOME CORP	773	MI	KEEGO HARBOR
AA	1400	PENNSYLVANIA ENGINEERING CORP	116	PA	PITTSBURGH
EW	1400	RYLAND GROUP INC.	497	MD	COLUMBIA
CL	1300	ATKINSON (GUY F.) CO.	928	CA	SOUTH SAN FRANCISCC
DHS	1200	STARRETT HOUSING CORP	84	NY	NEW YORK
AA	1200	DEVELOPMENT CORP OF AMERICA	174	FL	HOLLYWOOD
AA	1100	WILSON BROTHERS	67	FL	MIAMI BEACH
PW	1100	OAKWOOD HOMES CORP	94	NC	GREENSBORO
MH	1075	MYERS (L.E.) GROUP	114	IL	OAK BROOK

48

Major Companies - Continued:

Auditor	#Emp	Company Name	Sales	ST	City
AA	1000	AMERICAN CONTINENTAL CORP.	647	AZ	PHOENIX
TR	1000	POLORON PRODUCTS INC	37	NY	HARRISON
EW	900	JAMAICA WATER PROPERTIES INC.	132	NY	LAKE SUCCESS
AY	900	BANK BUILDING & EQUIPMENT CORP.	119	MO	ST LOUIS
PW	875	VAUGHAN JACKLIN CORP	79	IL	DOWNERS GROVE
PMM	850	HEIST (C.H.) CORP.	41	FL	CLEARWATER
AA	846	CENTEX CORP	1215	TX	DALLAS
AA	819	GENERAL HOMES CORPORATION	350	TX	HOUSTON
EW	810	SPW CORP.	265	TX	DALLAS
AA	800	MC DOWELL ENTERPRISES INC.	91	TN	NASHVILLE
CL	760	J.P. INDUSTRIES INC.	133	MI	ANN ARBOR
AA	740	AMREP CORP	89	NY	NEW YORK
PW	690	CGA COMPUTER INC.	26	NJ	HOLMDEL
PW	650	AM CABLE TV INDUSTRIES INC.	27	PA	Quakertown
PW	650	NEWBERY ENERGY CORP	73	AZ	TEMPE
PMM	620	AMELCO CORP	85	MI	Chesterfield
PMM	615	GEMCO NATIONAL INC	16	NY	NEW YORK
AY	606	ERNST (E.C.) INC	30	VA	FAIRFAX
TR	600	TEAM INC.	50	TX	HOUSTON
AA	560	KASLER CORP.	132	CA	SAN BERNARDINO
DHS	529	DYCOM INDUSTRIES INC.	28	FL	WEST PALM BEACH
PMM	389	PACIFIC CONSTRUCTION CORPORATION	70	HI	HONOLULU

Industry Strengths - Mining

Industry Segment: Mining (extractive industries and services)

Four Digit SIC Codes Included: 1000 to 1499

Total Public Companies In This Segment: 482

Leading Firms Serving This Segment
(client assets and sales in millions):

Firm	# of Clients	Client Assets	Client Sales
Arthur Andersen	109	$ 36,019	$ 27,266
Price Waterhouse	40	58,855	49,932
Coopers & Lybrand	80	30,727	23,123

Analysis: The three firms above dominate this segment based on assets and sales of clients. In terms of just number of clients Peat Marwick (71) and Arthur Young (45) deserve mention.

Major Companies In This Segment:

Auditor	#Emp	Company Name	Sales	ST	City
PW	144000	ALLIED-SIGNAL INC.	9115	NJ	MORRISTOWN
PW	80000	SCHLUMBERGER LTD	6119	NY	NEW YORK
AA	66000	HALLIBURTON CO	4779	TX	DALLAS
PW	50000	AMOCO CORP.	26922	IL	CHICAGO
EW	42000	STANDARD OIL COMPANY (OHIO)	13002	OH	CLEVELAND
AA	42000	OCCIDENTAL PETROLEUM CORP	14534	CA	LOS ANGELES
CL	40000	ALUMINUM COMPANY OF AMERICA	5163	PA	PITTSBURGH
AY	25000	PHILLIPS PETROLEUM CO	15636	OK	BARTLESVILLE
CL	20000	UNOCAL CORP	10738	CA	LOS ANGELES
CL	12000	NL INDUSTRIES INC	1423	NY	NEW YORK
CL	12000	AMAX INC	1789	CT	GREENWICH
CL	7600	CABOT CORP.	1408	MA	BOSTON
AA	7200	EASTERN ASSOCIATED COAL CORP	428	PA	PITTSBURGH
AA	6800	EASTERN GAS & FUEL ASSOCIATES	1325	MA	BOSTON
AA	6600	NEWMONT MINING CORP	684	NY	NEW YORK
PW	6400	PHELPS DODGE CORP.	887	NY	NEW YORK
DHS	6200	VULCAN MATERIALS CO	981	AL	BIRMINGHAM
PW	6200	INSPIRATION RESOURCES CORP.	1122	NY	NEW YORK
EW	5700	CLEVELAND CLIFFS IRON CO.	344	OH	CLEVELAND
DHS	5600	MAPCO INC	1908	OK	TULSA
PW	5300	WESTERN CO OF NORTH AMERICA	594	TX	FORT WORTH
EW	4800	KANEB SERVICES INC	584	TX	HOUSTON
PW	4700	CYPRUS MINERALS COMPANY	706	CO	ENGLEWOOD
AA	4600	ZAPATA CORP	289	TX	HOUSTON
CL	4500	FREEPORT-MCMORAN INC.	722	NY	NEW YORK
PW	4500	TOTAL PETROLEUM (N. AMERICA) LTD	2372	CO	DENVER
PMM	4200	OCEAN DRILLING & EXPLORATION CO.	648	LA	NEW ORLEANS
PMM	4100	TITANIUM METALS CORP. OF AMERICA	219	PA	PITTSBURGH

Major Companies - Continued:

Auditor	#Emp	Company Name	Sales	ST	City
EW	4100	NORTH AMERICAN COAL CORP	542	OH	CLEVELAND
AY	3600	CRUTCHER RESOURCES CORP	98	TX	HOUSTON
EW	3600	ROCHESTER & PITTSBURGH COAL CO	404	PA	INDIANA
EW	3600	HANNA (M.A.) COMPANY	265	OH	CLEVELAND
AA	3500	MITCHELL ENERGY & DEVELOPMENT CORP	844	TX	WOODLANDS
PW	3400	NATIONAL FUEL GAS CO	1011	NY	NEW YORK

Industry Strengths - Agriculture

Industry Segment: Agriculture, Forestry and Fisheries

Four Digit SIC Codes Included: 0 to 999

Total Public Companies In This Segment: 268

Leading Firms Serving This Segment
(client assets and sales in millions):

Firm	# of Clients	Client Assets	Client Sales
Peat Marwick	48	$ 4,202	$ 1,000
Coopers & Lybrand	35	2,996	1,185
Arthur Andersen	34	2,403	2,616
Ernst & Whinney	32	3,006	2,282

Analysis: The four firms above are accountants for 81% of all the assets in this industry segment. Based strictly on number of clients Touche Ross (33) should also be mentioned.

Major Companies In This Segment:

Auditor	#Emp	Company Name	Sales	ST	City
AA	35000	CASTLE & COOKE INC	1601	HI	HONOLULU
CL	5700	DEKALB AGRESEARCH INC	487	IL	DEKALB
AA	4600	SOUTHEASTERN PUBLIC SERVICE CO	497	FL	MIAMI BEACH
EW	3600	MONFORT OF COLORADO INC	1463	CO	GREELEY
CL	3100	CHEMLAWN CORP.	333	OH	COLUMBUS
DHS	1100	BEAR CREEK CORP	112	OR	MEDFORD
TR	890	CAL MAINE FOODS INC	116	MS	JACKSON MISS.
PMM	600	ENVIRONMENTAL INDUSTRIES INC.	60	CA	CALABASAS
PMM	500	KAU- AGRIBUSINESS CO. INC.	20	HI	HONOLULU
PMM	470	NEWHALL LAND & FARMING CO	149	CA	VALENCIA
MH	400	ST. LOUIS NATIONAL STOCK YARDS	1	IL	NAT'L.STOCK YARDS
PMM	400	AMERICAN AGRONOMICS CORP.	88	FL	TAMPA
AA	378	UNITED STOCKYARDS CORP.	25	NY	NEW YORK
EW	220	FARM FISH INC.	1	MS	BELZONI
DHS	113	MOLECULAR GENETICS INC.	1	MN	MINNETONKA

Major Domestic Offices

Please Note: The professional staff figures we indicate are conservative estimates. We would expect that actual number of staff would rather consistently exceed these estimates.

Major Domestic Offices

Arthur Andersen

Number of Domestic Offices: 69

Number of US Professional Staff: 14,337

Average Office Size: 208

Firm	City	# Prof Staff
AA	Chicago	2000
AA	New York	1100
AA	Houston	775
AA	Los Angeles	650
AA	Dallas	600
AA	Atlanta	550
AA	San Francisco	550
AA	Washington DC	550
AA	Boston	400
AA	Milwaukee	325
AA	Philadelphia	325
AA	Detroit	300
AA	Denver	275
AA	Hartford	250
AA	Minneapolis	250

Arthur Young

Number of Domestic Offices: 94

Number of US Professional Staff: 6,397

Average Office Size: 68

Firm	City	# Prof Staff
AY	New York	1050
AY	Chicago	430
AY	Dallas	410
AY	Washington DC	300
AY	Los Angeles	270
AY	San Francisco	225
AY	San Jose	175
AY	Atlanta	150
AY	Tulsa	140
AY	Milwaukee	130
AY	Boston	110
AY	Denver	110
AY	Houston	110
AY	Kansas City	110
AY	Toledo	110

Coopers & Lybrand

Number of Domestic Offices: 96

Number of US Professional Staff: 9,530

Average Office Size: 100

Firm	City	# Prof Staff
CL	New York	1300
CL	Boston	450
CL	Philadelphia	450
CL	Chicago	425
CL	Detroit	300
CL	Los Angeles	300
CL	Washington DC	300
CL	Dallas	250
CL	San Francisco	250
CL	Atlanta	200
CL	Hartford	175
CL	Houston	175
CL	Columbus	150
CL	Denver	150
CL	Miami	150
CL	Minneapolis	150
CL	Newark	150
CL	Pittsburgh	150

Deloitte Haskins & Sells

Number of Domestic Offices: 106

Number of US Professional Staff: 6,892

Average Office Size: 65

Firm City	# Prof Staff
DHS New York	885
DHS Chicago	290
DHS Los Angeles	285
DHS Houston	255
DHS San Francisco	250
DHS Morristown	205
DHS Atlanta	200
DHS Dallas	190
DHS Miami	180
DHS Cincinnati	170
DHS Detroit	165
DHS Costa Mesa	160
DHS Minneapolis	160
DHS Washington DC	160
DHS Denver	150

Ernst & Whinney

Number of Domestic Offices: 119

Number of US Professional Staff: 9,435

Average Office Size: 79

Firm	City	# Prof Staff
EW	New York	900
EW	Chicago	525
EW	Cleveland	500
EW	Washington DC	400
EW	Los Angeles	375
EW	Dallas	300
EW	Boston	275
EW	Houston	275
EW	Atlanta	200
EW	San Francisco	200
EW	Indianapolis	175
EW	Baltimore	150
EW	Detroit	150
EW	St. Louis	150
EW	Philadelphia	125

KMG Main Hurdman

Number of Domestic Offices: 86

Number of US Professional Staff: 3,000

Average Office Size: 35

Firm City	# Prof Staff
KMG New York	350
KMG San Francisco	165
KMG Philadelphia	125
KMG Harrisburg	110
KMG Los Angeles	100
KMG Decatur	85
KMG Washington DC	75
KMG Roseland (NJ)	70
KMG Atlanta	60
KMG Houston	60
KMG Sacramento	60
KMG Chicago	50
KMG Salt Lake City	50
KMG Dallas	45
KMG Boston	45

Peat Marwick Mitchell

Number of Domestic Offices: 113

Number of US Professional Staff: 10,732

Average Office Size: 95

Firm City	# Prof Staff
PMM New York	1200
PMM Chicago	600
PMM Los Angeles	450
PMM Dallas	400
PMM Houston	400
PMM Washington DC	400
PMM Boston	300
PMM Short Hills (NJ)	300
PMM San Francisco	275
PMM Atlanta	225
PMM Minneapolis	225
PMM Philadelphia	225
PMM St. Louis	200
PMM Denver	175
PMM Cleveland	150

Price Waterhouse

Number of Domestic Offices: 96

Number of US Professional Staff: 7,990

Average Office Size: 83

Firm	City	# Prof Staff
PW	New York	1300
PW	Washington DC	525
PW	Los Angeles	300
PW	Boston	250
PW	Chicago	250
PW	Philadelphia	250
PW	St. Louis	250
PW	Dallas	200
PW	San Francisco	200
PW	Atlanta	175
PW	Detroit	175
PW	Houston	175
PW	Pittsburgh	175
PW	Cleveland	150
PW	Hartford	150

Touche Ross

Number of Domestic Offices: 87

Number of US Professional Staff: 6,132

Average Office Size: 71

Firm	City	# Prof Staff
TR	New York	750
TR	Chicago	250
TR	Washington DC	250
TR	Detroit	225
TR	Los Angeles	225
TR	Newark	225
TR	Boston	175
TR	Houston	175
TR	Minneapolis	175
TR	Atlanta	150
TR	Dallas	150
TR	San Francisco	150
TR	Denver	125
TR	Philadelphia	125
TR	Seattle	125

Personnel, Offices and Public Clients
By Region

Regional Definitions

Region #1 – Northeast Region
Any office, personnel, or client in RI, MA, VT, NH, and ME

Region #2 – Greater New York Region
Any office, personnel, or client in NY, NJ, PA and CT

Region #3 – Mid-Atlantic Region
Any office, personnel, or client in DC, DE, MD, WV, VA, NC, and SC

Region #4 – Southeast Region
Any office, personnel, or client in FL, GA, AL, MS, and TN

Region #5 – Central Region
Any office, personnel, or client in OH, IN, MI and KY

Region #6 – Midwest Region
Any office, personnel, or client in IL, KS, NB, WI, MN, IA, ND, SD and MO

Region #7 – Southwest Region
Any office, personnel, or client in TX, CO, OK, NM, AR and LA

Region #8 – Western Region
Any office, personnel, or client in CA, HI, AZ, UT, and NV

Region #9 – Northwest Region
Any office, personnel, or client in WA, OR, ID, MT, WY, and and AK

Personnel By Region

Region	AA	AY	CL	DHS	EW	KMG	PMM	PW	TR
Northeast	400	225	640	165	400	160	475	300	200
Greater New York	2425	1600	2750	1600	1950	875	2300	2200	1400
Mid-Atlantic	875	525	675	725	975	175	1025	830	375
Southeast	1150	375	800	700	875	275	850	640	575
Central	1075	400	1100	625	1575	125	600	640	750
Midwest	3600	900	975	650	1050	400	1650	900	950
Southwest	2525	1150	925	925	1125	375	1875	900	675
Western	2000	1150	1275	1300	1250	550	1475	1375	1000
Northwest	400	175	400	200	250	100	300	225	350
Total Estimated Professional Staff	14450	6500	9540	6890	9450	3035	10550	8010	6275

Offices By Region

Region	AA	AY	CL	DHS	EW	KMG	PMM	PW	TR
Northeast	1	5	4	3	4	4	4	3	3
Greater New York	8	15	13	15	18	14	16	15	11
Mid-Atlantic	6	9	9	16	11	7	12	11	8
Southeast	11	12	15	15	18	10	13	13	13
Central	9	9	14	12	22	7	9	11	11
Midwest	9	11	10	10	7	15	16	8	11
Southwest	11	14	11	13	17	13	20	13	13
Western	11	16	13	18	18	12	17	18	12
Northwest	3	3	7	4	4	4	6	4	5
Total Offices	**69**	**94**	**96**	**106**	**119**	**86**	**113**	**96**	**87**

Public Clients By Region

Region	AA	AY	CL	DHS	EW	KMG	PMM	PW	TR
Northeast	80	36	92	28	49	13	63	32	34
Greater New York	235	105	230	115	226	106	256	191	201
Mid-Atlantic	70	28	46	44	78	13	75	53	43
Southeast	116	41	71	74	89	26	93	54	67
Central	97	37	115	80	165	9	69	69	43
Midwest	200	62	86	58	119	21	169	79	121
Southwest	215	116	113	96	108	30	207	81	96
Western	232	172	114	172	110	56	177	125	130
Northwest	25	19	29	23	16	1	31	21	40
Total Public Clients	**1270**	**616**	**896**	**690**	**960**	**275**	**1140**	**705**	**775**

Market Share Leadership

Market Share Leadership

Since we are continually asked questions about market share leadership on a city by city basis, we have analyzed the fifty- nine major cities of the country and identified the two firms which appear to be leaders in terms of market share. A city was considered major if a minimum of six Big Eight firms had offices located there. When there were not two clear leaders in an area, we identified additional firms. The firms are listed alphabetically for each city. We have not attempted to differentiate among the leaders.

You will note that Arthur Andersen is listed as being a market share leader in more cities than any other firm. You might say that if the other firms had their personnel concentrated in the major cities, as is Andersen's philosophy, the results would have been different. In a very few cases you would probably be correct. More often, however, this would have little affect on the results. You must keep in mind that Arthur Andersen has almost 50% more professional staff in the US than most of its competitors.

For purposes of this analysis market share was defined in two ways. First, market share was based on which firm has the most professional staff in the city. Under this measure a firm could, for example, have one major client and be the market share leader. The second method defined market share as the unit penetration leader or, in other words, which firm has the largest number of clients. For this measure we asked Services Rating Organization, Inc. to provide their opinion and input. A firm which is considered a market share leader under either definition has been listed.

Note for accounting firms: While our analysis provides an opinion regarding market share leadership for the major US metropolitan areas, individual practices will no doubt also find more detailed market information necessary. Research regarding name recognition, industry strengths, etc. may be particularly helpful in developing and/or revising the office marketing plan. For these types of more specific needs, a company such as Services Rating Organization can provide valuable input. Their personnel are well acquainted with the informational needs of the major public accounting firms.

Market Share Leadership

Anchorage	AK	PMM	PW		
Atlanta	GA	AA	EW	PMM	
Austin	TX	AA	CL	EW	PMM
Baltimore	MD	EW	PMM		
Birmingham	AL	AA	EW	PMM	
Boston	MA	AA	CL	PMM	
Buffalo	NY	EW	PMM	PW	
Charlotte	NC	AA	DHS	EW	
Chicago	IL	AA	PMM		
Cincinnati	OH	AA	DHS		
Cleveland	OH	AA	EW	PMM	
Columbia	SC	AA	PW		
Columbus	OH	AA	CL	DHS	
Dallas/Fort Worth	TX	AA	AY	PMM	
Dayton	OH	DHS	EW	TR	
Denver	CO	AA	PMM		
Detroit	MI	AA	CL	TR	
Fort Lauderdale	FL	CL	DHS	PMM	
Hartford	CT	AA	CL	PMM	PW
Honolulu	HI	CL	DHS	PMM	
Houston	TX	AA	EW	PMM	
Indianapolis	IN	AA	EW	PW	
Jacksonville	FL	CL	PMM	TR	
Kansas City	MO	AA	AY	PMM	TR
Los Angeles/Century City	CA	AA	EW	PMM	PW

Market Share Leadership

Louisville	KY	CL	EW	TR	
Memphis	TN	AA	EW	TR	
Miami	FL	AA	CL	DHS	PMM
Milwaukee	WI	AA	AY	TR	
Minneapolis	MN	AA	DHS	PMM	TR
Nashville	TN	AA	EW	PMM	TR
New Orleans	LA	AA	PMM	TR	
New York City	NY	AA	CL	PMM	PW
Oakland	CA	AA	PW		
Oklahoma City	OK	AA	AY	PMM	PW
Omaha	NB	AA	DHS	PMM	TR
Orlando	FL	AA	EW	PMM	PW
Philadelphia	PA	AA	CL	PMM	
Phoenix	AZ	AA	CL	PMM	TR
Pittsburgh	PA	AA	EW	PW	TR
Portland	OR	AA	CL	DHS	PMM
Raleigh	NC	EW	PMM		
Richmond	VA	AY	CL	EW	PMM
Rochester	NY	AA	PMM	PW	
Sacramento	CA	CL	KMG	PMM	PW
Salt Lake City	UT	AA	DHS	PMM	
San Antonio	TX	EW	PMM		
San Diego	CA	AY	DHS	PMM	PW
San Francisco	CA	AA	AY	CL	PMM
San Jose	CA	AA	AY	PMM	

Market Share Leadership

Seattle/Tacoma	WA	AA	EW	TR	
St. Louis	MO	AA	PMM	PW	
Stamford	CT	AA	CL	PW	TR
Tampa	FL	AA	PW		
Toledo	OH	AY	EW		
Tucson	AZ	CL	DHS	PMM	
Tulsa	OK	AA	AY	PMM	
Washington	DC	AA	EW	PMM	PW
West Palm Beach	FL	CL	DHS	EW	

Planning and Preparing For Your Interviews

Planning and Preparing For Your Interviews

You have just spent 4 or more years in higher education studying for a career in public accounting. Assuming you are properly prepared for your profession, many firms could desire your services. The number of choices you have will be largely dependent on your interviewing ability, strategy and preparation. This planning and preparing for interviews can mean the difference between receiving the offer you consider ideal and accepting what you may feel is second best. We encourage you to take full advantage of the services of your career plannning and placement offices and the guidance of your counselor.

Having been involved in the recruiting process with a Big Eight firm for years I am convinced the following factors are critical in obtaining the most attractive job offers. We encourage you to improve your understanding and skills in these areas.

Factor One - Assume Your Share of Responsibility for the Interview

Though you may find it hard to believe, many students go into interviews expecting to be asked all the questions. This is, by far, the most significant and common mistake made by recruits. No interviewer wishes to ask 30 to 45 minutes of questions and few recruits are prepared to answer them. It is absolutely key to remember that an interview is a conversation or discussion during which both parties are equally responsible for its success. You must also keep in mind that this is your opportunity to get to know the firm as much as they are getting to know you. Recruiters are ready with information about their firm and generally enjoy discussing their organization and its merits. They just need someone to show a genuine interest. Questions are obviously a way to show that interest.

Some of you may be wondering how the firm will find out enough about you if you are asking questions. First of all, you have already given the firm your resume, which we assume you prepared carefully and effectively. Secondly, the firm may have already discussed your qualifications with faculty and career placement personnel. (If they didn't, they certainly could and often do.) And, the recruiter can make some judgement about you and what is important to you from the questions you ask.

Developing an ability to ask questions and assume some responsbility for the interview discusssion is the first and most important step in successful interviewing.

Factor Two - Ask Effective Questions

If you accept the premise that assuming some responsibility for the interview is important, you must be prepared with effective questions. We would rate a question as effective if it meets one of the following criteria:

    1. Demonstrates you are knowledgeable about the firm.

2. Demonstrates you are knowledgeable about the business of public accounting and current events or issues.

3. Demonstrates you are viewing your career and firm choice as long term.

4. Is interesting and/or fun.

Let's review why each is important, since this may be helpful in preparing questions.

1. If you cannot show you are knowlegeable about the firm the recruiter may assume that either you did not have enough sense to prepare or are not seriously considering his firm. Either assumption is detrimental to your chances of success.

2. Public accounting is in the process of more change than ever in its history. Demonstrating you understand the business and are aware of current events/issues indicates you may also be adaptable and willing to creatively participate in the challenge of change - important traits.

3. Whether you plan to be in public accounting for your entire career or not isn't important. It is important that you convey the idea that you plan to give this opportunity your full attention now. With this attitude the firm can expect to receive an appropriate and fair effort from you. You also demonstrate maturity by indicating you understand that performing at the highest level at every job is the best long-term career decision. Opportunities are always available to high achievers, in or out of public accounting.

4. The recruiter's job is easy or difficult depending on how hard it is to develop a discussion with you. Attempt to intersperse questions throughout the conversation as they follow naturally from the recruiters questions and statements. Anyone who is able to make the interview interesting without getting off-point will benefit. It is a rare quality to be able to make the conversation fun, but if you are able to do it, you will definitely be remembered favorably.

There is no simple way to make sure your questions meet these criteria other than preparation and practice. And remember, you can always convey additional information about yourself by prefacing a question with a statement about yourself, your goals, etc. Find a friend with whom you feel comfortable practicing and spend some time on your questions and techniques. The effort should pay handsome dividends.

Factor Three - Dress Appropriately

As I'm sure you are aware, the interview process is largely a matter of first impressions. I happen to believe that clothes make a difference in the short and long term. However, for the purposes of this discussion, please recognize their importance during the interview. You must keep in mind that recruiters want to be proud they picked you to visit with their partners in the office and dress plays a critical part in that decision. It is simply much easier to choose someone who looks appropriate for an office interview than an individual whose appearance is a concern.

There are, of course, the old jokes about accountants, bankers and other corporate executives and the so-called Brooks Brothers look. Though the remarks may be humorous, accountants and other successful business professionals do dress in a manner best described as traditional and conservative. The reasons for this phenomenon are varied. Professionals are not trying to distinguish themselves on appearance, but rather on the value of their ideas, and services. And, perhaps more important, the traditional, conservative look will generally inspire the confidence of one's clients and colleagues.

Make it easy for the recruiter. The cost of one proper interviewing outfit is small by most any measure and yet it can be a very critical factor in your ultimate success. Have some fun while taking the time to search out the appropriate dress.

Factor Four - Attack the Marketing Issue

Five to ten years ago recruiters were not evaluating one area which today has become extremely important. Firms must try to answer the question, "Will this individual someday be able to effectively market our services?" Certainly a difficult assessment to make in light of the fact that the recruiter may himself have limited experience in this area. Nonetheless the question must be answered and the result could be negative if you do not demonstrate some confidence in discussing the subject.

We strongly recommend that you initiate the discussion, explaining you understand the importance of marketing and have tried to prepare yourself for this challenging activity. You might ask the recruiter what training the firm offers. You might also relate some future activities which seem to help to prepare professionals and ask the recruiter their opinion on the value. The purpose of the discussion is to demonstrate you accept marketing as part of the business and are confident that with training and effort you will succeed.

Some of you may be thinking that recruiters are looking for social activities as an indication of marketing abilities. They are not. An extremely social profile may indicate only that adjustment to the everyday rigors of public accounting could be difficult.

Marketing requires being socially comfortable and understanding that there is a business purpose to the interaction. The recruiter is looking for indications that you may have some success or experience in this activity. Examples might be leading a charity fund drive, making a successful presentation, organizing a fraternity/sorority activity, etc.

It is likely that the recruiter will bring up this area for discussion if you do not. A considered response should allay any concerns an interviewer may have about your abilities or willingness to someday be a part of firm marketing activities.

The recruiting process can be one of the most rewarding times of your entire college experience. Effective preparation, planning and practice are the primary ingredients to success. The basic suggestions we have provided should supplement professional counseling you are receiving from your placement center.

Some of you may have read Rollo Hester's "Foundation Stones" for building a firm basis for career success. In conclusion let us just mention that too many graduates forget or ignore Mr. Hester's first stone of advice.

Foundation Stones

1. The wisdom of preparation.
2. The value of confidence.
3. The worth of honesty.
4. The privilege of working.
5. The discipline of struggle.
6. The magnetism of character.
7. The radiance of health.
8. The forcefulness of simplicity.
9. The winsomeness of courtesy.
10. The attractiveness of modesty.
11. The inspiration of cleanliness.
12. The satisfaction of serving.
13. The power of suggestion.
14. The buoyancy of enthusiasm.
15. The advantage of initiative.
16. The virtue of patience.
17. The rewards of co-operation.
18. The fruitfulness of perseverance.
19. The sportsmanship of losing.
20. The joy of winning.

Selecting Audit, Tax or MCS

Selecting Audit, Tax or MCS

Many of you may have read "Inside Track - How To Get Into And Succeed In America's Prestige Companies". This recent Random House publication discusses the personality of Arthur Andersen, Coopers & Lybrand, Ernst & Whinney and Price Waterhouse (as well as companies in other industries) attempting to differentiate among organizations based on an overall analysis of firm style, firm leadership, and firm personality (people). I suggest you take the time to read this book, however, I challenge you to reach beyond a soft analysis of personality in making your important career choice.

"Inside Track" suggests, as have previous comparisons, that on whole Arthur Andersen is very structured and super hustling, that Coopers & Lybrand is very informal, almost casual, that Ernst & Whinney is laid-back and relaxed, and that Price Waterhouse is not the biggest, but is the best and super polished. Should your career choice be based on matching your personality and abilities to these loose observations? I hope not. For the following three reasons, I am going to suggest that analyzing and matching your personality is important, but not in the above context.

First, even if Price Waterhouse overall were accurately described as the best and most polished, you are joining a region and an office of the firm. The local office is far more likely to reflect the personality of the managing partner than a firm stereotype. For instance, during my eleven years with Ernst & Whinney I visited at least thirty of the firm's offices and never found one I would describe as laid-back and relaxed. Secondly, within any large organization there exist all types of personalities and styles. Regardless of your style it is very likely you can and will find a group with shared values and interests. And lastly, in my opinion the matching of your personality and abilities should first be made against the framework of the traditional public accounting disciplines and not a soft oversimplification of the firms' personalities.

Very early in your public accounting experience I believe you will appreciate that audit, tax and MCS disciplines require slightly different personality traits, abilities and formulas for success. I strongly suggest you begin your analysis now on which of these disciplines best suits your abilities and manner. I personally believe ultimate success as an executive in the three traditional public accounting disciplines is dependant on different factors.

Audit Executive - There are essentially two types of activities for audit partners in a Big Eight firm. First is to be a client service executive directing the audit process and enlisting other firm resources as needed by the client. The other activity is to be in a technical accounting and auditing role in either the local/regional review department or a staff position in the national office. By comparison there are few technical accounting/auditing roles within a firm and therefore our comments relate to the client service activity only. We believe that to be successful at this activity it is important to possess or develop the following skills/traits:

> 1. Must be extremely well organized as numerous engagements are in process at one time.

2. Must have excellent supervision and training skills. An audit executive is likely to have more staff under his supervision at any given time than any other discipline. Must also be willing to train staff.

3. Must have superior communication ability. There is constant contact with clients and staff. Must at times be very persuasive and at other times be very firm.

4. Must be impressive in written and oral presentations. The audit executive is often the lead individual in presentations to existing and potential clients.

5. Must be good judge of character and ability as performance of subordinates is critical to success. Character judgement also critical in evaluation of client and potential client integrity.

6. Must be able to identify additional service opportunities with existing clients and develop other relationships into new firm engagements.

Tax Executive - The function of tax executive can also be in either a technical or client service role. Technical tax staff, however, are more often geographically in the Washington DC national tax office than the firm national, regional or local office. Again for purposes of this discussion we will focus on the executive serving clients from the local office.

1. Must have superior technical knowledge of the law. Many lawyers would confess that if you have a highly technical tax problem consult a Big Eight tax partner.

2. Must be able to relate well one on one, by comparison to audit and MCS partners, much more work is with individual versus corporate clients.

3. Must be intellectually creative as many tax assignments involve using the law in a planning manner. Skills in compliance activities are only critical at the initial staff levels.

4. Must also have ability to identify new service opportunities in a similar manner to audit and MCS executives.

Training abilities are not as critical as staff usually have some prior audit experience or advanced technical training. Supervision skills are not as critical as most assignments are more solitary than group oriented. Partner staff ratios typically lower in tax departments as many engagements require more senior technical skills. These activities are not as conducive to a staff pyramid.

Management Consulting Executive - In contrast to the audit and tax departments, most MCS executives have a very specific technical specialty. Many are initially hired with special training (information sciences, industrial engineering, valuation analysis, personnel, strategic planning, etc.) and gain further expertise in their area through experience and additional training. While some generalists may still exist in the firms, their numbers are being reduced rapidly. To be successful at this activity we believe it is important to possess or develop the following skills/traits:

1. Must excel at identifying opportunities and marketing of services. MCS services are project oriented. While some have repetitive aspects, many are one-time engagements. To maintain staff utilization in a MCS department, the marketing/selling activity is constant.

2. Must be superior in technical specialty. Most larger corporations have become far more sophisticated internally in recent years. As the companies have increased their own technical capabilities, bringing in someone from the outside is done only when the need is very narrow technically.

3. Must be able to estimate costs on projects even though the activity is often unique. MCS engagements are not loss leaders. And more importantly you cannot make up a loss next year because in MCS there is likely to be no next time.

4. Must be excellent listener. In audit and tax the basic result of many engagements is often straightforward. By contrast the end result of a MCS project is seldom as clear. To make sure the client receives the product they expect you must have the ability to probe and always be listening for input. The most common complaint from clients regarding MCS engagements, is that they did not get what they thought they bought. Being a good listener is absolutely essential in management consulting.

5. Must have excellent supervision skills as projects can involve large numbers of staff

(somewhat dependant on specialty). Training abilities not as important as in audit department as staff typically has prior experience or advanced academic credentials.

It is hardest to categorize the MCS activity since it can be so varied depending on the specialty. It is fair to say, however, that MCS executives must possess superior marketing, technical and supervision skills - a unique combination.

A personal assessment of your abilities and personality traits will naturally and objectively lead you to one of the above disciplines. If the matching of personality and abilities has a place in the recruiting/career planning process it is in this context. We encourage you to make this important personal assessment as early as possible in your career. Public accounting is not unlike most other professions. It tends to move rather quickly and, therefore, it is to your advantage to be in the correct lane. Regarding the role of labels like "most polished firm", "most relaxed", "casual", "stuffy", "sleepy", etc. in the career decision we can only offer that, in our opinion, absolutely all other considerations would have to be equal for them to come into play.

Partnership Agreements and Partner Compensation

Partnership Agreements and Partner Compensation

No matter how enjoyable and rewarding client service activities are in the long term, one of the main attractions of Big Eight public accounting is the expected level of partner compensation. For a period in the 1960s and 1970s compensation among senior Big Eight partners made public accounting with a major firm one of the most attractive and lucrative of all business and professional careers. As competition has heated up in recent years it has been more and more difficult for the major firms to keep up with compensation levels in some other industries. Currently, investment banking, venture capital, money center commercial banking and specialized management consulting are industries which have done particularly well. Big Eight partners continue, however, to be well compensated and are among the highest paid business professionals.

Traditionally the firms have been reluctant to discuss in any detail the terms of their partnership agreement or the levels of partner compensation. To the best of our knowledge this posture continues today. The purpose of this section is to give you some sense of the key elements of the partnership agreement and average partner compensation. Since very few people switch employment among the Big Eight firms, we believe graduates should at least understand the basic elements of a public accounting partnership agreement and consider the potential compensation differences among firms.

Partnership Agreements

Before becoming a partner or participating principal (an individual who is not a CPA, but participates in firm profits) each firm requires that you sign their standard partnership agreement. Some of the firms are organized as professional corporations, but for purposes of this discussion there is no substantive difference. The basic elements of the partnership agreement for any of the Big Eight firms are as follows:

> **Capital Contribution** - The agreement specifies the amount of capital you must contribute initially. Figure a cash requirement of about $40,000, which most first year partners borrow from their banker and pay back out of future earnings over about three years. Subsequent capital contributions are based on performance. It may sound strange, but the higher your performance level the more the firm will require you contribute in capital. The advantage over time is that the primary factor in your annual earnings is how much you have in your capital account. Some firms pay a form of interest to their partners for use of capital contributed. From a personal cash flow standpoint the initial years of partnership can be the toughest. Making capital contributions with after-tax dollars can reduce available cash significantly.

Distribution of Profits - Each firm has its own method of distributing annual profits to their individual partners. Two key factors are part of this distribution process. First, performance is evaluated. In this area some firms tend to emphasize individual achievements over office performance while others tend to place greater importance on office and regional results. Firms using the latter approach would argue it stimulates and emphasizes a team versus individual effort. The second factor considered is the partner capital accounts which in essence is a measure of cumulative performance. The higher your capital account balance the greater your distribution. It is our understanding that the capital account balance, or (in other words) your tenure based investment in the partnership, is significantly more influential in the distribution process than current performance. It will be interesting whether the traditional distribution methods we have described can survive the changes occurring within the profession. As subsequently discussed, we may see a movement toward more individual performance based distribution systems to coincide with the competitive nature of the marketplace.

Non-Compete - The partnership agreement includes a non- compete clause which typically indicates that if you leave the firm you agree not to practice public accounting, or your consulting specialty, for a period of three to five years. While these agreements are largely untested, it is generally understood they carry a certain degree of force. Some of the firms even require a similar non-compete before the partner level.

Termination - In one way or another most partnership agreements require that the firm retain the full authority regarding your continued association. You also typically agree that termination need not be for any specific reason or cause.

Retirement - To insure opportunity will always exist for capable young professionals most firms have adopted a mandatory retirement age of 62 or younger. Upon retirement you receive your original capital back. To cushion the reduction in earnings during retirement many firms provide an annual consulting fee to retired partners of $30,000 to $50,000 for about five years.

Pension Plans - The firms handle pension planning for partners in various ways. Some have retirement plans for partners and contribute to these plans before dividing up the profits. Others have partners establish individual plans. When we discuss earnings we are referring to earnings before pension plan contributions. This approach makes the figures for all firms comparable.

The firms do vary some in the decision-making participation of individual partners. Some firms, in essence, give most decision- making authority to a managing committee. Others leave some power at the individual partner level. You might remember that when Price Waterhouse and Deloitte Haskins & Sells were considering merger, the firms had to receive some form of majority support from individual partners. In other firms the merger and other decisions are granted to the managing committee through the partnership agreement. Inquiry regarding these types of differences would be worthwhile.

Partner Compensation

As you are considering a career with one of the major firms it seems natural for you to want to know approximate initial partner compensation, average partner compensation, and whether there are any significant differences between firms. Based on our knowledge of the business and analysis of key firm operating data, we have estimated both initial and average partner compensation levels for each firm (these figures are for 1985 and intended to coincide with other financial statistics presented in this comparison).

Regarding the figures for Touche Ross and KMG we estimate that on the average the partner level is achieved about 1-2 years before the partner level in the other firms (promotion to partner requires about 11 years at the other firms). This would affect the comparability of the figures to some minor degree.

Estimated First Year Partner Compensation

Price Waterhouse	$120,000
Arthur Andersen	110,000
Ernst & Whinney	100,000
Coopers & Lybrand	95,000
Peat Marwick Mitchell	95,000
Arthur Young	90,000
Deloitte Haskins & Sells	85,000 *
Touche Ross	70,000
KMG Main Hurdman	60,000

Due to the growth in number of new partners for most of the firms in recent years, the average age of partners in the firms is now relatively young. We estimate that it would take being a partner for 7 to 10 years to reach average compensation in most of the firms. This variance in number of years to reach the average, makes estimating average compensation more difficult than intial compensation. We therefore have stated the average compensation of firm partners in terms of a range.

Estimated Average Partner Compensation

Price Waterhouse	$200,000 to $220,000
Arthur Andersen	190,000 to 210,000
Ernst & Whinney	180,000 to 200,000
Arthur Young	160,000 to 190,000
Coopers & Lybrand	160,000 to 190,000
Deloitte Haskins & Sells	160,000 to 190,000
Peat Marwick Mitchell	160,000 to 190,000
Touche Ross	130,000 to 160,000
KMG Main Hurdman	110,000 to 130,000

* See subsequent discussion on the 1986 changes in the distribution system at Deloitte Haskins & Sells.

The Effect of Performance on Compensation

As previously mentioned, capital accounts and other measures of partner tenure have traditionally played a key role in the annual distribution of firm profits. In the current competitive environment this time and grade emphasis is being challenged within some firms since it may not give proper recognition to individual performance. It is our understanding that Deloitte Haskins & Sells has taken a leadership role in adopting a performance based system in 1986. Under this system it will be possible for new partners to achieve higher initial compensation and, based on superior achievement reach the average partner distribution well before the traditional 7 to 10 years. It is our understanding that for the new Deloitte partners admitted in 1986, their average compensation was $115,000 (compensation ranging from $85,000 to $145,000). This represents an almost 35% increase for new partners under the performance based system versus $85,000 (shown above) under the previous tenure system in 1985. Though average compensation for all partners would not change, the average becomes less important.

While the significance of this bold departure from tradition by Deloitte Haskins & Sells and their new chairman, J. Michael Cook, on future performance of the firm remains to be seen, certainly a couple of initial observations are appropriate. The principal challenge of the system will be to maintain a "we" attitude and team effort toward a common good. The principal opportunity is that Deloitte may be able to attract top personnel and harness the energy and vitality of its younger partners. In a competitive environment talent, energy and vitality do tend to play a rather significant role. It will be interesting to follow developments in the compensation arena in future periods.

While compensation is just one factor to be considered in your career/firm evaluation, we believe the above analysis confirms our previous comments that differences do indeed exist among firms. It also points out that as changes are occuring within the profession, compensation systems are adjusting to assist firms to meet new challenges. We trust this background on partnership agreements and estimates on compensation is helpful to you.

Marketing Expertise and Visibility Success

Marketing Expertise and Visibility Success

Nearly ten years ago the Supreme Court, in a landmark decision, struck down the ethical restrictions accountants had placed on the marketing of their services. Initially some professionals and firms took a wait-and-see attitude as to how this ruling would affect their firm and practice. It didn't take long, however, to realize that significant change would take place. Two new disciplines have evolved in the practice of public accounting: marketing and visibility. We believe you need to understand the role these functions play in the profession and how the firms have faired in terms of developing their skills in these areas.

Keep in mind that it is the growth and vitality of new business activity that will provide career opportunity for you.

Marketing Expertise

When we refer to an accounting firm's marketing expertise we are actually referring to the firm's ability to sell its services. Those firms which have been successful during the initial stages of this deregulated environment have expected their partners and senior staff to develop new business relationships, identify new professional opportunities, make effective proposals and presentations, and obtain new engagements, all selling activities. As the firms equalize in their selling skills, the other more sophisticated aspects of marketing will begin to differentiate the firms. You must realize that the initial step of mobilizing the partnership in selling activities has been a giant and often painful experience for most of the Big Eight firms. Based on our contact with the firms and the profession it appears that the following firms were the first to emphasize selling skills among their partners and staff. While the other major firms are moving quickly to develop similar skills, these firms appear to currently have a certain marketing (selling) advantage.

Arthur Andersen

Coopers & Lybrand

Ernst & Whinney

Peat Marwick Mitchell

Over the last eight years these four firms have grown at a faster rate than other members of the Big Eight, with Arthur Andersen leading the way. In Public Accounting Report's monthly tally of public client gains and losses, Arthur Young has over the last two years given very strong indication that it would like to join the above group. While statistics from a single year can be misleading there is very recent evidence that Deloitte Haskins & Sells is also making a move. It seems attitudes can also move in the other direction. In Fortune's article on the Big Eight firms in 1978, Coopers & Lybrand was described as the most aggressive of the firms. I do not believe that would be an accurate description of the firm today. For whatever reason Coopers & Lybrand seems to currently be moving forward with more caution.

During the interview process/office visit process you must obtain a sense of marketing/selling expertise. Ask questions. What has been the office growth rate in recent years? Does the firm have marketing training for you? Does the office have a marketing plan? How does the plan allow younger staff members to get involved? What are projected growth rates for the office? What industries does the plan emphasize? Etc., Etc.

Many of you may be wondering if marketing and selling activities are likely to continue intensifying among firms. While there are professionals within the firms who wish the more genteel days would return, I am convinced competition will remain very strong. During these next two to three years the firms will continue to perfect their selling skills and begin developing more marketing related expertise. To this extent I think you could also describe future competition as likely to be more sophisticated and perhaps creative. The firms will dabble in advertising, refine planning skills, establish marketing goals, identify target companies, develop new services, repackage old services, develop market research skills, hire inside strategic planning experts, become much more involved in marketing training for staff members, and as we discuss next, stress visibility for their firm and partners to complement the marketing effort. Yes, marketing is here to stay.

Visibility Success

While it is difficult to quantify the direct benefits of visibility for a major accounting firm, there is growing evidence and belief that this discipline is a critical part of an overall marketing effort for professional services. With regard to visibility, firms typically have two primary objectives. First is to create a desired image for their firm which will complement their other more direct efforts. An excellent recent example is the national advertising campaign of Arthur Young. The idea is that Arthur Young will serve your business in a very, very personal way. The second objective is simply to build name recognition. If a company needs accounting services name recognition will increase the chances the organization will at least think of your firm. To obtain this recognition firms are increasingly emphasizing the need for their personnel to develop relationships with the media as experts in a particular area. Editors of the major financial publications use Big Eight partners constantly to assist them in explaining complex financial or tax situations. When you consider the national exposure for the individual and firm the benefits are tremendous.

You may be saying these discussions regarding visibility are far too intangible for me. Do the firms really expend that much effort and does it really make that much difference? Let me relate to you an example which I hope will demonstrate that effort does make a difference and visibility is vitally important.

In connection with our monthly newsletter we monitor the amount of positive media coverage each firm receives in the major US financial publications. Up until mid-1984 the well recognized names such as Peat Marwick, Price Waterhouse and Arthur Andersen seemed to consistently receive most of the attention by our measure. In the summer of 1984, however, we noticed that Arthur Young was receiving more attention. At the time, we didn't know whether the increase was momentary or the result of a continuing effort and plan on the part of the firm. Within months the firm announced

their plan to publish a tax guide for individuals at the end of the year. By this time it was quite clear that Arthur Young was indeed executing a plan with precision to increase the recognition and visibility for their firm. Throughout 1985 the momentum continued. By 1986 Arthur Young was not just improving, they were winning. Public Accounting Report announced the firm had obtained more new public clients in the last year than any other firm. In only its second year the Arthur Young Tax Guide had replaced J.K. Lasser as the nation's favorite reference. And in June, 1986 we announced in our Annual Report that Arthur Young had received more attention from the media than any other firm. With the publication of two books since June the firm isn't resting. Do firms really make an effort to increase visibility for their organization and does it really make a difference? Ask someone from Arthur Young.

We hope the above example makes the point that regardless of how intangible visibility may seem, it is not a matter of chance. Peat Marwick has been a leader in this area as long as we have monitored the news. They are particularly strong in the tax area and have numerous partners who have become favorites of the media. We believe this is another instance of how a plan and organized effort can make a difference.

From time to time I catch myself discussing the new competition aspect of our profession as if it is too bad it was allowed. Public accounting used to be such a gentlemenly sport. In the long term, however, I sincerely believe everyone will benefit. The firms which accept that marketing and visibility are here to stay and are aggressively perfecting their skills, will not only be survivors, but will significantly increase the opportunities for their staff. We cannot emphasize enough the importance of obtaining a sense of a firm's national and local marketing/visibility expertise and success during your interviews.

Professional Liability Problems

Professional Liability Problems

Some of you may be thinking that much of the material we have presented suggests that faster growth, greater diversification, more aggressive marketing, etc. are the most important attributes to consider when selecting a firm. The "bigger is better" philosophy is certainly receiving considerable support these days, however, there are other factors which must be considered in your analysis. We are currently seeing evidence that the existing environment is taking a certain toll on the firms. We do not know exactly how each firm has been affected, but some have or will pay a price. In this section we would like to bring you up to date on the area of professional liability. The information regarding settlements was provided by the firms to the SEC in 1985. The information regarding pending suits is our summary based on newspaper, newsletter, trade journal, etc. accounts of the various problems. This summary is likely to be incomplete in some way, however, we believe it includes most major matters outstanding.

Please understand we are not presenting this information to indicate we in any way have a crystal ball regarding the outcome of these matters. Since the firms and profession are dealing with the liability issue as a major problem for the first time, it will take considerably more time for anyone to sort out and assess the damage. We do, however, believe it is important to make you aware of facts for your consideration and future discusssions.

Settlements

In connection with the Congressional hearings lead by Rep. Dingell the SEC asked the major US firms for the total amount of audit-related payouts to settle professional liability actions. This information was provided in early 1985 and covers a period of approximately five years ending December, 1984. To the best of our knowledge this information is the only data of its kind which the firms have made public.

Firm	# of Payouts	$ of Payouts	Major Cases
Arthur Andersen	16	$137 million	Fund of Funds Chase Manhattan Marsh McLennan Frigitemp Biatron
Peat Marwick	2	19 "	Nat'l Student Marketing Itel
Ernst & Whinney	n/p	6 "	Franklin Nat'l Bank US Surgical
Deloitte Haskins	23	5 "	Iowa Premium Service

Firm	# of Payouts	$ of Payouts	Major Cases
Coopers & Lybrand	26	4 million	All Small Amts
Price Waterhouse	2	3 "	All Small Amts
Touche Ross	1	2 "	Brokerage Firm
Arthur Young	2	1 "	All Small Amts

n/p - not provided

Since the above data was submitted there have been at least two major settlements. First, Grant Thornton (Grant Thornton is not a Big Eight firm, however, this situation must be mentioned since it is major and could affect suits the Big Eight are involved with) has settled for $50 million with the municipalities which invested in ESM. While the firm has expressed satisfaction that it was able to negotiate this settlement, many more major suits remain which relate to ESM. In addition, Peat Marwick has settled the FDIC portion of its problems related to an audit of Penn Square Bank. The agency sought nearly $100 million in damages and while no amount has been disclosed, industry experts have estimated they settled for about $50 million or less. Again, this is just the first step for Peat Marwick in resolving the problems related to Penn Square. You may remember that the losses for banks which invested in Penn Square loans were in the billions. The reason these two settlements are mentioned is that they present a more realistic picture of what the future year(s) may hold for the accounting firms and professional liability.

Suits In Process

The following is a list of the actions which are currently outstanding (in process) by firm. Since the dollar amount of the suits often has little to do with the later settlement amount, we have not shown the amount claimed. We have, however, noted with an asterisk any suit which, based on the accounts we have read, is more than a nuisance or minor scuffle. As we have mentioned previously this list may not be complete, but we believe it includes all major actions.

Firm	Suit In Process Involves
Arthur Andersen	Bell National Corp. S & L (CA)
	*Delorean Motor Company (NY and UK)
	*Financial Corp. of America (CA)
	Home State Savings (OH)
	Nucorp (CA)
	*SeaFirst Corp. (WA)

Note: Most recently Arthur Andersen lost their appeal of the $17 million Manufacturers Hanover decision. While another appeal may be possible, settlement at this point would seem more likely.

Firm	Suit In Process Involves
Arthur Young	Alexander & Howden (UK)
	*Bank of England (UK - JMB Ltd)
	Osborne Computer (CA)
Coopers & Lybrand	Ambassador Insurance Co. (NJ)
	Crime Control Inc. (IN)
	Hasbro Bradley
	Longhorn Oil Drilling Partnerships (TX)
	Security America Corp. (IL)
	Sun Diamond Co-op (CA)
	USF&G (MD)
Ernst & Whinney	Arrays, Inc. (CA)
	*Continental Illinois National Bank (IL)
	First Peoples Bank of New Jersey
	*United American Bank (TN)
	*Washington Public Power Supply System
Deloitte Haskins	American Savings & Loan (FL)
KMG Main Hurdman	Technical Equities (CA)
Peat Marwick	*Baldwin-United (OH)
	Borg-Warner Finance (IL)
	Control Data Corp. (MN)
	McKinney Cos. (OK)
	*Penn Square Bank (OK)
	Republic Finance Corp.
Price Waterhouse	none noted
Touche Ross	Beverly Hills S & L (CA)
	Giant Stores
	Inter-Regional Financial Group (MN)
	Media General Inc. (VA)

One of the major suits pending which is not mentioned above involves Fell & Starkey, an Australian firm, which is now a part of Ernst & Whinney. A judgement stands against the firm in the amount of $95 million (US) which is now under appeal. Australian industry experts speculate that if the judgement does stand on appeal the firm had only about $20 million in insurance coverage during the year in which the claim applies. This could be the first situation where a firm, in essence, fails and the individual partners are required to be financially involved. We assume this situation does not involve Ernst & Whinney because it pre-dates their merger, however, it is mentioned to illustrate that accounting firms can fail, partners can be individually liable and just because this has not occurred on a large scale as yet, doesn't mean it won't occur. The ESM litigation

involving Grant Thorton could be described in a similar manner as the Fell & Starkey situation.

Industry Concerns and Solutions

Observers of the profession have consistently commented that the professional liability area for accountants involves at least three major issues. First, users of financial statements seem to have a misunderstanding as to the assurance being provided by the accountant, often referred to as the "perception gap" problem. Secondly, the public seems to be asking the profession to expand its audit role to include an evaluation of "business risks". And lastly the existing peer review program is being challenged on the basis that the results of the system need greater public exposure.

If we somehow knew today the outcome of every suit in process, the mystery behind the professional liability problem would be far from over. Until the leadership of the profession wrestles with and resolves the three more philosophical problems described above, additional misunderstandings are going to occur. In our opinion the Big Eight firms must take a leadership role in the resolution of these broader liability issues. Some astute observer of our profession may soon conclude that continuing to issue audit reports with the present gaps in expectations is paramount to self destruction.

In an interview with the International Accounting Bulletin, J. Michael Cook, managing partner of Deloitte Haskins & Sells, expressed concern that if litigation does destroy one or more firms, the real cost will be the difficulty in attracting top people to the profession.

The firms are currently paying a price. Defense costs are mounting. Liability insurance premiums are astronomical and rising. Reputations are being injured. We believe it is important that you be at least aware of the current situation by firm and feel comfortable discussing both the specific situations and broader issues during your visits with the firms.

Summary

Summary

We hope in some way this comparison will help you make a considered choice among firms, and so begin an exciting career in public accounting. Never before have the profession and firms been subjected to such change, but with this change will come increased opportunity and challenge for you. As you begin your career let me offer just one brief and final thought that Placement Director Lars Johnson gave to me as I was leaving the University of Illinois in 1972. It went something like this.

> "Jim, you are very fortunate. Having chosen to study accounting and then being given the opportunity to work for one of the world's largest firms is an honor. You should be proud. Before you start work, though, let me tell you a little secret about the Big Eight firms. There are no other organizations in the world where ability and a lot of hard work will get you further."

Good luck and best regards.

James C. Emerson

October, 1986
Redmond, Washington

Regional Data

Regional Definitions

Region #1 – Northeast Region
   Any office, personnel, or client in RI, MA, VT, NH, and ME

Region #2 – Greater New York Region
   Any office, personnel, or client in NY, NJ, PA and CT

Region #3 – Mid-Atlantic Region
   Any office, personnel, or client in DC, DE, MD, WV, VA, NC, and SC

Region #4 – Southeast Region
   Any office, personnel, or client in FL, GA, AL, MS, and TN

Region #5 – Central Region
   Any office, personnel, or client in OH, IN, MI and KY

Region #6 – Midwest Region
   Any office, personnel, or client in IL, KS, NB, WI, MN, IA, ND, SD and MO

Region #7 – Southwest Region
   Any office, personnel, or client in TX, CO, OK, NM, AR and LA

Region #8 – Western Region
   Any office, personnel, or client in CA, HI, AZ, UT, and NV

Region #9 – Northwest Region
   Any office, personnel, or client in WA, OR, ID, MT, WY, and and AK

Offices By Firm - Northeast Region

CITY	ST	AA	AY	CL	DHS	EW	KMG	PMM	PW	TR
Bennington	VT						1			
Boston	MA	1	1	1	1	1	1	1	1	2
Burlington	MA							1		
Manchester	NH		1	1	1	1				
Newton	MA								1	
Portland	ME		1	1		1		1		
Providence	RI		1		1	1		1	1	
Springfield	MA			1			1			
Worcester	MA		1				1			1
TOTALS		1	5	4	3	4	4	4	3	3

Market Share Leadership
Northeast Region

```
CITY or AREA                              ST    Firm Firm Firm Firm
--------------------------------------    --    ---- ---- ---- ----
Boston                                    MA    AA   CL   PMM
```

Personnel By Region

Northeast Region

Region	AA	AY	CL	DHS	EW	KMG	PMM	PW	TR
Northeast	400	225	640	165	400	160	475	300	200

Major Clients By Firm
Northeast Region

Aud1 = Principal Accountants

Trd = Shows the where traded status of company shares
       A - American Stock Exchange
       N - New York Stock Exchange
       O - Over the Counter
       B - Company in some condition of bankruptcy
       C - Co-op or mutual
       L - Company in liquidation
       S - Subsidiary which reports separately
       U - Subsidiary whose auditor is different from parent
       X - Company which has gone private

Emp = Number of employees

Name = Company name

SIC = Four digit Standard Industrial Classification

Sta = State

Ast = Assets

Sls = Sales

Arthur Andersen

Aud1	Trd	Emp	Ast	Sls	Cty	Sta	Name
AA	N	23000	430	1145	WELLESLEY	MA	EG&G INC
AA	N	8100	597	770	NATICK	MA	PRIME COMPUTER INC.
AA	N	6800	1210	1325	BOSTON	MA	EASTERN GAS & FUEL ASSOCIATES
AA	N	6500	770	546	Providence	RI	NORTEK INC
AA	N	4571	330	401	WILMINGTON	MA	COMPUGRAPHIC CORP
AA	O	3300	258	296	CHELMSFORD	MA	APOLLO COMPUTER INC.
AA	A	2800	323	810	FRAMINGHAM	MA	PERINI CORP
AA	N	2700	194	235	WALTHAM	MA	THERMO ELECTRON CORP
AA	N	2511	727	678	CAMBRIDGE	MA	COMMONWEALTH ENERGY SYSTEM
AA	O	2400	187	328	WESTFIELD	MA	STANHOME INC.
AA	O	2400	2543	262	WORCESTER	MA	CONIFER GROUP INC.
AA	N	2200	74	105	WOBURN	MA	UNIFIRST CORP.
AA	N	2100	1153	536	AUGUSTA	ME	CENTRAL MAINE POWER CO
AA	A	2000	285	367	BOSTON	MA	AFFILIATED PUBLICATIONS INC
AA	S	1700	401	596	BOSTON	MA	BOSTON GAS CO
AA	A	1500	36	75	TAUNTON	MA	ARLEY MERCHANDISE CORPORATION
AA	O	1200	88	92	SALEM	NH	HADCO CORPORATION
AA	S	1100	229	163	CAMBRIDGE	MA	NEW BEDFORD GAS & EDISON LIGHT
AA	S	1070	205	246	CAMBRIDGE	MA	COMMONWEALTH ELECTRIC CO.
AA	N	969	625	200	BOSTON	MA	XTRA CORP
AA	O	899	27	62	WILMINGTON	MA	DYNAMICS RESEARCH CORP
AA	O	890	23	51	BROCKTON	MA	OFFICIAL INDUSTRIES INC
AA	O	854	27	72	BALTIMORE	MA	LUSKIN'S INC.
AA	S	800	891	274	WEST SPRINGFIELD	MA	WESTERN MASSACHUSETTS ELECTRIC CO.
AA	O	790	734	80	PORTLAND	ME	CASCO NORTHERN CORP
AA	S	782	185	263	CAMBRIDGE	MA	COMMONWEALTH GAS CO.
AA	N	726	62	46	WALTHAM	MA	REECE CORP
AA	O	722	1287	122	BOSTON	MA	UST CORP.
AA	N	628	374	169	RUTLAND	VT	CENTRAL VERMONT PUBLIC SERVICE
AA	O	625	117	133	WESTWOOD	MA	LTX CORP
AA	X	592	15	29	PROVIDENCE	RI	CUMMINGS INC INTL SIGN SERVICE
AA	A	590	113	156	PROVIDENCE	RI	PROVIDENCE ENERGY CO.
AA	O	570	192	71	PORTLAND	ME	CONSUMERS WATER CO
AA	O	530	21	43	CAMBRIDGE	MA	INTERMETRICS INC
AA	O	526	69	38	CONCORD	MA	NUCLEAR METALS INC.
AA	O	460	30	30	WILMINGTON	MA	ALTRON INCORPORATED
AA	O	434	23	33	CAMBRIDGE	MA	ORION RESEARCH INC
AA	O	432	805	89	MANCHESTER	NH	NUMERICA FINANCIAL CORP.
AA	B	430	13	31	CAMBRIDGE	MA	ADVENT CORP
AA	O	400	187	98	BANGOR	ME	BANGOR HYDRO ELECTRIC CO
AA	B	370	1	6	BURLINGTON	MA	COMPUTER DEVICES INC
AA	O	325	12	20	HYANNIS	MA	SENTINEL
AA	O	325	280	28	BROCKTON	MA	CHARTERBANK INC.
AA	O	325	12	20	HYANNIS	MA	SENTINEL TECHNOLOGIES

Arthur Young

Aud1	Trd	Emp	Ast	Sls	Cty	Sta	Name
AY	N	56000	4337	4991	PROVIDENCE	RI	TEXTRON INC
AY	N	18000	1002	1193	WORCESTER	MA	NORTON CO
AY	N	16000	1387	1559	HANOVER	NH	AMCA INTERNATIONAL LTD.
AY	N	4800	348	322	NORWOOD	MA	ANALOG DEVICES INC
AY	N	2600	296	309	BEDFORD	MA	GCA CORP
AY	O	2500	138	922	WORCESTER	MA	IDLE WILD FOODS INC
AY	N	1900	211	278	BOSTON	MA	HOUGHTON MIFFLIN CO
AY	O	1100	21	44	WOBURN	MA	GREENERY REHABILITATION GROUP INC.
AY	O	781	35	38	BURLINGTON	MA	SEMICON INC
AY	O	600	1100	117	PORTLAND	ME	ONE BANCORP (THE)
AY	Z	485	52	59	COHASSET	MA	ESKEY INC.
AY	O	432	60	42	NATICK	MA	STRATUS COMPUTER INC.
AY	O	380	97	69	CAMBRIDGE	MA	SYMBOLICS
AY	O	360	25	23	WEST WARWICK	RI	MICROBIOLOGICAL SCIENCES INC
AY	O	329	15	16	STURBRIDGE	MA	GALILEO ELECTRO-OPTICS CORP
AY	O	309	33	33	MERRIMACK	NH	CHEMICAL FABRICS CORPORATION
AY	O	284	33	33	MERRIMACK	NH	CHEMFAB
AY	A	283	664	213	COHASSET	MA	YANKEE COMPANIES INC.
AY	A	241	14	32	STOUGHTON	MA	SYSTEMS ENGINEERING & MFG. CORP.
AY	O	180	160	18	PROVIDENCE	RI	NATIONAL COLUMBUS BANCORP INC
AY	O	172	35	35	STAMFORD	VT	PATTEN CORPORATION
AY	O	156	676	78	BOSTON	MA	UNION WARREN SAVINGS BANK
AY	O	135	19	22	PROVIDENCE	RI	BEVIS INDUSTRIES INC
AY	O	120	133	123	FITCHBURG	MA	SAFETY FUND CORP
AY	O	80	1	1	AMHERST	NH	SANTEC CORP
AY	O	76	1	1	WORCESTER	MA	ARTEL COMMUNICATIONS CORP.
AY	O	60	1	1	CONCORD	NH	BREW (RICHARD D.) & CO. INC.
AY	N	39	229	32	BOSTON	MA	BAY FINANCIAL CORP
AY	O	28	12	13	NASHUA	NH	BKW INCORPORATED
AY	O	25	126	11	PROVIDENCE	RI	NARRAGANSETT CAPITAL CORP.
AY	A	15	183	23	BOSTON	MA	PROPERTY CAPITAL TRUST
AY	O	8	1	1	NATICK	MA	MEDIVIX INC.
AY	O	0	787	81		ME	MAINE SAVINGS BANK
AY	O	0	17	1	PROVIDENCE	RI	PROVIDENCE INVESTORS CO.
AY	O	0	157	42	MANCHESTER	NH	AMOSKEAG CO
AY	O	0	1	1	HANOVER	MA	SPECTRA PHARMACEUTICAL SERVICES

Coopers & Lybrand

Aud1	Trd	Emp	Ast	Sls	Cty	Sta	Name
CL	N	87000	6369	6686	MAYNARD	MA	DIGITAL EQUIPMENT CORP
CL	N	73000	3441	6409	LEXINGTON	MA	RAYTHEON CO
CL	N	53000	1582	4036	FRAMINGHAM	MA	ZAYRE CORP
CL	S	29000	6595	3086	BOSTON	MA	NEW ENGLAND TELEPHONE & TELEGRAPH
CL	N	20000	28296	3436	BOSTON	MA	BANK OF BOSTON CORP
CL	C	9000	10908	2300	BOSTON	MA	NEW ENGLAND MUTUAL LIFE INSURANCE
CL	N	8000	181	277	CAMBRIDGE	MA	STRIDE RITE CORP.
CL	C	8000	15579	2421	SPRINGFIELD	MA	MASSACHUSETTS MUTUAL LIFE INS.
CL	N	7600	1595	1408	BOSTON	MA	CABOT CORP.
CL	N	5000	3687	1444	WESTBOROUGH	MA	NEW ENGLAND ELECTRIC SYSTEM
CL	N	5000	350	389	BOSTON	MA	TERADYNE INC
CL	O	4400	346	367	BEDFORD	MA	MILLIPORE CORP
CL	N	4300	2288	1204	BOSTON	MA	BOSTON EDISON CO
CL	O	4100	18	1	FRAMINGHAM	MA	UNITED EDUCATORS INC
CL	O	3400	436	388	WORCESTER	MA	WYMAN-GORDON CO
CL	N	3000	94	140	ATTLEBORO	MA	SWANK INC
CL	N	2700	123	129	NEEDHAM HEIGHTS	MA	DAMON CORP
CL	O	2600	154	257	BURLINGTON	MA	DYNATECH CORP
CL	O	2500	195	307	BOSTON	MA	HEALTHCO INTERNATIONAL INC.
CL	A	2300	220	807	SCARBOROUGH	ME	HANNAFORD BROS CO
CL	N	2100	169	168	LEXINGTON	MA	UNITRODE CORP
CL	O	2100	69	104	LOWELL	MA	COURIER CORP
CL	O	2000	2070	215	Dedham	MA	MULTIBANK FINANCIAL CORP.
CL	N	2000	134	121	NORTH KINGSTOWN	RI	BROWN & SHARPE MFG CO
CL	N	2000	140	216	HUDSON	NH	CENTRONICS DATA COMPUTER CORP
CL	O	1900	2265	263	PROVIDENCE	RI	RIHT FINANCIAL CORP
CL	N	1832	96	138	CAMBRIDGE	MA	BOLT BERANEK & NEWMAN INC
CL	A	1600	143	129	WALTHAM	MA	ADAMS-RUSSELL CO. INC.
CL	N	1600	194	184	WESTWOOD	MA	CULLINET SOFTWARE INC.
CL	N	1500	86	92	BURLINGTON	MA	HIGH VOLTAGE ENGINEERING CORP
CL	O	1350	88	55	NEWTON	MA	MEDIPLEX GROUP INC.
CL	O	1200	110	139	READING	MA	ADDISON WESLEY PUBLISHING CO INC.
CL	O	1100	38	52	WEST WARREN	MA	WRIGHT (WILLIAM E.) CO.
CL	N	1100	714	334	BOSTON	MA	EASTERN UTILITIES ASSOCIATES
CL	O	1100	93	115	HOLYOKE	MA	AMPAD CORPORATION
CL	S	980	270	316	PROVIDENCE	RI	NARRAGANSETT ELECTRIC CO.
CL	S	807	2014	1016	WESTBOROUGH	MA	NEW ENGLAND POWER CO
CL	O	741	186	226	CAMBRIDGE	MA	LOTUS DEVELOPMENT CORPORATION
CL	O	680	25	41	BRAINTREE	MA	JONES & VINING INC
CL	O	619	824	91	MANCHESTER	NH	BANKEAST CORP
CL	O	601	14	40	BOSTON	MA	KEANE INC.
CL	A	600	59	60	MELROSE	MA	ARMATRON INTERNATIONAL INC
CL	A	579	66	65	WATERTOWN	MA	IONICS INC
CL	O	560	56	43	BILLERCIA	MA	ADAGE INC

Deloitte Haskins & Sells

Aud1	Trd	Emp	Ast	Sls	Cty	Sta	Name
DHS	N	5700	219	379	SALEM	NH	STANDEX INTERNATIONAL CORP
DHS	N	3500	267	255	MANSFIELD	MA	AUGAT INC
DHS	O	2000	104	191	ACTON	MA	CML GROUP INC.
DHS	O	1800	82	158	GROTON	MA	NEW ENGLAND BUSINESS SERVICE INC
DHS	O	1600	68	117	WOBURN	MA	TRANSITRON ELECTRONIC CORP
DHS	9	1100	1374	139	MANCHESTER	NH	FIRST NEW HAMPSHIRE BANKS INC.
DHS	O	950	354	134	BOSTON	MA	MOSELEY HOLDING CORP.
DHS	A	800	14	28	MANCHESTER	NH	SHAER SHOE CORP
DHS	O	553	33	32	MARION	MA	SIPPICAN INC.
DHS	O	490	23	26	METHUEN	MA	PARLEX CORPORATION
DHS	O	484	653	72	BRATTLEBORO	VT	FIRST VERMONT FINANCIAL CORP
DHS	O	230	1	1	CAMBRIDGE	MA	TSC CORP
DHS	L	160	1	12	CONCORD	NH	MERRIMACK FARMERS EXCHANGE INC.
DHS	O	159	12	12	WESTWOOD	MA	EPSCO INC
DHS	A	157	115	40	PRESQUE ISLE	ME	MAINE PUBLIC SERVICE CO
DHS	O	150	15	20	AVON	MA	KIDDIE PRODUCTS INC
DHS	O	148	40	37	PITTSFIELD	MA	BERKSHIRE GAS CO
DHS	O	138	64	15	FRAMINGHAM	MA	EATON FINANCIAL CORPORATION
DHS	O	130	1	13	CHARLESTOWN	MA	CPU COMPUTER CORP
DHS	A	123	41	41	MIDDLETOWN	RI	NEWPORT ELECTRIC CORP
DHS	O	70	1	1	BOSTON	MA	CAMBRIDGE ANALYTICAL ASSOCIATES
DHS	O	50	1	1	BILLERICA	MA	CAMBRIDGE MEDICAL TECHNOLOGY
DHS	O	37	1	1	BILLERICA	MA	CAMBRIDGE NUCLEAR CORP
DHS	O	24	1	1	BEDFORD	MA	AVIATION SIMULATION TECHNOLOGY
DHS	O	14	1	1	BOSTON	MA	KEWEENAW LAND ASSOCIATION LTD.
DHS	O	14	11	1	SALEM	NH	NEW HAMPSHIRE JOCKEY CLUB INC
DHS	O	14	1	1	CANTON	MA	FLEXWATT CORPORATION
DHS	O	2	1	1	BOSTON	MA	LO-JACK CORPORATION

Ernst & Whinney

Aud1	Trd	Emp	Ast	Sls	Cty	Sta	Name
EW	A	32000	2376	2352	BOSTON	MA	WANG LABORATORIES INC
EW	C	19000	26256	2351	BOSTON	MA	HANCOCK (JOHN) MUTUAL LIFE INSUR.
EW	O	12000	17804	1710	BOSTON	MA	BANK OF NEW ENGLAND CORP
EW	N	8300	463	662	WALTHAM	MA	DENNISON MANUFACTURING CO
EW	O	4300	6653	546	BOSTON	MA	STATE STREET BOSTON CORP.
EW	C	3400	3504	527	PORTLAND	ME	UNION MUTUAL LIFE INSURANCE CO.
EW	N	2900	227	218	Concord	MA	GENRAD INC.
EW	O	2600	114	233	CAMBRIDGE	MA	LITTLE (ARTHUR D.) INC.
EW	N	2500	240	267	BOSTON	MA	TOWLE MANUFACTURING CO
EW	N	2300	150	199	NEWTON LOWER FALLS	MA	BARRY WRIGHT CORP
EW	O	2200	113	100	RANDOLPH	MA	DUNKIN' DONUTS INC.
EW	N	1900	2486	774	SPRINGFIELD	MA	MONARCH CAPITAL CORP
EW	O	1800	46	80	BRISTOL	NH	INTERNATIONAL PACKINGS CORP.
EW	O	1800	3705	339	PROVIDENCE	RI	OLD STONE CORP.
EW	A	1600	119	139	LINCOLN	RI	CROSS (A.T.) CO.
EW	A	1470	67	97	FARMINGHAM	MA	ARROW AUTOMOTIVE INDUSTRIES INC
EW	O	1100	23	66	NORTH DIGHTON	MA	MARS STORES INC
EW	O	800	687	74	PORTLAND	ME	MAINE NATIONAL BANK
EW	O	740	1342	142	NASHUA	NH	INDIAN HEAD BANKS INC
EW	A	730	56	96	WELLESLEY HILLS	MA	AMERICAN BILTRITE INC
EW	A	700	25	27	QUINCY	MA	PNEUMATIC SCALE CORP.
EW	O	689	1237	121	MANCHESTER	NH	AMOSKEAG BANK SHARES INC.
EW	O	600	693	74	BANGOR	ME	MERRILL BANKSHARES CO
EW	O	550	23	53	CHARLESTOWN	MA	DUDDYS INC
EW	O	490	13	24	WOONSOCKET	RI	ACS INDUSTRIES INC
EW	O	410	339	55	BURLINGTON	VT	HOWARD BANCORP
EW	O	304	1	15	MILLBURY	MA	FELTERS CO.
EW	O	291	19	28	BILLERICA	MA	AUTOMATIX INC
EW	O	289	578	59	BURLINGTON	VT	BANKVERMONT CORP.
EW	O	270	86	46	PROVIDENCE	RI	GTECH CORPORATION
EW	O	266	573	54	MANCHESTER	NH	BANK OF NEW HAMPSHIRE CORP
EW	A	240	11	1	NORTH SPRINGFIELD	VT	VERMONT RESEARCH CORP
EW	A	190	45	104	LEOMINSTER	MA	VERTIPILE INC
EW	O	180	1	1	BOSTON	MA	DI-AN CONTROLS INC
EW	O	138	395	44	MANCHESTER	NH	UNITED FEDERAL BANK
EW	O	130	170	26	PROVIDENCE	RI	GREATER PROVIDENCE DEPOSIT CORP
EW	O	130	1	1	NEWTON	MA	HYGEIA SCIENCES INC.
EW	O	127	11	18	WESTBORO	MA	ALDEN ELECTRONIC INC.
EW	O	115	1	10	POCASSET	MA	DATAMARINE INTERNATIONAL INC.
EW	O	110	20	11	NALTHAM	MA	BGS SYSTEMS INC
EW	O	101	103	1	AUGUSTA	ME	BANC OF MAINE CORP.
EW	O	100	1	1	BURLINGTON	MA	PROGRAMS & ANALYSIS INC
EW	O	98	363	42	BOSTON	MA	CAPITOL BANCORPORATION
EW	O	40	20	1	NASHUA	NH	PENNICHUCK CORP.

KMG Main Hurdman

Aud1	Trd	Emp	Ast	Sls	Cty		Sta	Name
MH	A	1500	81	69	WOBURN		MA	ALPHA INDUSTRIES INC
MH	O	540	34	46	WOBURN		MA	CHOMERICS INC
MH	O	289	32	15	STURBRIDGE		MA	SPECTRAN CORP
MH	O	280	20	27	GLOUCESTER		MA	RULE INDUSTRIES INC.
MH	O	250	11	13	SOUTH NATICK		MA	EALING CORP.
MH	O	143	13	1	BEDFORD		MA	CONCORD COMPUTING CORPORATION
MH	O	122	1	1	WELLESLEY HILLS		MA	COMPUTER TELEPHONE CORP.
MH	O	69	1	1	STOUGHTON		MA	VANZETTI SYSTEMS INC.
MH	O	17	1	1	CHESTER		VT	IMTEC INC.
MH	O	15	1	1	ATHOL		MA	U.S. ELECTRICAR CORP
MH	O	4	1	1	WORCESTER		MA	IVY MICROCOMPUTER CORPORATION
MH	O	0	1	1	BOSTON		MA	LANDVEST PROPERTIES 1973 LTD
MH	O	0	1	1	CONCORD		MA	TECHNICAL COMMUNICATIONS CORP

Peat Marwick Mitchell

Aud1	Trd	Emp	Ast	Sls	Cty	Sta	Name
PMM	N	44000	1112	3689	BOSTON	MA	STOP & SHOP COMPANIES INC
PMM	N	31000	2425	2400	BOSTON	MA	GILLETTE CO
PMM	B	18000	77	281	NEWTON	MA	KDT INDUSTRIES INC.
PMM	N	13000	1385	1295	CAMBRIDGE	MA	POLAROID CORP
PMM	A	7000	846	1220	PAWTUCKET	RI	HASBRO INC.
PMM	N	6200	390	353	ANNAPOLIS	MA	UNC RESOURCES INC.
PMM	N	5900	430	638	BEVERLY	MA	KENNER PARKER TOYS INC.
PMM	O	5300	6269	614	BOSTON	MA	BAYBANKS INC.
PMM	N	5100	256	541	CANTON	MA	MORSE SHOE INC
PMM	N	5000	7122	794	PROVIDENCE	RI	FLEET FINANCIAL GROUP
PMM	O	3800	1490	898	WORCESTER	MA	HANOVER INSURANCE CO
PMM	B	2800	1	119	BOSTON	MA	BOSTON & MAINE CORP.
PMM	N	2400	2662	520	MANCHESTER	NH	PUBLIC SERVICE CO OF NEW HAMP.
PMM	O	2000	104	69	BOSTON	MA	SONESTA INTERNATIONAL HOTELS CORP
PMM	O	1500	16	51	NEW BEDFORD	MA	HEMINGWAY TRANSPORT
PMM	O	1500	54	66	GUILFORD	ME	GUILFORD INDUSTRIES INC
PMM	O	1400	1	12	CAMBRIDGE	MA	CAMBRIDGE RUBBER CO.
PMM	O	1300	31	61	BOSTON	MA	MORTON COMPANIES
PMM	N	1100	321	314	CANTON	MA	BAY STATE GAS CO
PMM	O	1000	19	28	DEDHAM	MA	HERSEY PRODUCTS INC.
PMM	O	879	1865	167	PROVIDENCE	RI	CITIZENS FINANCIAL GROUP INC.
PMM	O	796	851	94	BURLINGTON	VT	CHITTENDEN CORP.
PMM	O	700	43	49	BEDFORD	MA	BAIRD CORP
PMM	A	694	903	132	LOWELL	MA	COMFED SAVINGS BANK
PMM	O	661	41	49	BOSTON	MA	BIW CABLE SYSTEMS INC.
PMM	A	600	221	353	CHESTNUT HILL	MA	SEABOARD CORP.
PMM	O	591	35	50	EAST LONGMEADOW	MA	PACKAGE MACHINERY CO.
PMM	O	500	1	39	AUBURNDALE	MA	RIX CORP
PMM	O	464	18	30	BOSTON	MA	SPORTO CORP.
PMM	O	418	1127	121	BOSTON	MA	NEWORLD BANK FOR SAVINGS
PMM	O	390	24	35	LEOMINSTER	MA	CONDUCTRON CORP.
PMM	O	306	127	16	FRAMINGHAM	MA	CHARTER FINANCIAL CORP.
PMM	S	285	342	119	BATTLEBORO	VT	VERMONT YANKEE NUCLEAR POWER
PMM	O	262	255	25	WATERTOWN	MA	FIRST COOLIDGE CORP
PMM	O	261	11	21	WALTHAM	MA	DATA ARCHITECTS INC
PMM	O	261	524	78	BOSTON	MA	HOME OWNERS FEDERAL SAV. & LOAN
PMM	O	192	329	40	BOSTON	MA	MERCHANTS BANK OF BOSTON
PMM	O	180	233	28	WESTERLY	RI	WASHINGTON TRUST BANCORP INC.
PMM	O	180	392	41	JOHNSON	VT	STERLING TRUST CORP.
PMM	O	169	385	39	LITTLETON	NH	SAVER'S BANCORP INC.
PMM	O	160	1	1	CAMBRIDGE	MA	PIEZO ELECTRIC PRODUCTS INC
PMM	O	130	169	17	WESTERLY	RI	WASHINGTON TRUST CO.
PMM	O	119	1	1	WESTFORD	MA	DISPLAY COMPONENTS INC.
PMM	O	115	201	24	CONCORD	MA	CO-OPERATIVE BANK OF CONCORD (THE)

Price Waterhouse

Aud1	Trd	Emp	Ast	Sls	Cty	Sta	Name
PW	N	17000	1262	1239	WESTBORO	MA	DATA GENERAL CORP
PW	N	12000	871	848	BURLINGTON	MA	M/A-COM INC
PW	N	11000	618	886	NASHUA	NH	SANDERS ASSOCIATES INC
PW	N	7000	346	674	EXETER	NH	TYCO LABORATORIES INC.
PW	O	5300	7823	721	BOSTON	MA	SHAWMUT CORP
PW	N	5200	264	622	NASHUA	NH	NASHUA CORP
PW	N	4800	439	441	BEDFORD	MA	COMPUTERVISION CORP
PW	C	4100	3464	1100	WORCESTER	MA	STATE MUTUAL
PW	C	3000	3101	644	MONTPELIER	VT	NATIONAL LIFE INSURANCE CO
PW	O	2312	172	220	North Reading	MA	CONVERSE INCORPORATED
PW	O	2100	117	191	E WALPOLE	MA	BIRD INC
PW	O	1800	46	48	KILLINGTON	VT	S-K-I LTD.
PW	A	1000	46	68	BOSTON	MA	INSTRON CORP
PW	O	694	28	48	BURLINGTON	MA	EPSILON DATA MANAGEMENT INC.
PW	Z	650	979	89	LAWRENCE	MA	ARLTRU BANCORPORATION
PW	O	500	36	43	KILLINGTON	VT	SHERBURNE CORP.
PW	A	500	22	52	CANTON	MA	PLYMOUTH RUBBER CO INC
PW	O	446	34	37	BILLERICA	MA	LEXIDATA CORP
PW	O	400	41	35	BOSTON	MA	COLONIAL GROUP INC. (THE)
PW	O	280	998	80	BOSTON	MA	PROVIDENT INSTITUTION FOR SAVINGS
PW	O	220	429	44	BURLINGTON	VT	BURLINGTON SAVINGS BANK
PW	A	210	39	148	HOLBROOK	MA	MOORE MEDICAL CORP.
PW	O	160	744	79	CONCORD	NH	NEW HAMPSHIRE SAVINGS BANK CORP.
PW	O	73	63	10	DERRY	NH	CORNERSTONE FINANCIAL CORP.
PW	O	50	1	1	NEWTON	MA	KEY-DATA CORP.
PW	O	18	1	1	LAWRENCE	MA	SOFTWARE SERVICES OF AMERICA INC.
PW	O	11	1	1	WOBURN	MA	MACROCHEM CORPORATION
PW	X	9	140	28	BOSTON	MA	REAL ESTATE INV.TRUST OF AMERICA
PW	O	8	1	1	NEWTON	MA	INTERACTION SYSTEMS INC.
PW	O	6	1	1	CAMBRIDGE	MA	POWER RECOVERY SYSTEMS INC.
PW	O	5	10	1	BOSTON	MA	WMI EQUITY INVESTORS
PW	O	0	15	1	BOSTON	MA	BRADLEY REAL ESTATE TRUST

Touche Ross

Aud1	Trd	Emp	Ast	Sls	Cty	Sta	Name
TR	N	13000	945	967	CHESTNUT HILL	MA	GENERAL CINEMA CORP
TR	N	8800	495	572	FOXBORO	MA	FOXBORO CO
TR	O	5300	3181	832	NEW BEDFORD	MA	BERKSHIRE HATHAWAY INC.
TR	N	2600	105	118	ATHOL	MA	STARRETT (L.S.) CO
TR	O	2500	48	93	BOSTON	MA	ALMY STORES INC.
TR	B	1900	25	47	BROCKTON	MA	GARLAND CORP
TR	C	1800	302	532	PLYMOUTH	MA	OCEAN SPRAY CRANBERRIES INC.
TR	N	1700	97	185	BOSTON	MA	CHELSEA INDUSTRIES INC
TR	B	1400	93	79	NEWTON	MA	AITS INC
TR	A	1000	95	47	CANTON	MA	DELMED INC.
TR	A	888	24	43	ACTON	MA	BOWMAR INSTRUMENT CORP.
TR	O	829	37	50	CAMBRIDGE	MA	COSTAR CORP.
TR	O	720	1	1	WALTHAM	MA	IPL SYSTEMS INC.
TR	O	520	231	344	NASHUA	NH	EDGCOMB STEEL OF NEW ENGLAND INC
TR	O	364	37	32	HUDSON	MA	ENTWISTLE CO
TR	O	334	34	25	HYANNIS	MA	FIBRONICS INTERNATIONAL INC.
TR	A	271	21	20	HOPKINTON	MA	MATEC CORP.
TR	B	200	1	1	LEXINGTON	MA	ARP INSTRUMENTS INC
TR	O	180	29	25	TEWKSBURY	MA	VISUAL TECHNOLOGY INC.
TR	O	150	1	1	WEST ROXBURY	MA	ARMSTRONG LABORATORIES INC
TR	O	118	15	8	WOBURN	MA	BIOASSAY SYSTEMS CORP.
TR	Z	74	1	1	WOBURN	MA	AMERICAN PACEMAKER CORP.
TR	O	71	14	1	CAMBRIDGE	MA	ENSECO INCORPORATED
TR	O	62	91	29	BOSTON	MA	CHANCELLOR CORP.
TR	O	44	1	1	NEW MARKET	NH	VITRONICS CORPORATION
TR	O	40	1	1	NASHUA	NH	TERMIFLEX CORPORATION
TR	O	35	1	1	CAMBRIDGE	MA	LASER DISC COMPUTER SYSTEMS INC
TR	O	32	1	5	WOBURN	MA	MEMTEK CORP
TR	O	29	1	1	NANTUCKET	MA	NANTUCKET ELECTRIC CO.
TR	O	11	4	1	WOBURN	MA	ADVANCED NMR SYSTEMS INC.
TR	O	4	1	1	HOPKINTON	MA	CAMBRIDGE BIOSCIENCE CORP
TR	O	3	1	1	WELLESLEY	MA	CONSULTANT CAPACITIES GROUP
TR	A	0	13	1	NEWTON	MA	WEDGESTONE REALTY INVESTORS TR
TR	O	0	1	1	BOSTON	MA	CHICAGO REAL ESTATE TRUSTEES

Offices By Firm - Greater New York Region

CITY	ST	AA	AY	CL	DHS	EW	KMG	PMM	PW	TR
Albany	NY		1	1		1		1		
Allentown	PA				1			1		
Astoria	NY		1							
Atlantic City	NJ		1							
Bridgeport	CT		1						1	
Buffalo	NY		1		1	1	1	1	1	1
Cherry Hill	NJ				1					
Danbury	CT						1			
Erie	PA					1				
Floral Park	NY			1	.					
Garden City	NY						1			
Glastonbury	CT								1	
Hackensack	NJ				1	1			1	
Harrisburg	PA			1		1	1	1		
Hartford	CT	1	1	1	1	1		1	1	1
Jericho	NY		1					1	1	1
Lancaster	PA						1			
Lawrenceville	NJ						1			
Lebanon	PA						1			
Melville	NY	1		1		1				
Morristown	NJ				1				1	
New Haven	CT				1	1				
New York	NY	1	2	1	2	1	1	1	3	2
Newark	NJ		1	1	1	1				1
Philadelphia	PA	1	1	1	1	1	1	1	1	1

CITY	ST	AA	AY	CL	DHS	EW	KMG	PMM	PW	TR
Pittsburgh	PA	1	1	1	1	1	1	1	1	1
Princeton	NJ		1							
Reading	PA					1				
Rochester	NY	1		1	1	1		1	1	1
Roseland	NJ	1					1			
Saddlebrook	NJ		1							
Short Hills	NJ							1		
Stamford	CT	1	1	1	1	1	1	1	1	1
State College	PA						1			
Syracuse	NY			1		1		1	1	
Trenton	NJ					1	1	1		1
Valley Forge	PA							1		
Waterbury	CT			1						
White Plains	NY					1		1		
Woodbury	NY				1					
TOTALS		8	15	13	15	18	14	16	15	11

Market Share Leadership

Greater New York Region

CITY or AREA	ST	Firm	Firm	Firm	Firm
Buffalo	NY	EW	PMM	PW	
Hartford	CT	AA	CL	PMM	PW
New York City	NY	AA	CL	PMM	PW
Philadelphia	PA	AA	CL	PMM	
Pittsburgh	PA	AA	EW	PW	TR
Rochester	NY	AA	PMM	PW	
Stamford	CT	AA	CL	PW	TR

Personnel By Region

Greater New York Region

Region	AA	AY	CL	DHS	EW	KMG	PMM	PW	TR
Greater New York	2425	1600	2750	1600	1950	875	2300	2200	1400

Major Clients By Firm

Greater New York Region

Audl = Principal Accountants

Trd = Shows the where traded status of company shares
        A - American Stock Exchange
        N - New York Stock Exchange
        O - Over the Counter
        B - Company in some condition of bankruptcy
        C - Co-op or mutual
        L - Company in liquidation
        S - Subsidiary which reports separately
        U - Subsidiary whose auditor is different from parent
        X - Company which has gone private

Emp = Number of employees

Name = Company name

SIC = Four digit Standard Industrial Classification

Sta = State

Ast = Assets

Sls = Sales

Arthur Andersen

Aud1	Trd	Emp	Ast	Sls	Cty	Sta	Name
AA	N	232000	14272	12715	NEW YORK	NY	ITT CORP.
AA	N	184000	26558	15732	STAMFORD	CT	GTE CORP.
AA	X	112000	1693	2652	PHILADELPHIA	PA	ARA SERVICES INC.
AA	S	105000	4493	4647	NEW YORK	NY	INTERNATIONAL STANDARD ELECTRIC
AA	N	54000	37703	46297	WHITE PLAINS	NY	TEXACO INC
AA	N	51000	6098	5770	STAMFORD	CT	CHAMPION INTERNATIONAL CORP
AA	N	47000	3395	4685	NEW YORK	NY	AMERICAN HOME PRODUCTS CORP
AA	N	41000	2814	4524	NEW YORK	NY	COLGATE PALMOLIVE CO
AA	N	33000	4902	3548	RAHWAY	NJ	MERCK & CO INC
AA	N	32000	6039	4502	NEW YORK	NY	INTERNATIONAL PAPER CO
AA	N	32000	1586	3049	BETHPAGE	NY	GRUMMAN CORP
AA	N	32000	1689	2164	SADDLE BROOK	NJ	KIDDE INC.
AA	S	28800	441	1472	RYE	NY	ITT CONTINENTAL BAKING CO.
AA	N	26000	2161	2408	STAMFORD	CT	COMBUSTION ENGINEERING INC
AA	N	23000	1549	1636	HARRISBURG	PA	AMP INC.
AA	N	20000	1251	1579	NEW YORK	NY	COLT INDUSTRIES INC
AA	N	19000	2593	1830	ALLENTOWN	PA	AIR PRODUCTS & CHEMICALS INC
AA	N	18000	1030	1368	NEW YORK	NY	MARSH & MCLENNAN COMPANIES INC
AA	N	17000	21749	3139	NEW YORK	NY	HUTTON (E.F.) GROUP INC
AA	N	15000	1197	2035	HERSHEY	PA	HERSHEY FOODS CORP
AA	N	14000	1968	1935	STAMFORD	CT	GREAT NORTHERN NEKOOSA CORP
AA	A	13000	78	236	WILTON	CT	FOTOMAT CORP
AA	N	11000	627	696	GARDEN CITY	NY	ESSELTE BUSINESS SYSTEMS
AA	A	11000	30	1	PHILADELPHIA	PA	CSS INDUSTRIES INC.
AA	N	9900	959	1013	PHILADELPHIA	PA	PENNWALT CORP
AA	N	9100	6148	2081	HARTFORD	CT	NORTHEAST UTILITIES
AA	A	9000	32	137	NEW YORK	NY	INTERNATIONAL SERVICE SYSTEM INC.
AA	S	8700	4899	1756	HARTFORD	CT	CONNECTICUT LIGHT & POWER CO.
AA	N	8000	671	884	NEW YORK	NY	SUN CHEMICAL CORP
AA	S	7200	320	428	PITTSBURGH	PA	EASTERN ASSOCIATED COAL CORP
AA	N	7200	311	296	DANBURY	CT	GROLIER INC
AA	O	6800	659	506	KING OF PRUSSIA	PA	UNIVERSAL HEALTH SERVICES INC
AA	N	6600	2085	684	NEW YORK	NY	NEWMONT MINING CORP
AA	N	6600	143	462	NEW YORK	NY	AMERICAN BAKERIES CO.
AA	N	6400	385	465	MURRAY HILL	NJ	BARD (C.R.) INC.
AA	N	6300	86601	27896	NEW YORK	NY	SALOMON INC.
AA	C	6300	7923	1392	HARTFORD	CT	CONNECTICUT MUTUAL LIFE INS. CO.
AA	S	6300	1325	763	STAMFORD	CT	ITT RAYONIER INC
AA	N	5400	393	537	NEW YORK	NY	BAIRNCO CORP.
AA	N	4900	327	341	LATROBE	PA	KENNAMETAL INC
AA	O	4800	390	1490	NEW YORK	NY	GRAYBAR ELECTRIC CO. INC.
AA	N	4300	879	732	WAYNE	NJ	GAF CORP
AA	N	4100	999	584	STAMFORD	CT	MOORE MCCORMACK RESOURCES INC
AA	O	3900	61	73	DANBURY	CT	BARDEN CORP

Arthur Young

Aud1	Trd	Emp	Ast	Sls	Cty	Sta	Name
AY	N	164000	41752	55960	NEW YORK	NY	MOBIL CORP.
AY	N	150000	5861	8057	PURCHASE	NY	PEPSICO INC
AY	N	76000	5773	5687	NEW YORK	NY	SPERRY CORP.
AY	N	68000	74777	11850	NEW YORK	NY	AMERICAN EXPRESS CO.
AY	N	41000	1012	3220	NEW YORK	NY	UNITED BRANDS CO
AY	N	41000	2270	2912	NEW YORK	NY	AMERICAN STANDARD INC
AY	N	26000	3008	2941	Westport	CT	CHESEBROUGH PONDS INC
AY	N	25000	2448	3484	NEW YORK	NY	PAN AM CORP.
AY	N	16000	13589	1885	NEW YORK	NY	PAINE WEBBER GROUP INC.
AY	N	14000	829	994	NEW YORK	NY	GENERAL INSTRUMENT CORP
AY	N	14000	1274	1491	NEW YORK	NY	MC GRAW-HILL INC.
AY	N	12000	7986	3350	JERSEY CITY	NJ	FIREMAN'S FUND CORP.
AY	O	12000	2007	1526	WESTPORT	CT	STAUFFER CHEMICAL CO
AY	N	11000	1066	1400	PITTSBURGH	PA	KOPPERS COMPANY INC.
AY	N	11000	177	704	HARTSDALE	NY	INTERSTATE BAKERIES CORP.
AY	N	11000	530	1040	NEW YORK	NY	COLLINS & AIKMAN CORP
AY	O	8300	124	139	PITTSBURGH	PA	PORTER (H.K.) COMPANY#INC.
AY	N	8000	2286	2235	NEW YORK	NY	WARNER COMMUNICATIONS INC
AY	N	8000	6219	7653	NEW YORK	NY	AMERADA HESS CORP
AY	N	8000	1885	1021	NEW YORK	NY	CAPITAL CITIES/ABC INC.
AY	N	8000	587	677	NEW YORK	NY	MACMILLAN INC
AY	O	7600	492	548	GREENWICH	CT	BANGOR PUNTA CORP
AY	N	7100	85	104	PEAPACK	NJ	FEDDERS CORP
AY	N	6600	401	503	NEW YORK	NY	AMETEK INC
AY	O	6500	11080	1043	PHILADELPHIA	PA	CORESTATES FINANCIAL CORP
AY	N	6500	5763	2394	WARREN	NJ	CHUBB CORP
AY	N	5300	406	507	NEW YORK	NY	TODD SHIPYARDS CORP
AY	O	5200	221	383	SECAUCUS	NJ	JONATHAN LOGAN INC
AY	N	4800	254	432	BRISTOL	CT	BARNES GROUP INC.
AY	N	4500	315	354	PITTSBURGH	PA	COPPERWELD CORP
AY	O	4100	162	300	WILLIMANTIC	CT	BRINTEC CORP.
AY	N	3850	269	280	NEW YORK	NY	CLUB MED INC.
AY	N	3800	342	276	ATLANTIC CITY	NJ	BALLY'S PARK PLACE INC
AY	O	3400	206	216	OLD GREENWICH	CT	CONDEC CORP
AY	N	2800	321	168	NEW YORK	NY	WESTERN PACIFIC INDUSTRIES INC
AY	O	2500	65	38	MCAFEE	NJ	GREAT AMERICAN RECREATION INC.
AY	N	2400	862	473	PITTSBURGH	PA	EQUITABLE RESOURCES INC.
AY	S	1800	298	136	CARLISLE	PA	UNITED TELEPHONE CO. OF PENN.
AY	N	1400	130	150	STAMFORD	CT	CONRAC CORP
AY	O	1300	382	196	NEW YORK	NY	LIN BROADCASTING CORP
AY	O	1200	2035	181	LINWOOD	NJ	NATIONAL COMMUNITY BANK OF NJ.
AY	N	1200	352	534	NEW YORK	NY	ARROW ELECTRONICS INC
AY	O	1200	84	105	MONTGOMERY	PA	AEL INDUSTRIES INC
AY	N	1100	176	41	OLD GREENWICH	CT	CLABIR CORP.

Coopers & Lybrand

Aud1	Trd	Emp	Ast	Sls	Cty	Sta	Name
CL	S	338000	40463	34910	BERKELEY HEIGHTS	NJ	AT & T TECHNOLOGIES INC.
CL	N	338000	40463	34910	BERKELEY HEIGHTS	NJ	AMERICAN TELEPHONE & TELEGRAPH
CL	N	114000	17429	15964	NEW YORK	NY	PHILIP MORRIS INC
CL	N	92000	21000	10314	NEW YORK	NY	NYNEX CORP.
CL	N	79000	19788	9084	PHILADELPHIA	PA	BELL ATLANTIC CORP.
CL	N	77000	4926	7308	NEW YORK	NY	AMERICAN BRANDS INC
CL	N	75000	5095	6421	NEW BRUNSWICK	NJ	JOHNSON & JOHNSON
CL	N	56000	2673	2772	NEW YORK	NY	DUN & BRADSTREET CORP.
CL	S	55000	13664	7055	NEW YORK	NY	NEW YORK TELEPHONE CO.
CL	N	46000	834	1026	NEW YORK	NY	OGDEN CORP
CL	N	45000	2474	4048	PITTSBURGH	PA	HEINZ (H J) CO
CL	O	43000	21284	28503	PITTSBURGH	PA	GULF CORP
CL	N	40000	6354	5163	PITTSBURGH	PA	ALUMINUM COMPANY OF AMERICA
CL	C	39000	6568	3208	PHILADELPHIA	PA	CONSOLIDATED RAIL CORP.
CL	N	38000	12923	13769	RADNOR	PA	SUN COMPANY INC
CL	S	33000	5365	2444	PHILADELPHIA	PA	BELL TELPHONE CO OF PA
CL	N	31000	41642	14594	HARTFORD	CT	TRAVELERS CORP
CL	N	28000	3509	4677	NEW YORK	NY	CBS INC.
CL	N	26000	3084	2855	GREENWICH	CT	AMERICAN CAN CO
CL	N	25000	15571	5782	NEW YORK	NY	AMERICAN INTERNATIONAL GROUP
CL	S	22000	5168	2504	NEWARK	NJ	NEW JERSEY BELL TELEPHONE CO.
CL	C	18000	1360	4067	Syracuse	NY	AGWAY INC
CL	N	15000	520	321	NEW YORK	NY	STONE & WEBSTER INC.
CL	N	15000	683	1449	ROCKY HILL	CT	AMES DEPARTMENT STORES INC
CL	N	14000	6176	2870	PARSIPPANY	NJ	GENERAL PUBLIC UTILITIES
CL	N	14000	2424	1304	NEW HAVEN	CT	SOUTHERN NEW ENGLAND TELEPHONE
CL	N	14000	1017	1228	LIVINGSTON	NJ	FOSTER WHEELER CORP
CL	N	12000	1597	1423	NEW YORK	NY	NL INDUSTRIES INC
CL	N	12000	824	1261	CAMP HILL	PA	HARSCO CORP
CL	N	12000	3561	1789	GREENWICH	CT	AMAX INC
CL	N	11000	10165	3014	PHILADELPHIA	PA	PHILADELPHIA ELECTRIC CO.
CL	N	8200	1745	1167	JERSEY CITY	NJ	ASARCO INC.
CL	C	7500	9284	1655	NEW YORK	NY	MUTUAL LIFE INSURANCE CO OF NY
CL	O	7200	10355	889	EDISON	NJ	MIDLANTIC BANKS INC
CL	N	6900	1177	1039	NEW YORK	NY	DOW JONES & COMPANY INC
CL	N	6800	936	2264	EDISON	NJ	ENGELHARD CORP
CL	N	6700	1313	872	GREENWICH	CT	LONE STAR INDUSTRIES INC
CL	N	6100	696	664	NEW YORK	NY	LORAL CORP
CL	N	6000	649	974	OIL CITY	PA	QUAKER STATE OIL REFINING CORP
CL	X	6000	324	333	ALBANY	NY	ALBANY INTERNATIONAL CORP
CL	N	5800	84	112	TRUMBULL	CT	RAYMARK CORP
CL	N	5500	485	633	WINDSOR LOCKS	CT	DEXTER CORP
CL	N	5200	207	290	NEWTON	PA	SPS TECHNOLOGIES INC.
CL	N	5200	188	252	ONEIDA	NY	ONEIDA LTD.

Deloitte Haskins & Sells

Aud1	Trd	Emp	Ast	Sls	Cty	Sta	Name
DHS	N	811000	63832	96372	NEW YORK	NY	GENERAL MOTORS CORP
DHS	N	123000	7333	11338	PITTSBURGH	PA	ROCKWELL INTERNATIONAL CORP
DHS	N	79000	1329	2152	NEW YORK	NY	TRANSWORLD CORP.
DHS	N	65000	1608	6615	MONTVALE	NJ	GREAT ATLANTIC & PACIFIC TEA CO
DHS	O	57000	2262	2183	NEW YORK	NY	RAPID AMERICAN CORP
DHS	N	44000	10710	7798	NEW YORK	NY	UNION PACIFIC CORP
DHS	N	44000	48117	7117	New York	NY	MERRILL LYNCH & CO INC
DHS	X	43000	3653	4942	STAMFORD	CT	CONTINENTAL GROUP
DHS	N	38000	4084	4346	PITTSBURGH	PA	PPG INDUSTRIES INC
DHS	C	38000	76494	7316	NEW YORK	NY	METROPOLITAN LIFE INSURANCE
DHS	S	32000	1565	1038	NEW YORK	NY	MC CRORY CORP.
DHS	N	31000	2874	2527	Greenwich	CT	PENN CENTRAL CORP.
DHS	C	30000	47990	2595	NEW YORK	NY	EQUITABLE LIFE ASSURANCE
DHS	N	30000	1523	1775	HARTFORD	CT	EMHART CORP
DHS	N	29000	2769	3725	NEW YORK	NY	TRANS WORLD AIRLINES INC.
DHS	N	24000	2773	1927	KENILWORTH	NJ	SCHERING-PLOUGH CORP
DHS	N	20000	1523	2115	MIDDLEBURY	CT	UNIROYAL INC
DHS	N	17000	2127	914	NEW YORK	NY	ALEXANDER & ALEXANDER SERVICES
DHS	O	14000	1062	2063	ALLENTOWN	PA	MACK TRUCKS INC.
DHS	N	14000	10487	4409	NEWARK	NJ	PUBLIC SERVICE ELECTRIC & GAS CO
DHS	N	12000	460	1099	NEW YORK	NY	CRANE CO
DHS	N	12000	533	1039	NEW YORK	NY	FISCHBACH CORP.
DHS	N	10000	382	640	NEW YORK	NY	LOWENSTEIN (M.) CORP.
DHS	A	10000	1296	1394	NEW YORK	NY	NEW YORK TIMES CO.
DHS	N	8400	6966	1977	ALLENTOWN	PA	PENNSYLVANIA POWER & LIGHT CO
DHS	N	7600	391	614	PITTSBURGH	PA	ROBERTSON (H.H.) CO.
DHS	S	7100	1252	1305	GREENWICH	CT	PENNSYLVANIA CO
DHS	N	5700	918	784	MONTVALE	NJ	FEDERAL PAPER BOARD CO INC
DHS	N	4700	3854	915	PITTSBURGH	PA	DUQUESNE LIGHT CO
DHS	C	4500	3172	1771	NEW YORK	NY	GUARDIAN OF AMERICA LIFE INSURANCE
DHS	N	4500	2019	2370	PITTSBURGH	PA	NATIONAL INTERGROUP INC
DHS	A	4500	63	164	NEW YORK	NY	RESTAURANT ASSOCIATES INDUSTRIES I
DHS	S	4100	113	269	NEW YORK	NY	NEWBERRY (J.J.) CO.
DHS	A	4000	203	439	SADDLE BROOK	NJ	MICHIGAN GENERAL CORP
DHS	N	3700	115	211	WHITE PLAINS	NY	IPCO CORP.
DHS	O	3200	297	324	New York	NY	GOULDS PUMPS INC
DHS	N	3200	268	408	NEW YORK	NY	CHICAGO PNEUMATIC TOOL CO
DHS	A	3100	846	150	NEW YORK	NY	FIDATA CORP.
DHS	N	3100	45531	2452	NEW YORK	NY	FIRST BOSTON INC.
DHS	A	2700	59	118	ROCHESTER	NY	CHAMPION PRODUCTS INC
DHS	N	2100	1300	580	PLEASANTVILLE	NJ	ATLANTIC CITY ELECTRIC CO
DHS	A	2100	151	247	MILFORD	CT	BIC CORP
DHS	N	1800	136	128	WHITE PLAINS	NY	SERVICE RESOURCES CORP.
DHS	A	1400	86	185	BUFFALO	NY	PRATT & LAMBERT INC.

Ernst & Whinney

Aud1	Trd	Emp	Ast	Sls	Cty	Sta	Name
EW	N	33000	860	1481	WYOMISSING	PA	VF CORP
EW	N	27000	1200	1858	NEW YORK	NY	STEVENS (J.P.) & CO.
EW	N	19000	3072	3404	NEW YORK	NY	TIME INC
EW	O	18000	3305	3267	PITTSBURGH	PA	JONES & LAUGHLIN STEEL CORP
EW	N	18000	1288	3823	VALLEY FORGE	PA	ALCO STANDARD CORP
EW	H	17000	1241	1144	PARAMUS	NJ	BECTON DICKINSON & CO.
EW	N	15000	778	1208	NEW BRITAIN	CT	STANLEY WORKS
EW	O	15000	689	1076	STAMFORD	CT	UNITED STATES INDUSTRIES INC
EW	N	15000	4064	3844	NEW YORK	NY	GULF & WESTERN INDUSTRIES INC.
EW	X	10000	106	342	NEW YORK	NY	SELIGMAN & LATZ INC
EW	N	8700	1966	1634	EDISON	NJ	SEA-LAND CORP.
EW	O	8400	18778	1790	PITTSBURGH	PA	PNC FINANCIAL CORP.
EW	N	8011	578	768	NEW HAVEN	CT	ARMSTRONG RUBBER CO.
EW	O	8000	309	410	NEW YORK	NY	VOLT INFORMATION SCIENCES INC
EW	N	8000	810	1449	NEW YORK	NY	WITCO CORP.
EW	N	7700	278	591	NEW YORK	NY	PHILLIPS VAN HEUSEN CORP
EW	N	7400	763	1110	VALLEY FORGE	PA	CERTAINTEED CORP
EW	S	7400	6815	1175	NEW YORK	NY	ASSOCIATES FIRST CAPITAL CORP.
EW	O	7000	362	1764	CENTRAL ISLIP	NY	WALDBAUM INC.
EW	O	6500	62	42	NEW YORK	NY	PANEX INDUSTRIES INC.
EW	N	6100	7122	707	ALBANY	NY	KEY CORP.
EW	N	6000	172	597	GREAT NECK	NY	PUEBLO INTERNATIONAL INC
EW	S	6000	6638	1151	NEW YORK	NY	ASSOCIATES CORP. OF NORTH AMER.
EW	O	5900	431	631	PHILADELPHIA	PA	STRAWBRIDGE & CLOTHIER
EW	N	5700	5620	547	ALBANY	NY	KEY BANKS INC.
EW	N	5600	7954	2034	MINEOLA	NY	LONG ISLAND LIGHTING CO
EW	S	5600	6862	729	HARTFORD	CT	CBT CORP.
EW	C	5600	9444	1423	NEWARK	NJ	MUTUAL BENEFIT LIFE INSURANCE
EW	S	4900	219	300	PRINCETON	NJ	DE LAVAL TURBINE
EW	N	4800	238	269	NEW YORK	NY	UNITED INDUSTRIAL CORP
EW	O	4100	186	266	NEW YORK	NY	AMERACE CORP
EW	N	3900	186	229	ROCHESTER	NY	GLEASON CORP
EW	N	3700	468	478	GREENWICH	CT	UNITED STATES TOBACCO CO
EW	O	3600	266	404	INDIANA	PA	ROCHESTER & PITTSBURGH COAL CO
EW	N	3600	301	345	ERIE	PA	ZURN INDUSTRIES INC
EW	S	3500	132	178	NEW YORK	NY	AMERICAN BANK NOTE CO.
EW	N	3300	87	148	PRINCETON	NJ	GULTON INDUSTRIES INC
EW	O	3000	183	392	CORNWELL HEIGHTS	PA	CHARMING SHOPPES INC
EW	A	2600	95	125	ROGERS	CT	ROGERS CORP
EW	B	2300	97	91	NEW YORK	NY	CROMPTON COMPANY
EW	A	2300	123	136	LAKE SUCCESS	NY	VERNITRON CORP
EW	O	2200	254	319	TREVOSE	PA	BETZ LABORATORIES INC
EW	A	2100	83	199	CARLISLE	PA	MASLAND INDUSTRIES
EW	O	2000	246	204	NEW YORK	NY	GREY ADVERTISING INC

KMG Main Hurdman

Aud1	Trd	Emp	Ast	Sls	Cty	Sta	Name
MH	N	91000	10581	9003	DANBURY	CT	UNION CARBIDE CORP
MH	N	52000	2643	4395	NEW YORK	NY	NORTH AMERICAN PHILIPS CORP
MH	N	39000	4463	4025	NEW YORK	NY	PFIZER INC
MH	N	39000	3017	4210	ENGLEWOOD CLIFFS	NJ	CPC INTERNATIONAL INC
MH	N	38000	2289	2470	NEW YORK	NY	AVON PRODUCTS INC
MH	N	17000	756	1543	SHIREMANSTOWN	PA	RITE AID CORP
MH	N	13000	729	795	NEW YORK	NY	UNITED MERCHANTS & MFGRS INC.
MH	N	13000	542	893	PITTSBURGH	PA	DRAVO CORP
MH	N	5700	471	557	NEW YORK	NY	HANDY & HARMAN
MH	N	5000	236	311	STAMFORD	CT	KOLLMORGEN CORP
MH	N	4400	112	50	NEW YORK	NY	LEHIGH VALLEY INDUSTRIES INC
MH	O	3100	49	163	BROOKLYN	NY	TSS-SEEDMAN'S INCORPORATED
MH	N	2500	175	243	LONG ISLAND CITY	NY	STANDARD MOTOR PRODUCTS INC
MH	A	2400	215	118	NEW YORK	NY	NATIONAL PATENT DEVELOPMENT CORP
MH	O	2300	53	164	SECAUCUS	NJ	NPS TECHNOLOGIES GROUP INC
MH	O	2000	98	163	DOWINGTON	PA	CHEMICAL LEAMAN CORP
MH	A	1850	455	501	SHELTON	CT	TIE COMMUNICATIONS INC.
MH	A	1700	46	68	NORTH BERGEN	NJ	DURO - TEST CORP.
MH	S	1700	103	170	BETHPAGE	NY	GRUMMAN AMERICAN AVIATION CORP
MH	N	1500	100	208	NEW YORK	NY	WILLCOX & GIBBS INC
MH	O	1500	2598	251	HARRISBURG	PA	DAUPHIN DEPOSIT CORP.
MH	B	1300	15	26	CARLSTADT	NJ	FRIER INDUSTRIES INC
MH	A	1300	51	31	NORWALK	CT	TRANS LUX CORP
MH	O	1200	15	34	LITTLE FERRY	NJ	VALLEY FAIR CORP
MH	A	1200	52	49	WOODBURY	NY	INTERNATIONAL HYDRON CORP.
MH	O	1100	3614	367	NEW YORK	NY	AMERICAN SAVINGS BANK-FSB
MH	O	1000	21	41	LYNDHURST	NJ	BLASIUS INDUSTRIES INC
MH	B	980	19	93	ALBANY	NY	TOBIN PACKING CO INC
MH	O	961	66	136	BROOKLYN	NY	CRAZY EDDIE
MH	A	900	309	32	WOODBURY	NY	CABLEVISION SYSTEMS CORP.
MH	O	798	75	160	STAMFORD	CT	PETROLEUM HEAT AND POWER CO. INC.
MH	O	758	77	54	LEBANON	PA	ARNOLD INDUSTRIES INC.
MH	O	710	58	244	SYOSSET	NY	MEENAN OIL CO INC
MH	A	610	32	35	GREAT NECK	NY	TECHNODYNE INC.
MH	C	600	538	297	HARLEYSVILLE	PA	HARLEYSVILLE MUTUAL INSURANCE
MH	O	580	54	43	PITTSBURGH	PA	UNION ELECTRIC STEEL CORP
MH	A	550	48	41	SYOSSET	NY	PORTA SYSTEMS CORP
MH	O	524	13	55	BASKING RIDGE	NJ	HOOPER HOLMES INC.
MH	A	475	33	33	GREAT NECK	NY	ELECTRO AUDIO DYNAMICS INC
MH	O	475	53	154	NEW YORK	NY	NICO INC.
MH	O	470	49	48	MERRICK	NY	TOP BRASS ENTERPRISES INC
MH	O	402	45	44	Darien	CT	ACTMEDIA INCORPORATED
MH	O	400	405	44	WOODBURY	NJ	COMMUNITY BANCSHARES CORP
MH	O	390	37	43	BLOOMFIELD	CT	ANDERSEN GROUP

Peat Marwick Mitchell

Aud1	Trd	Emp	Ast	Sls	Cty	Sta	Name
PMM	N	304000	26432	28285	FAIRFIELD	CT	GENERAL ELECTRIC CO
PMM	N	179000	10522	13747	NEW YORK	NY	PENNEY (J.C.) COMPANY INC
PMM	N	102000	9817	8948	STAMFORD	CT	XEROX CORP
PMM	N	81000	173597	22504	NEW YORK	NY	CITICORP
PMM	N	76000	1807	4775	HARRISON	NY	MELVILLE CORP
PMM	L	63000	2678	169	NEW YORK	NY	CITY INVESTING CO. LIQ. TRUST
PMM	N	48000	1392	2416	STAMFORD	CT	SINGER CO
PMM	N	41000	58294	18612	HARTFORD	CT	AETNA LIFE & CASUALTY CO
PMM	N	37000	3405	3536	WAYNE	NJ	AMERICAN CYANAMID CO
PMM	N	33000	1507	2057	PITTSBURGH	PA	ALLEGHENY INTERNATIONAL INC
PMM	N	32000	3733	3257	PHILADELPHIA	PA	SMITHKLINE BECKMAN CORP
PMM	N	32000	75224	8385	NEW YORK	NY	MANUFACTURERS HANOVER CORP
PMM	N	24000	2453	2042	PRINCETON	NJ	SQUIBB CORP
PMM	N	23000	1483	1801	STAMFORD	CT	GENERAL SIGNAL CORP
PMM	N	21000	1093	1679	LANCASTER	PA	ARMSTRONG WORLD INDUSTRIES
PMM	N	20000	2809	3046	NEW YORK	NY	CELANESE CORP
PMM	N	20000	444	800	PISCATAWAY	NJ	PUROLATOR COURIER INC.
PMM	N	17000	11495	5092	NEW YORK	NY	CONTINENTAL CORP
PMM	N	16000	1598	1751	STAMFORD	CT	OLIN CORP
PMM	N	16000	1017	1440	NEW YORK	NY	DOVER CORP
PMM	N	16000	33406	3222	PITTSBURGH	PA	MELLON BANK CORP.
PMM	N	14000	925	1251	GREENWICH	CT	PITTSTON CO
PMM	Z	13000	2335	0	NEW YORK	NY	AMERICAN BROADCASTING COMPANIES
PMM	N	13000	399	760	AMSTERDAM	NY	MOHASCO CORP
PMM	N	12000	1734	2051	PHILADELPHIA	PA	ROHM & HAAS CO
PMM	N	12000	428	1017	SUNBURY	PA	WEIS MARKETS INC
PMM	N	9600	21651	2028	NEW YORK	NY	IRVING BANK CORP.
PMM	O	7500	1066	978	NEWARK	NJ	PEOPLE EXPRESS AIRLINES INC.
PMM	N	7400	8998	882	ALBANY	NY	NORSTAR BANCORP INC.
PMM	B	7200	187	378	NEW YORK	NY	SAXON INDUSTRIES INC
PMM	S	6800	22469	2918	NEW YORK	NY	GENERAL ELECTRIC CREDIT CORP
PMM	A	6000	85	301	PHILADELPHIA	PA	CDI CORP.
PMM	O	5000	6230	658	READING	PA	MERIDIAN BANCORP INC
PMM	O	5000	226	556	BLOOMFIELD	CT	KAMAN CORP
PMM	O	4600	1311	533	SECAUCUS	NJ	METROMEDIA INC
PMM	N	4600	496	823	WHITE PLAINS	NY	REICHHOLD CHEMICALS INC
PMM	O	4500	17153	1537	PHILADELPHIA	PA	PHILADELPHIA SAVINGS FUND SOCIETY
PMM	N	4400	1315	904	DARREN	CT	BOWATER INC.
PMM	O	4300	75	118	STAMFORD	CT	AMERICAN THREAD CO.
PMM	O	4100	328	420	LAKE SUCCESS	NY	TAMBRANDS INC.
PMM	O	4100	150	219	PITTSBURGH	PA	TITANIUM METALS CORP. OF AMERICA
PMM	N	3800	1812	1184	NEW YORK	NY	MC LEAN INDUSTRIES INC.
PMM	N	3800	195	244	STAMFORD	CT	GEO INTERNATIONAL CORP
PMM	S	3800	7967	1084	LIVINGSTON	NJ	C.I.T. FINANCIAL CORPORATION

Price Waterhouse

Aud1	Trd	Emp	Ast	Sls	Cty	Sta	Name
PW	N	406000	52634	50056	ARMONK	NY	INTERNATIONAL BUSINESS MACHINES
PW	N	185000	10528	15749	HARTFORD	CT	UNITED TECHNOLOGIES CORP
PW	N	146000	69160	91620	NEW YORK	NY	EXXON CORP
PW	N	144000	13271	9115	MORRISTOWN	NJ	ALLIED-SIGNAL INC.
PW	N	129000	12143	10631	ROCHESTER	NY	EASTMAN KODAK CO
PW	N	126000	9682	10700	PITTSBURGH	PA	WESTINGHOUSE ELECTRIC CORP
PW	N	118000	2535	5958	NEW YORK	NY	WOOLWORTH (F W) CO
PW	N	117000	5421	7260	NEW YORK	NY	GRACE (W.R.) & CO.
PW	N	80000	11282	6119	NEW YORK	NY	SCHLUMBERGER LTD
PW	N	80000	18446	18429	PITTSBURGH	PA	UNITED STATES STEEL CORP
PW	N	49000	45000	16197	PHILADELPHIA	PA	CIGNA CORP.
PW	N	45000	4743	5118	BETHLEHEM	PA	BETHLEHEM STEEL CORP
PW	N	45000	87685	9733	NEW YORK	NY	CHASE MANHATTAN CORP
PW	N	45000	2438	3989	CAMDEN	NJ	CAMPBELL SOUP CO
PW	N	40000	3870	4815	MIAMI	NY	EASTERN AIR LINES INC
PW	N	40000	2358	3200	MORRIS PLAINS	NJ	WARNER-LAMBERT CO
PW	N	36000	3721	4444	NEW YORK	NY	BRISTOL MYERS CO
PW	N	34000	2243	2637	WOODCLIFF LAKE	NJ	INGERSOLL-RAND CO.
PW	N	33000	2932	4716	NEW YORK	NY	BORDEN INC
PW	O	31000	585	2529	ELMWOOD PARK	NJ	GRAND UNION CO
PW	N	30000	2313	2209	WASHINGTON	NY	GANNETT CO INC
PW	N	29000	1763	1832	STAMFORD	CT	PITNEY BOWES INC
PW	N	26000	2032	1691	CORNING	NY	CORNING GLASS WORKS
PW	N	22000	3517	3050	PHILADELPHIA	PA	SCOTT PAPER CO.
PW	N	22000	8945	5498	NEW YORK	NY	CONSOLIDATED EDISON CO OF N.Y.
PW	N	21000	1618	1848	NEW YORK	NY	STERLING DRUG INC
PW	S	21000	624	2529	NORTH DARIEN	CT	CAVENHAM (USA) INC
PW	N	20000	56990	5651	NEW YORK	NY	CHEMICAL NEW YORK CORP
PW	C	19000	27978	3830	NEW YORK	NY	NEW YORK LIFE INSURANCE
PW	N	18000	2661	1866	WAYNE	NJ	UNION CAMP CORP
PW	N	16000	1135	1305	NORWALK	CT	PERKIN ELMER CORP
PW	N	15000	1923	1722	NEW YORK	NY	WESTVACO CORP
PW	N	14000	2259	1134	UPPER SADDLE RIVE	NJ	WESTERN UNION CORP
PW	N	13000	69375	6575	NEW YORK	NY	MORGAN (J.P.) & CO. INC.
PW	N	13000	866	1487	PHILADELPHIA	PA	CROWN CORK & SEAL CO INC
PW	N	12200	802	691	NEW YORK	NY	INTERPUBLIC GROUP OF COMPANIES
PW	N	12000	23386	2495	BUFFALO	NY	MARINE MIDLAND BANKS INC
PW	N	12000	1278	1877	ERIE	PA	HAMMERMILL PAPER CO
PW	S	12000	22246	3922	BLOOMFIELD	CT	CONNECTICUT GENERAL LIFE
PW	N	11000	7014	2695	SYRACUSE	NY	NIAGARA MOHAWK POWER CORP
PW	N	11000	2020	2289	NEW YORK	NY	NATIONAL DISTILLERS & CHEMICAL
PW	N	11000	307	591	BRIDGEPORT	CT	WARNACO INC
PW	N	11000	50581	4699	NEW YORK	NY	BANKERS TRUST NEW YORK CORP
PW	N	11000	546	564	STAMFORD	CT	GENERAL HOST CORP

Touche Ross

Aud1	Trd	Emp	Ast	Sls	Cty	Sta	Name
TR	X	152000	4162	7687	GREENWICH	CT	UNITED PARCEL SERVICE
TR	N	97000	87000	8972	NEW YORK	NY	RCA CORP
TR	N	64000	2772	4135	NEW YORK	NY	ALLIED STORES CORP
TR	N	64000	2289	4385	NEW YORK	NY	ASSOCIATED DRY GOODS CORP
TR	C	61000	91139	14332	NEWARK	NJ	PRUDENTIAL INS. CO. OF AMERICA
TR	N	55000	2357	4368	NEW YORK	NY	MACY (R.H.) & CO. INC.
TR	N	49000	1104	5123	WOODBRIDGE	NJ	SUPERMARKETS GENERAL CORP
TR	N	22000	16120	6700	NEW YORK	NY	LOEWS CORP
TR	N	18000	1018	1030	ROSELAND	NJ	AUTOMATIC DATA PROCESSING INC.
TR	N	12000	1478	1693	NEW BRUNSWICK	NJ	TRIANGLE INDUSTRIES INC
TR	S	12000	267	700	NEW YORK	NY	LERNER STORES CORP.
TR	N	11000	178	520	NEW YORK	NY	ALEXANDERS INC
TR	N	10000	960	772	STAMFORD	CT	ERBAMONT N.V.
TR	O	9800	5057	2517	NEW YORK	NY	RELIANCE GROUP HOLDINGS INC.
TR	N	8100	554	982	NEW YORK	NY	BLAIR (JOHN) & CO.
TR	S	7700	3436	2064	NEW YORK	NY	RELIANCE FINANCIAL SERVICES CORP.
TR	N	7500	18486	1594	NEW YORK	NY	BANK OF NEW YORK COMPANY INC
TR	N	7000	1219	417	BRIARCLIFF MANOR	NY	HALL (FRANK B.) & CO. INC.
TR	N	6800	27	69	JERSEY CITY	NJ	MARCADE GROUP INC.
TR	N	6100	214	472	NEW YORK	NY	MANHATTAN INDUSTRIES INC
TR	A	4900	67	117	HILLSIDE	NJ	SERVISCO
TR	A	4900	34	56	Plainview	NY	PROFESSIONAL CARE INC.
TR	A	4200	109	557	BRONX	NY	SHOPWELL INC
TR	N	3828	215	219	NORWALK	CT	BURNDY CORP
TR	N	3600	1283	440	NEW YORK	NY	INTEGRATED RESOURCES INC
TR	O	3600	201	435	DUNDEE	NY	PIERCE (S.S.) CO. INC.
TR	O	3400	118	64	GREENWICH	CT	NATIONAL (THE) GUARDIAN CORP.
TR	O	3300	141	469	DANBURY	CT	COMSTOCK GROUP INC.
TR	X	3200	163	768	TARRYTOWN	NY	KANE MILLER CORP
TR	N	3100	132	367	LIVERPOOL	NY	FAYS DRUG COMPANY INC
TR	O	3000	13	48	PITTSBURGH	PA	ALLIED SECURITY INC
TR	N	2700	93	144	NEW YORK	NY	SALANT CORP
TR	N	2700	180	390	PITTSBURGH	PA	GENERAL NUTRITION INC
TR	N	2500	117	314	MONTVALE	NJ	BUTLER INTERNATIONAL INC
TR	O	2500	39	73	BALA CYNWYD	PA	VESPER CORP.
TR	N	2400	71	129	SHELTON	CT	FRIGITRONICS INC
TR	N	2300	149	224	FORT WASHINGTON	PA	SAFEGUARD BUSINESS SYSTEMS INC
TR	A	2300	145	143	PENNSAUKEN	NJ	MEDIQ INC.
TR	O	2200	45	55	NEW YORK	NY	VISTA RESOURCES INC.
TR	A	2200	75	138	NEW CASTLE	PA	UNIVERSAL RUNDLE CORP
TR	O	1900	119	148	JACKSON HEIGHTS	NY	BULOVA WATCH CO INC
TR	A	1800	55	97	NEW YORK	NY	EAGLE CLOTHES INC.
TR	O	1800	206	156	TEANECK	NJ	GRAPHIC SCANNING CORP
TR	O	1800	30	103	STAMFORD	CT	DRESS BARN INC.

Offices By Firm - Mid-Atlantic Region

CITY	ST	AA	AY	CL	DHS	EW	KMG	PMM	PW	TR
Baltimore	MD	1	1	1	1	1	1	1	1	1
Bethesda	MD								1	
Boone	NC				1					
Charleston	SC		1							
Charleston	WV					1	1			
Charlotte	NC	1	1	1	1	1	1	1	1	1
Clarksburg	WV						1			
Columbia	MD							1		
Columbia	SC	1	1	1	1	1			1	
Durham	NC									1
Greensboro	NC	1			1			1		1
Greenville	SC		1		1	1		1	1	
Hagerstown	MD						1			
Hickory	NC				1					
Lenoir	NC				1					
Lynchburg	VA			1						
Morgantown	NC				1					
Newport News	VA			1						
Norfolk	VA		1	1		1		1	1	
Raleigh	NC	1		1	1	1		1	1	1
Reston	VA		1							
Richmond	VA		1	1	1	1		1	1	1
Roanoke	VA				1			1		
Salisbury	MD							1		
Sanford	NC				1					

CITY	ST	AA	AY	CL	DHS	EW	KMG	PMM	PW	TR
Southern Pines	NC				1					
Spartanburg	NC					1				
Vienna	VA							1		
Washington	DC	1	1	1	1	1	1	1	1	1
Wilmington	DE				1			1	1	
Winston-Salem	NC					1			1	1
TOTALS		6	9	9	16	11	7	12	11	8

Market Share Leadership
Mid-Atlantic Region

CITY or AREA	ST	Firm	Firm	Firm	Firm
Baltimore	MD	EW	PMM		
Charlotte	NC	AA	DHS	EW	
Columbia	SC	AA	PW		
Raleigh	NC	EW	PMM		
Richmond	VA	AY	CL	EW	PMM
Washington	DC	AA	EW	PMM	PW

Personnel By Region

Mid-Atlantic Region

Region	AA	AY	CL	DHS	EW	KMG	PMM	PW	TR
Mid-Atlantic	875	525	675	725	975	175	1025	830	375

Major Clients By Firm

Mid-Atlantic Region

```
Audl = Principal Accountants

Trd  = Shows the where traded status of company shares
            A - American Stock Exchange
            N - New York Stock Exchange
            O - Over the Counter
            B - Company in some condition of bankruptcy
            C - Co-op or mutual
            L - Company in liquidation
            S - Subsidiary which reports separately
            U - Subsidiary whose auditor is different from parent
            X - Company which has gone private

Emp  = Number of employees

Name = Company name

SIC  = Four digit Standard Industrial Classification

Sta  = State

Ast  = Assets

Sls  = Sales
```

Arthur Andersen

Aud1	Trd	Emp	Ast	Sls	Cty	Sta	Name
AA	N	137000	3664	4242	BETHESTA	MD	MARRIOTT CORP
AA	N	22000	1151	1880	WILMINGTON	DE	MERCANTILE STORES CO INC
AA	N	18000	579	454	SILVER SPRING	MD	MANOR CARE INC
AA	N	12000	5835	4053	WILMINGTON	DE	COLUMBIA GAS SYSTEM INC
AA	N	11000	1178	1276	YORKLYN	DE	NVF CO
AA	N	8600	277	640	MCLEAN	VA	DYNALECTRON CORP
AA	N	8200	250	523	CHERRYVILLE	NC	CAROLINA FREIGHT CORP
AA	O	5800	207	350	PRESTON	MD	PRESTON CORP.
AA	S	5600	997	425	DURHAM	NC	GENERAL TELEPHONE CO OF SOUTHEAST
AA	O	5300	185	255	GRANITEVILLE	SC	GRANITEVILLE CO
AA	N	5100	167	541	BALTIMORE	MD	EASCO CORP
AA	N	4700	1557	1872	Mclean	VA	PRIMARK
AA	O	4300	119	669	ARLINGTON	VA	SMITHFIELD FOODS INC
AA	O	4200	5726	551	WASHINGTON	DC	FIRST AMERICAN BANKSHARES
AA	A	4200	227	730	CHARLOTTE	NC	RUDDICK CORP
AA	A	3800	118	250	MCLEAN	VA	BDM INTERNATIONAL INC.
AA	N	3400	759	801	WASHINGTON	DC	WASHINGTON GAS LIGHT CO
AA	S	3000	541	211	DURHAM	NC	GENERAL TELEPHONE CO OF KENTUCKY
AA	N	2400	269	305	Washington	DC	DANAHER CORP.
AA	N	2100	225	357	GREENSBORO	NC	GUILFORD MILLS INC
AA	A	1900	91	191	SPRUCE PINE	NC	RAGAN BRAD INC
AA	O	1900	5434	471	WASHINGTON	DC	RIGGS NATIONAL CORP.
AA	N	1900	109	144	MCLEAN	VA	FLOW GENERAL INC
AA	O	1500	73	118	WASHINGTON	DC	SYSCON CORP
AA	O	1400	46	87	ALEXANDRIA	VA	VSE CORP
AA	O	1300	1467	154	LUMBERTON	NC	SOUTHERN NATIONAL CORP
AA	O	1100	4073	457	ALEXANDRIA	VA	PERPETUAL AMERICAN BANK F.S.B.
AA	O	957	226	215	GASTONIA	NC	PUBLIC SERVICE CO OF NORTH CAR.
AA	O	850	103	120	LANDOVER	MD	CROWN BOOKS CORPORATION
AA	O	800	2337	235	MCLEAN	VA	FIRST AMERICAN BANK OF VIRGINIA
AA	O	650	30	38	CHAPEL HILL	NC	KENAN TRANSPORT CO.
AA	O	640	135	270	CHARLESTON	WV	ALLEGHENY & WESTERN ENERGY CORP.
AA	O	591	40	67	COLUMBIA	MD	GENERAL PHYSICS CORP.
AA	O	470	18	38	JESSUP	MD	CLASSIC CORP.
AA	O	400	98	164	FAYETTEVILLE	NC	NORTH CAROLINA NATURAL GAS CORP
AA	O	389	9509	20	ALEXANDRIA	VA	BOAT AMERICA CORPORATION
AA	O	366	16	31	SPARKS	MD	E.I.L. INSTRUMENTS INC.
AA	O	356	29	33	CHARLOTTE	NC	SYSTEMS ASSOCIATES INC.
AA	O	340	75	79	LANDOVER	MD	TRAK AUTO CORP
AA	O	325	1104	215	WASHINGTON	DC	UNITED SERVICES LIFE INSURANCE COS
AA	O	224	10	11	ANDREWS	SC	PHOENIX MEDICAL TECHNOLOGY INC.
AA	O	192	261	32	WILMINGTON	DE	TSO FINANCIAL CORP.
AA	O	141	1	1	RESTON	VA	SCOPE INC
AA	O	134	20	18	VIENNA	VA	VM SOFTWARE INC.

Arthur Young

Aud1	Trd	Emp	Ast	Sls	Cty	Sta	Name
AY	N	14000	488	1070	RICHMOND	VA	UNIVERSAL LEAF TOBACCO CO INC
AY	N	10000	373	586	EDEN	NC	FIELDCREST MILLS INC
AY	N	8600	301	470	RICHMOND	VA	OVERNITE TRANSPORTATION CO
AY	A	7000	688	579	RICHMOND	VA	MEDIA GENERAL INC
AY	S	4400	836	439	TARBORO	NC	CAROLINA TELEPHONE & TELEGRAPH
AY	A	4000	441	645	ALEXANDRIA	VA	KAY CORP
AY	O	1700	200	382	BALTIMORE	MD	NOXELL CORP
AY	A	1400	225	168	HUNT VALLEY	MD	GENERAL DEFENSE CORP
AY	O	1400	979	182	RICHMOND	VA	HOME BENEFICIAL CORP
AY	A	1400	158	208	ALEXANDRIA	VA	KAY JEWELERS INC.
AY	N	800	14450	1283	WASHINGTON	DC	SALLIE MAE
AY	O	680	71	56	WASHINGTON	DC	TRT COMMUNICATIONS INC.
AY	B	606	9	30	FAIRFAX	VA	ERNST (E.C.) INC
AY	O	515	57	67	BLUEFIELD	WV	BLUEFIELD SUPPLY CO.
AY	O	507	27	39	SILVER SPRING	MD	COMPUTER ENTRY SYSTEMS CORP.
AY	O	390	28	51	ROCKVILLE	MD	MBI BUSINESS CENTERS INC.
AY	O	265	636	69	CHARLESTON	SC	FIRST FEDERAL S & L OF CHARLESTON
AY	O	170	1	17	Mechaniesville	VA	CONSUMAT SYSTEMS INC.
AY	O	138	32	21	WINSTON SALEM	NC	SALEM NATIONAL CORP.
AY	O	41	1	1	ALEXANDRIA	VA	SPORTING (THE) LIFE INC.
AY	S	27	6708	1150	WILMINGTON	DE	AMERICAN EXPRESS CREDIT CORP
AY	O	22	1	1	KENSINGTON	MD	APPLIED OPTICS
AY	O	8	1	1	BALTIMORE	MD	TOXICOM TECHNOLOGIES INC.
AY	O	0	1	1	CHANTILLY	VA	VERDIX CORP.
AY	O	0	1	1	WASHINGTON	DC	WESTERN CENTERS EQUITY TRUST
AY	O	0	131	1	RICHMOND	VA	UNITED DOMINION REALTY TRUST
AY	O	0	101	11	MARTINSBURG	WV	SHENANDOAH FEDERAL SAVINGS BANK
AY	O	0	149	16	VIENNA	VA	PROVIDENCE SAVINGS & LOAN ASSOC.

Coopers & Lybrand

Aud1	Trd	Emp	Ast	Sls	Cty	Sta	Name
CL	N	26000	2659	2587	WILMINGTON	DE	HERCULES INC
CL	N	22000	1741	2492	RICHMOND	VA	JAMES RIVER CORPORATION OF VA.
CL	S	16000	2747	1211	BALTIMORE	MD	CHESAPEAKE & POTOMAC TEL CO (MD)
CL	O	15000	440	1866	SALISBURY	NC	FOOD LION INC
CL	N	13000	8481	2712	RICHMOND	VA	DOMINION RESOURCES INC. (VA)
CL	S	12000	2804	1260	RICHMOND	VA	CHESAPEAKE & POTOMAC TEL CO (VA)
CL	O	12000	7678	2612	RICHMOND	VA	VIRGINIA ELECTRIC & POWER CO
CL	O	12000	501	870	HARTSVILLE	SC	SONOCO PRODUCTS CO
CL	N	11000	1556	1548	RICHMOND	VA	ETHYL CORP
CL	N	9100	4183	1755	BALTIMORE	MD	BALTIMORE GAS & ELECTRIC CO
CL	N	9100	7674	3556	BALTIMORE	MD	USF & G CORP.
CL	N	5600	186	372	MCLEAN	VA	PLANNING RESEARCH CORP
CL	N	4500	618	454	WEST POINT	VA	CHESAPEAKE CORP OF VIRGINIA
CL	O	4400	893	406	WASHINGTON	DC	CHESAPEAKE & POTOMAC TEL. CO. (DC)
CL	S	4200	1046	457	CHARLESTON	WV	CHESAPEAKE & POTOMAC TEL CO OF WVA
CL	N	2600	1675	723	WILMINGTON	DE	DELMARVA POWER & LIGHT CO
CL	O	2600	59	98	MARTINSVILLE	VA	AMERICAN FURNITURE CO INC
CL	O	2400	2568	283	BALTIMORE	MD	MERCANTILE BANKSHARES CORP
CL	C	2100	292	677	RICHMOND	VA	SOUTHERN STATES COOPERATIVE INC
CL	O	1500	170	381	NEWPORT NEWS	VA	NOLAND CO
CL	O	1200	42	85	RICHMOND	VA	CADMUS COMMUNICATIONS CORP.
CL	O	1100	15	31	MYRTLE BEACH	SC	SANDS INVESTMENTS INC.
CL	O	1000	1102	61	CHARLESTON	WV	KEY CENTURION BANCSHARES INC.
CL	O	970	61	131	HIGH POINT	NC	CULP INCORPORATED
CL	O	921	305	77	CHARLOTTE	NC	INTERSTATE SECURITIES INC.
CL	N	630	158	73	BALTIMORE	MD	LEGG MASON INC.
CL	B	500	24	82	WASHINGTON	DC	GILPIN (HENRY B) CO.
CL	O	372	24	26	GASTONIA	NC	RAUCH INDUSTRIES INC
CL	O	300	14	33	ELIZABETH	WV	RAVENS METAL PRODUCTS INC
CL	O	270	15	25	BELTSVILLE	MD	MICROS SYSTEMS INC.
CL	N	262	75	51	COLUMBIA	SC	GIANT PORTLAND & MASONRY CEMENT CO
CL	O	248	14	1	ROCKVILLE	MD	QUANTA SYSTEMS CORP
CL	O	228	13	14	RESEARCH TRIAGLE PRK	NC	COMPUCHEM CORP.
CL	O	180	18	30	STERLING	VA	SYSTEMATICS GENERAL CORP
CL	O	115	1	1	CHEVY CHASE	MD	WAPORA INC.
CL	O	100	23	23	BALTIMORE	MD	PENTA SYSTEMS INTERNATIONAL INC
CL	O	88	1	1	ROCKVILLE	MD	BIOTECH RESEARCH LABORATORIES
CL	O	75	40	46	DOVER	DE	CHESAPEAKE UTILITIES CORP
CL	O	62	12	18	FLORENCE	SC	PEOPLES NATURAL GAS CO OF S.C.
CL	O	54	13	25	LYNCHBURG	VA	LYNCHBURG GAS CO.
CL	B	51	1	1	CHARLOTTE	NC	ENVIRONMENTAL CONTROL PRODUCTS
CL	O	33	11	1	FEDERALSBURG	MD	AMERICAN FUEL TECHNOLOGIES INC.
CL	N	27	439	17	BALTIMORE	MD	ADAMS EXPRESS COMPANY
CL	N	11	268	17	BALTIMORE	MD	PETROLEUM & RESOURCES

Deloitte Haskins & Sells

Aud1	Trd	Emp	Ast	Sis	Cty	Sta	Name
DHS	X	27000	709	1229	GREENSBORG	NC	BLUE BELL INC.
DHS	N	25000	1013	1013	FORT MILL	SC	SPRINGS INDUSTRIES INC
DHS	N	20000	8024	2899	CHARLOTTE	NC	DUKE POWER CO
DHS	N	12000	857	2073	NORTH WILKESBORO	NC	LOWE'S COMPANIES INC.
DHS	N	9300	6655	1935	RALEIGH	NC	CAROLINA POWER & LIGHT CO
DHS	N	8200	8709	2059	WILMINGTON	DE	BENEFICIAL CORP
DHS	S	6700	2716	1323	ROANOKE	VA	APPALACHIAN POWER CO
DHS	O	5400	227	355	CHARLOTTE	NC	LANCE INC.
DHS	N	3900	2544	1110	COLUMBIA	SC	SCANA CORP.
DHS	N	3100	1162	459	WASHINGTON	DC	COMMUNICATIONS SATELLITE CORP
DHS	N	2600	154	213	Charlotte	NC	REXHAM CORP
DHS	O	2400	132	127	MORGANTON	NC	HENREDON FURNITURE INDUSTRIES
DHS	O	2100	118	125	CHARLOTTESVILLE	VA	COMDIAL CORP
DHS	O	1500	31	45	CLAREMONT	NC	WESTERN STEER-MOM'N'POPS
DHS	O	1500	27	55	ROCKVILLE	MD	COMPUTER DATA SYSTEMS INC
DHS	O	1300	48	79	SALEM	VA	ROWE FURNITURE CORP
DHS	O	1100	50	78	LUTHERVILLE	MD	SCHENUIT INVESTMENTS INC
DHS	N	1100	376	406	CHARLOTTE	NC	PIEDMONT NATURAL GAS CO INC
DHS	O	1000	39	64	HUDSON	NC	KINCAID FURNITURE CO. INC.
DHS	O	1000	12	20	ROCKVILLE	MD	FAMILY ENTERTAINMENT CENTERS
DHS	O	820	25	82	RALEIGH	NC	GOODMARK FOODS INC.
DHS	A	700	13	28	Alexandria	VA	HALIFAX ENGINEERING INC.
DHS	A	620	47	41	TARBORO	NC	EMPIRE OF CAROLINA IC.
DHS	O	415	140	84	WILMINGTON	DE	AMERICAN INDEMNITY FINANCIAL CORP.
DHS	O	260	13	26	Fairfax	VA	HADRON INC.
DHS	O	255	6	11	LINCOLNTON	NC	BURRIS INDUSTRIES INC
DHS	O	245	1	1	WINSTON-SALEM	NC	PEANUT (THE) SHACK OF AMERICA INC.
DHS	O	190	1	1	ROCKVILLE	MD	BIOSPHERICS INC
DHS	O	179	18	21	CHARLOTTE	NC	DATASOUTH COMPUTER CORPORATION
DHS	O	154	186	21	ROCK HILL	SC	RHNB CORPORATION
DHS	O	145	24	43	ROANOKE	VA	ROANOKE GAS CO
DHS	O	100	1	1	NEWARK	DE	SPECIALTY COMPOSITES CORP
DHS	O	59	1	1	COLUMBIA	SC	DENTAL MANAGEMENT SERVICES INC
DHS	O	29	1	29	MCLEAN	VA	IVERSON TECHNOLOGY CORPORATION
DHS	O	28	55	1	Rockville	MD	FIRST WOMEN'S BANK
DHS	O	26	1	1	COLUMBIA	SC	TELECOMMUNICATIONS SYSTEMS INC.
DHS	O	11	1	1	LAUREL	MD	DIAGNON CORP.
DHS	O	3	1	1	MORRISVILE	NC	IMUTECH INC
DHS	O	0	83	9	SANFORD	NC	MID-SOUTH BANCSHARES (N.C.) INC.
DHS	O	0	1	1	FOUNTAIN INN	SC	PALMETTO REAL ESTATE TRUST
DHS	O	0	68	31	RALEIGH	NC	GOLDEN CORRAL CORP.
DHS	O	0	1	1	ROSSLYN	VA	ENERGY CAPITAL DVLP. CORP
DHS	O	0	41	56	COLUMBIA	MD	COLUMBIA DATA PRODUCTS INC.
DHS	Z	0	141	222	MARTINSVILLE	VA	BASSETT-WALKER INC.

Ernst & Whinney

Aud1	Trd	Emp	Ast	Sls	Cty	Sta	Name
EW	N	148000	16930	16595	WINSTON-SALEM	NC	REYNOLDS (R.J.) INDUSTRIES INC.
EW	N	67000	2258	4410	BETHESDA	MD	MARTIN MARIETTA CORP.
EW	N	52000	11494	7320	RICHMOND	VA	CSX CORP.
EW	N	27000	3647	3416	RICHMOND	VA	REYNOLDS METALS CO
EW	N	22000	1452	1732	TOWSON	MD	BLACK & DECKER CORP.
EW	N	16000	1487	1527	WINSTON-SALEM	NC	PIEDMONT AVIATION INC
EW	N	12000	17707	1753	WINSTON-SALEM	NC	FIRST WACHOVIA CORP.
EW	N	12000	702	856	GERMANTOWN	MD	FAIRCHILD INDUSTRIES INC
EW	O	11000	2107	1064	Baltimore	MD	BALTIMORE & OHIO RAILROAD CO
EW	O	10807	2380	255	Rockymount	NC	PEOPLES BANCORPORATION (NC)
EW	O	8200	9672	1037	NORFOLK	VA	SOVRAN FINANCIAL CORP.
EW	N	7900	236	413	RICHMOND	VA	ROBERTSHAW CONTROLS CO
EW	O	7500	582	873	HUNT VALLEY	MD	MC CORMICK & CO. INC.
EW	O	6600	266	409	BASSETT	VA	BASSETT FURNITURE INDUSTRIES INC.
EW	O	6000	215	439	NORFOLK	VA	FARM FRESH INC.
EW	O	5700	197	305	GASTONIA	NC	TI-CARO INC
EW	A	5600	484	1473	BALTIMORE	MD	CROWN CENTRAL PETROLEUM CORP.
EW	N	5300	7745	813	RICHMOND	VA	BANK OF VIRGINIA CO
EW	O	5300	7792	879	BALTIMORE	MD	MARYLAND NATIONAL CORP
EW	N	5300	2378	1219	WASHINGTON	DC	GEICO CORP.
EW	O	4400	169	382	DANVILLE	VA	DIBRELL BROTHERS INC
EW	A	4000	72	117	CHARLOTTE	NC	STANWOOD CORP.
EW	N	3400	3144	356	FALLS CHURCH	VA	FIRST VIRGINIA BANKS INC.
EW	O	3200	58	85	LYNCHBURG	VA	CRADDOCK-TERRY SHOE CORP.
EW	O	3200	2765	282	RALEIGH	NC	FIRST CITIZENS CORP
EW	O	2700	3804	267	BALTIMORE	MD	EQUITABLE BANCORPORATION
EW	Z	2700	2870	269	COLUMBIA	SC	CITIZENS & SOUTHERN CORP
EW	N	2300	884	294	GREENVILLE	SC	LIBERTY CORP
EW	S	2300	3391	501	CHARLOTTE	NC	BARCLAYS AMERICAN CORP.
EW	O	2100	1867	101	BALTIMORE	MD	UNION TRUST BANCORP
EW	O	1827	138	131	CAMDEN	SC	BUILDERS TRANSPORT INC.
EW	O	1800	2906	290	BETHESDA	MD	SUBURBAN BANCORP.
EW	O	1800	19	44	MOUNT AIRY	NC	QUALITY MILLS INC
EW	O	1700	472	204	RALEIGH	NC	MCM CORP
EW	O	1700	213	68	GREENVILLE	SC	U.S. SHELTER CORP.
EW	O	1700	1031	245	BALTIMORE	MD	MONUMENTAL CORP
EW	O	1600	42	69	ANDREWS	SC	ONEITA KNITTING MILLS
EW	O	1600	17	127	BALTIMORE	MD	SCHLUDERBERG KURDLE CO INC
EW	O	1500	2328	227	WILMINGTON	DE	WILMINGTON TRUST CO.
EW	O	1500	45	51	GREENVILLE	SC	STEEL HEEDLE MFG. CO.
EW	N	1400	173	497	COLUMBIA	MD	RYLAND GROUP INC.
EW	O	1400	63	74	PULASKI	VA	PULASKI FURNITURE CORP
EW	O	1400	147	239	COCKEYSVILLE	MD	EASTMET CORP
EW	O	1300	618	232	RALEIGH	NC	DURHAM CORP.

KMG Main Hurdman

Aud1	Trd	Emp	Ast	Sls	Cty	Sta	Name
MH	O	12000	229	791	ALEXANDRIA	VA	PEOPLES DRUG STORES INC
MH	N	5800	303	523	NITRO	WV	HECKS INC
MH	O	4000	118	93	BALTIMORE	MD	FAIR LANES INC
MH	O	840	291	94	WILMINGTON	DE	ROGERS CABLESYSTEMS OF AMERICA INC
MH	S	562	12	18	RALEIGH	NC	CAROLINA COACH CO.
MH	A	140	68	23	CLARKSBURG	WV	ALAMCO INC.
MH	B	92	1	1	POCA	WV	MED-PAK CORP.
MH	O	87	29	14	BRIDGEPORT	WV	PETROLEUM DEVELOPMENT CORP
MH	O	25	1	1	GREENBELT	MD	DURATEK CORP.
MH	O	4	1	1	CHEVY CHASE	MD	DASI INC.
MH	L	0	1	1	FAIRFAX	VA	P.C. TELEMART INC.
MH	S	0	1	1	CHARLOTTE	NC	JONES GROUP INC.
MH	S	0	340	1041	CHARLOTTE	NC	JONES (J.A.)CONSTRUCTION CO

Peat Marwick Mitchell

Aud1	Trd	Emp	Ast	Sls	Cty	Sta	Name
PMM	N	45000	2139	2802	GREENSBORO	NC	BURLINGTON INDUSTRIES INC
PMM	N	40000	9769	3825	Roanoke	VA	NORFOLK SOUTHERN CORP.
PMM	N	23000	1	1878	WILMINGTON	DE	IU INTERNATIONAL CORP.
PMM	N	18000	1332	2235	RICHMOND	VA	BEST PRODUCTS CO INC
PMM	S	17000	4682	1795	NORFOLK	VA	SOUTHERN RAILWAY CO.
PMM	O	17000	612	958	Cheverly	MD	ALLEGHENY BEVERAGE CORP
PMM	N	14000	1951	1765	ARLINGTON	VA	USAIR GROUP INC.
PMM	O	14000	313	1009	HENDERSON	NC	ROSES STORES INC
PMM	O	12000	16567	1688	CHARLOTTE	NC	FIRST UNION CORP
PMM	S	9400	7373	1320	BALTIMORE	MD	COMMERCIAL CREDIT CO.
PMM	O	5900	8100	728	RICHMOND	VA	UNITED VIRGINIA BANKSHARES INC
PMM	O	4500	106	247	HIGH POINT	NC	LADD FURNITURE INC.
PMM	N	3800	191	519	RICHMOND	VA	CIRCUIT CITY STORES INC.
PMM	N	3700	480	374	WILMINGTON	DE	RLC CORP
PMM	O	3700	4493	468	BALTIMORE	MD	FIRST MARYLAND BANCORP
PMM	O	3600	1191	247	COLUMBIA	MD	ROUSE CO
PMM	O	3200	4689	506	ROANOKE	VA	DOMINION BANKSHARES CORP
PMM	O	2900	399	336	GREENVILLE	SC	MULTIMEDIA INC
PMM	O	2900	44	55	GREENVILLE	SC	RYAN'S FAMILY STEAK HOUSES INC
PMM	N	2800	2754	866	HUNT VALLEY	MD	PHH GROUP INC.
PMM	O	2800	3511	364	RICHMOND	VA	CENTRAL FIDELITY BANKS INC
PMM	O	2700	59	164	TOWSON	MD	MERRY-GO-ROUND ENTERPRISES INC.
PMM	O	2500	2766	289	WILSON	NC	BRANCH CORP
PMM	N	2000	110	357	RICHMOND	VA	WARDS COMPANY INC.
PMM	O	2000	13	16	ROCKY MOUNT	NC	GUARDIAN CORP
PMM	N	1800	99087	10342	WASHINGTON	DC	FEDERAL NATL. MORTGAGE ASSOC.
PMM	O	1726	1058	135	Greenville	SC	SOUTHERN BANCORPORATION INC
PMM	N	1600	79	69	VIENNA	VA	HAZLETON LABORATORIES CORP.
PMM	O	1400	1461	165	WHITEVILLE	NC	UNITED CAROLINA BANCSHARES CORP
PMM	O	1200	510	171	BALTIMORE	MD	BROWN (ALEX) INC.
PMM	O	962	960	100	DURHAM	NC	CENTRAL CAROLINA BANK & TRUST CO.
PMM	O	858	1356	145	WILMINGTON	DE	BANK OF DELAWARE
PMM	O	826	1101	202	CHARLOTTESVILLE	VA	JEFFERSON BANKSHARES INC
PMM	A	810	77	119	NEWPORT	NC	CONNER CORP.
PMM	O	778	215	51	RICHMOND	VA	RICHMOND FREDERICKSBURG & POTOMAC
PMM	O	774	963	104	WILMINGTON	DE	DELAWARE TRUST CO
PMM	O	700	268	82	CLAYMONT	DE	GWC CORPORATION
PMM	O	696	651	68	ROCKY MOUNT	NC	PLANTERS CORP
PMM	O	593	51	69	WINSTON-SLAEM	NC	MANUFACTURED HOMES INC.
PMM	O	538	925	95	WASHINGTON	DC	NS & T BANKSHARES INC
PMM	N	460	80	105	WILMINGTON	DE	ROLLINS ENVIRONMENTAL SERVICES
PMM	A	387	642	81	CHARLESTON	WV	MAGNET BANK F.S.B.
PMM	Z	370	12	37	LINTHICUM	MD	SCOTTS SEABOARD CORP.
PMM	A	370	75	66	ROANOKE	VA	UNIVERSAL COMMUN. SYSTEMS INC

Price Waterhouse

Aud1	Trd	Emp	Ast	Sls	Cty	Sta	Name
PW	N	146000	25140	29483	WILMINGTON	DE	DU PONT (E.I.) DE NEMOURS & CO.
PW	C	12000	4510	2542	WASHINGTON	DC	MCI COMMUNICATIONS CORP
PW	N	9700	19754	1936	CHARLOTTE	NC	NCNB CORP
PW	N	8100	174	260	MARTINSVILLE	VA	TULTEX CORP
PW	A	6300	885	1079	WASHINGTON	DC	WASHINGTON POST CO.
PW	N	5400	3020	1316	WASHINGTON	DC	POTOMAC ELECTRIC POWER CO
PW	O	4100	4212	415	COLUMBIA	SC	SOUTH CAROLINA NATIONAL CORP
PW	O	3900	55	167	MATTHEWS	NC	PCA INTERNATIONAL INC.
PW	N	3700	1383	430	GREENVILLE	DE	AMERICAN WATER WORKS CO INC
PW	C	3200	44834	3372	N.W. WASHINGTON	DC	INTERNATIONAL BANK FOR RECONSTRC
PW	O	2900	169	234	ALEXANDRIA	VA	ATLANTIC RESEARCH CORP
PW	B	2800	33	73	WHEELING W	WV	GOOD (L.S.) & CO.
PW	O	2600	85	276	WINSTON SALEM	NC	SALEM CARPET MILLS INC
PW	O	2200	440	427	CHARLOTTE	NC	COCA COLA BOTTLING CO CONSOLIDATED
PW	O	2100	1660	274	COLUMBIA	SC	BANKERS TRUST OF SOUTH CAROLINA
PW	S	2000	966	499	FAIRMONT	WV	MONONGAHELA POWER CO.
PW	O	1800	137	148	CLAYTON	DE	PHOENIX STEEL CORP
PW	O	1500	4155	379	WASHINGTON	DC	AMERICAN SECURITY CORP
PW	O	1400	50	112	ARLINGTON	VA	AMERICAN MANAGEMENT SYSTEMS INC.
PW	O	1300	38	63	MCLEAN	VA	VIE DE FRANCE
PW	O	1300	24	39	ASHEBORO	NC	WALKER (B.B.) CO.
PW	S	1100	961	532	HAGERSTOWN	MD	POTOMAC EDISON CO
PW	A	1100	66	94	GREENSBORO	NC	OAKWOOD HOMES CORP
PW	O	1000	49	65	BALTIMORE	MD	WAVERLY PRESS INC
PW	O	862	1439	146	WASHINGTON	DC	WASHINGTON BANCORPORATION
PW	O	850	97	367	RICHMOND	VA	OWENS & MINOR INC.
PW	A	750	45	65	CHARLOTTE	NC	AERONCA INC
PW	O	700	20	37	RICHMOND	VA	S & K FAMOUS BRANDS INC
PW	O	660	671	72	COLUMBIA	SC	FIRST CIT. BANCORP.OF S.C. INC.
PW	O	333	13	52	PORTSMOUTH	VA	DOUGHTIE'S FOODS INC.
PW	O	275	655	80	CHARLOTTE	NC	NORTH CAROLINA FEDERAL S & L
PW	O	250	93	29	CHARLESTON	WV	WEST VIRGINIA WATER CO.
PW	O	250	21	27	BETHESDA	MD	SURVIVAL TECHNOLOGY INC
PW	C	230	1673	173	WASHINGTON	DC	INTERNATIONAL FINANCE CORP.
PW	O	200	28	16	Gaithersburg	MD	GENEX CORP
PW	O	150	27	1	VIRGINIA BEACH	VA	TVX BROADCAST GROUP INC.
PW	A	136	19	32	GREENSBORO	NC	KEY COMPANY
PW	O	130	19	31	WINSTON-SALEM	NC	BRENNER COMPANIES INC.
PW	O	120	454	38	WASHINGTON	DC	DC NATIONAL BANCORP INC
PW	O	95	40	11	NEWARK	DE	ARTESIAN RESOURCES
PW	S	89	196	17	BECKLEY	WV	SUMMIT HOLDING CORP.
PW	O	49	3	1	RALEIGH	NC	DAY TELECOMMUNICATIONS INC.
PW	O	25	17	10	HARRISBURG	NC	CHARLOTTE MOTOR SPEEDWAY INC
PW	O	19	1	1	Lanham-Seabrook	MD	CHEUNG LABORATORIES INC.

Touche Ross

Aud1	Trd	Emp	Ast	Sls	Cty	Sta	Name
TR	O	8800	302	404	WASHINGTON	DC	WOODWARD & LOTHROP INC
TR	N	3900	560	758	CHARLOTTE	NC	NUCOR CORP
TR	O	3400	353	489	LANDOVER	MD	HECHINGER CO
TR	A	2900	84	163	KINSTON	NC	HAMPTON INDUSTRIES INC
TR	N	1600	304	182	RICHMOND	VA	HEILIG MEYERS CO
TR	O	1500	44	98	ARLINGTON	VA	CACI INC
TR	O	1100	33	93	CHARLOTTE	NC	CATO CORP
TR	L	830	30	49	ROCKVILLE	MD	DIVERSITRON INC
TR	A	800	75	82	BALTIMORE	MD	ARUNDEL CORP
TR	A	730	69	74	ROCKVILLE	MD	PENRIL CORP
TR	O	723	36	7	WASHINGTON	DC	PRESIDENTIAL AIRWAYS INC.
TR	O	679	43	82	MOUNT AIRY	NC	EXPOSAIC INDUSTRIES INC.
TR	N	650	28	63	VIENNA	VA	ERC INTERNATIONAL INC.
TR	A	600	14	17	Alexandria	VA	BOWL AMERICA INC
TR	O	413	46	33	STERLING	VA	RADIATION SYSTEMS INC
TR	O	395	22	31	RALEIGH	NC	ATHEY PRODUCTS CORP.
TR	A	390	1	15	HAZELWOOD	NC	WELLCO ENTERPRISES INC
TR	O	367	1	14	DURHAM	NC	BLACK INDUSTRIES INC
TR	C	300	13	33	SAVAGE	MD	GREENBELT COOPERATIVE INC.
TR	O	300	1	1	ARLINGTON	VA	STANWICK CORP
TR	O	243	21	36	BAILEY'S CROSSROADS	VA	CERBERONICS INC.
TR	O	237	431	77	MC LEAN	VA	FINALCO GROUP INC.
TR	O	187	264	28	PRINCETON	WV	FIRST COMMUNITY BANCSHARES INC.
TR	O	180	22	64	LANHAM	MD	SCHWARTZ BROTHERS INC.
TR	O	166	74	57	VIENNA	VA	ENTRE COMPUTER CENTERS INC.
TR	O	130	1	13	Falls Church	VA	TECHNALYSIS CORP.
TR	O	130	26	31	FALLS CHURCH	VA	WILLIAMS INDUSTRIES INC
TR	O	127	1	11	BALTIMORE	MD	PHARMAKINETICS LABORATORIES INC.
TR	O	110	70	17	BALTIMORE	MD	CHESAPEAKE LIFE INS. CO.
TR	O	110	1	1	MCLEAN	VA	TESDATA SYSTEMS CORP.
TR	O	70	13	10	DENVER	NC	AIR TRANSPORTATION HOLDING CO. INC
TR	A	64	35	54	OXON HILL	MD	WASHINGTON HOMES INC
TR	O	63	1	1	ROCKVILLE	MD	INDUSTRIAL TRAINING CORP.
TR	O	49	5	6	GAITHERSBURG	MD	DATA MEASUREMENT CORP
TR	S	46	9943	1030	WILMINGTON	DE	SEARS ROEBUCK ACCEPTANCE CORP.
TR	O	40	71	19	BALTIMORE	MD	BTR REALTY INC.
TR	O	40	1	1	Rockville	MD	AUTOSCOPE INC.
TR	O	30	1	1	Washington	DC	CAMPTOWN INDUSTRIES INC
TR	O	11	1	1	CHAPEL HILL	NC	PIZZA TRANSIT AUTHORITY INC.
TR	O	0	239	102	WASHINGTON	DC	NATIONAL HOUSING PARTNERSH
TR	O	0	1	1	CHEVY CHASE	MD	SMITH COLLINS PHARMACEUTICAL INC.
TR	O	0	1	1	ALEXANDRIA	VA	INTERLEUKIN-2 INC.
TR	O	0	1	1	WILMINGTON	DE	AMERICAN SPECIALTY FOODS

Offices By Firm - Southeast Region

CITY	ST	AA	AY	CL	DHS	EW	KMG	PMM	PW	TR
Atlanta	GA	1	2	1	2	2	1	2	2	1
Birmingham	AL	1	1	1	1	1		1	1	1
Boca Raton	FL			1		1				
Chattanooga	TN	1			1	1	1			
Clearwater	FL						1			
Columbus	GA					1				
Daytona Beach	FL		1							
Duluth	GA			1						
Fort Lauderdale	FL	1	1	1	1	1	1	1	1	1
Fort Myers	FL			1						
Greeneville	TN						1			
Jackson	MS	1				1		1		1
Jacksonville	FL	1	1	1	1	1		1	1	1
Johnson City	TN							1		
Knoxville	TN				1	1	1			
Marietta	GA									1
Melbourne	FL			1						
Memphis	TN	1		1	1	1		1	1	1
Miami	FL	1	1	1	1	1	1	1	1	1
Mobile	AL				1	1				
Naples	FL			1						
Nashville	TN	1	1		1	1		1	1	2
Orlando	FL	1	1	1	1	1	1	1	1	1
Punta Gorda	FL			1						
Sarasota	FL									1

CITY	ST	AA	AY	CL	DHS	EW	KMG	PMM	PW	TR
St. Petersburg	FL		1		1	1	1		1	
Tallahassee	FL		1							
Tampa	FL	1	1	1	1	1		1	1	1
Vero Beach	FL							1		
West Palm Beach	FL			1	1	1	1	1	1	
TOTALS		11	12	15	15	18	10	13	13	13

Market Share Leadership

Southeast Region

CITY or AREA	ST	Firm	Firm	Firm	Firm
Atlanta	GA	AA	EW	PMM	
Birmingham	AL	AA	EW	PMM	
Fort Lauderdale	FL	CL	DHS	PMM	
Jacksonville	FL	CL	PMM	TR	
Memphis	TN	AA	EW	TR	
Miami	FL	AA	CL	DHS	PMM
Nashville	TN	AA	EW	PMM	TR
Orlando	FL	AA	EW	PMM	PW
Tampa	FL	AA	PW		
West Palm Beach	FL	CL	DHS	EW	

Southeast Region

Region	AA	AY	CL	DHS	EW	KMG	PMM	PW	TR
Southeast	1150	375	800	700	875	275	850	640	575

Major Clients By Firm
Southeast Region

Aud1 = Principal Accountants

Trd = Shows the where traded status of company shares
      A - American Stock Exchange
      N - New York Stock Exchange
      O - Over the Counter
      B - Company in some condition of bankruptcy
      C - Co-op or mutual
      L - Company in liquidation
      S - Subsidiary which reports separately
      U - Subsidiary whose auditor is different from parent
      X - Company which has gone private

Emp = Number of employees

Name = Company name

SIC = Four digit Standard Industrial Classification

Sta = State

Ast = Assets

Sls = Sales

Arthur Andersen

Aud1	Trd	Emp	Ast	Sls	Cty	Sta	Name
AA	N	50000	2448	1804	MEMPHIS	TN	HOLIDAY CORP.
AA	N	39000	3627	4684	ATLANTA	GA	DELTA AIR LINES INC
AA	N	38000	4866	6716	ATLANTA	GA	GEORGIA PACIFIC CORP
AA	N	31000	16531	6814	ATLANTA	GA	SOUTHERN CO
AA	N	27000	1900	2031	MEMPHIS	TN	FEDERAL EXPRESS CORP. (THE)
AA	N	23300	238	453	WINTER HAVEN	FL	SCOTTYS INC
AA	N	22000	5074	2557	ATLANTA	GA	CONTINENTAL TELECOM
AA	N	19000	618	1191	ATLANTA	GA	NATIONAL SERVICE INDUSTRIES INC
AA	N	19000	104	279	CORAL GABLES	FL	WACKENHUT CORP
AA	A	17000	918	1046	Miami Beach	FL	DWG CORP
AA	N	16000	19406	1819	ORLANDO	FL	SUNTRUST BANKS INC.
AA	S	15000	9031	3444	ATLANTA	GA	GEORGIA POWER CO
AA	S	11000	2056	863	TAMPA	FL	GENERAL TELEPHONE CO. OF FLORIDA
AA	N	11000	803	819	Orlando	FL	HARCOURT BRACE JOVANOVICH INC
AA	N	11000	381	1268	MEMPHIS	TN	FEDERAL CO. (THE)
AA	N	11000	221	564	ATLANTA	GA	EQUIFAX INC
AA	S	9900	5722	2414	BIRMINGHAM	AL	ALABAMA POWER CO
AA	N	9000	120	281	ATLANTA	GA	ROLLINS INC
AA	A	6400	771	898	MIAMI BEACH	FL	SHARON STEEL CORP
AA	N	6400	3494	1653	ST PETERSBURG	FL	FLORIDA PROGRESS CORP
AA	N	6100	196	532	CHATTANOOGA	TN	DORSEY CORP
AA	A	5500	725	542	MACON	GA	CHARTER MEDICAL CORP
AA	S	5200	3169	1505	ST. PETERSBURG	FL	FLORIDA POWER CORP.
AA	S	5100	6165	647	ATLANTA	GA	TRUST COMPANY OF GEORGIA
AA	O	4800	237	887	BIRMINGHAM	AL	BRUNO'S INCORPORATED
AA	N	4600	310	497	MIAMI BEACH	FL	SOUTHEASTERN PUBLIC SERVICE CO
AA	O	4460	130	214	ATLANTA	GA	CRAWFORD & CO
AA	N	4300	236	519	DALTON	GA	SHAW INDUSTRIES INC.
AA	O	4200	98	143	NASHVILLE	TN	PO FOLKS INCORPORATED
AA	N	4200	281	437	ATLANTA	GA	SCIENTIFIC ATLANTA INC
AA	O	4100	5249	527	MEMPHIS	TN	FIRST TENNESSEE NATIONAL CORP
AA	N	3700	319	253	LARGO	FL	PARADYNE CORP.
AA	O	3500	118	92	MURFREESBORO	TN	NATIONAL HEALTH CORPORATION
AA	A	2100	34	133	ATLANTA	GA	CAGLES INC
AA	O	2100	135	189	ATLANTA	GA	HBO & CO
AA	O	2000	179	167	ATLANTA	GA	RHODES INC.
AA	O	1900	1730	177	FORT MYERS	FL	SOUTHWEST FLORIDA BANKS INC
AA	N	1900	99	112	BOAZ	AL	RIVER OAKS INDUSTRIES
AA	O	1800	55	69	MADISON	GA	WELLINGTON INDUSTRIES INC
AA	O	1800	436	201	ATLANTA	GA	GREAT AMERICAN MANAGEMENT & INVEST
AA	O	1500	922	518	PENSACOLA	FL	GULF POWER CO
AA	O	1500	680	447	GULFPORT	MS	MISSISSIPPI POWER CO
AA	N	1400	115	95	ATLANTA	GA	RPC ENERGY SERVICES INC
AA	N	1400	120	194	TAMPA	FL	AMERICAN SHIP BUILDING CO

Arthur Young

Aud1	Trd	Emp	Ast	Sls	Cty	Sta	Name
AY	N	21000	783	1204	WEST POINT	GA	WEST POINT PEPPERELL INC
AY	N	6800	3570	2498	BIRMINGHAM	AL	SONAT INC.
AY	A	4700	176	238	SYLACAUGA	AL	AVONDALE MILLS
AY	O	3900	132	265	ATLANTA	GA	INTERMET CORP.
AY	O	2700	213	202	MIAMI	FL	CORDIS CORP
AY	N	2600	130	203	WEST PALM BEACH	FL	STEEGO CORP.
AY	A	2300	198	271	JACKSONVILLE	FL	FLORIDA ROCK INDUSTRIES INC
AY	O	1800	191	253	MOBILE	AL	MARION CORP
AY	N	1500	455	153	ST AUGUSTINE	FL	FLORIDA EAST COAST INDUSTRIES INC.
AY	O	1200	51	32	DOTHAN	AL	NATIONAL HEALTHCARE INC.
AY	O	988	89	91	BIRMINGHAM	AL	BIRMINGHAM STEEL CORP.
AY	O	920	244	72	BOCA RATON	FL	SENSORMATIC ELECTRONICS CORP
AY	O	680	47	170	FOREST PARK	GA	RTC TRANSPORTATION INC.
AY	O	600	40	101	TAMPA	FL	TREASURE ISLE INC
AY	O	547	10	38	ORLANDO	FL	FLORIDA EXPRESS
AY	O	400	150	65	FORT LAUDERDALE	FL	SAFECARD SERVICES
AY	O	356	34	61	ATLANTA	GA	COMPUTONE SYSTEMS INC
AY	O	350	10	18	JACKSONVILLE	FL	INDUSTRIAL-AMERICA CORP.
AY	A	320	49	36	CLEARWATER	FL	AMBRIT INC.
AY	O	275	13	14	AUSTELL	GA	OLD FASHION FOODS INC.
AY	O	254	15	14	SANFORD	FL	INFRARED INDUSTRIES INC.
AY	O	246	11	79	HOLLYWOOD	FL	LOREN INDUSTRIES INC.
AY	O	232	27	46	ATLANTA	GA	ADVANCED TELECOMMUNICATIONS CORP.
AY	O	165	12	41	Decatur	GA	STEREO VILLAGE INC.
AY	O	130	1	1	MOBILE	AL	SUPER STORES INC.
AY	O	75	1	1	ALBANY	GA	NORSUL OIL & MINING LTD.
AY	O	69	1	1	Deerfield Beach	FL	DATAVISION INC.
AY	O	59	1	1	ORLANDO	FL	LASER PHOTONICS INC
AY	O	45	1	1	LARGO	FL	UNIVERSITY OPTICAL PRODUCTS CO.
AY	O	45	1	1	PALM CITY	FL	BIO ANALYTIC LABORATORIES INC.
AY	O	20	1	1	ROSWELL	GA	VISIONTECH INC.
AY	O	14	1	1	DEERFIELD BEACH	FL	CHECK ROBOT INC.
AY	O	13	1	1	BOCA RATON	FL	MICRO-SYSTEMS SOFTWARE INC.
AY	O	9	1	1	ATLANTA	GA	CHEM-TECHNICS INC.
AY	O	7	1	1	NORCROSS	GA	21ST CENTURY ROBOTICS INC.
AY	O	5	1	1	PLANTATION	FL	DENTIST PLACE INC.
AY	O	5	1	1	NORTH MIAMI	FL	HEALTH INTEGRATED SERVICES INC
AY	O	2	15	1	Jackson	MS	SEAXE ENERGY CORP.
AY	O	0	469	239	JACKSONVILLE	FL	ST. JOE PAPER COMPANY
AY	O	0	1	1	OCALA	FL	WIRESAT CORPORATION
AY	O	0	1	1	TAMPA	FL	DATA DYNAMICS INC

Coopers & Lybrand

Aud1	Trd	Emp	Ast	Sls	Cty	Sta	Name
CL	N	94000	25008	10664	ATLANTA	GA	BELLSOUTH
CL	S	53000	13516	5784	ATLANTA	GA	SOUTHERN BELL TEL. & TEL. CO.
CL	S	38000	10193	4014	BIRMINGHAM	AL	SOUTH CENTRAL BELL TELEPHONE
CL	O	16000	195	471	TAMPA	FL	MORRISON INC
CL	A	11000	648	1166	MONTGOMERY	AL	BLOUNT INC
CL	X	4800	1242	537	MIAMI	FL	STORER COMMUNICATIONS INC.
CL	N	4200	386	496	MELBOURNE	FL	HARRIS GRAPHICS CORPORATION
CL	N	4100	2039	886	TAMPA	FL	TECO ENERGY INC.
CL	s	3800	3588	435	FT. LAUDERALE	FL	LANDMARK BANKING CORP.`
CL	N	3600	78	64	LAKE HAMILTON	FL	ORANGE-CO. INC.
CL	S	3300	1664	694	TAMPA	FL	TAMPA ELECTRIC COMPANY
CL	O	2400	312	275	CLEWISTON	FL	UNITED STATES SUGAR CORP
CL	A	2200	275	271	BIRMINGHAM	AL	SAUNDERS SYSTEMS INC.
CL	X	2100	125	99	PALM BEACH	FL	COOK INTERNATIONAL INC.
CL	O	1700	134	184	BIRMINGHAM	AL	PARISIAN INC
CL	N	1500	72	118	KNOXVILLE	TN	CLAYTON HOMES INC
CL	B	1400	189	58	MIAMI	FL	MAULE INDUSTRIES INC.
CL	O	1100	971	289	BIRMINGHAM	AL	PROTECTIVE LIFE CORP.
CL	N	1100	194	374	BIRMINGHAM	AL	ENERGEN
CL	O	937	1	14	PALM BEACH	FL	APPLIED DEVICES CORP
CL	O	780	884	89	MIAMI	FL	FLORIDA COMMERCIAL BANKS INC
CL	O	642	76	92	ATLANTA	GA	HYPONEX CORPORATION
CL	N	633	367	159	SAVANNAH	GA	SAVANNAH ELECTRIC & POWER CO
CL	O	557	39	42	TAMPA	FL	REFLECTONE INC.
CL	O	554	37	27	OCALA	FL	MICRODYNE CORP.
CL	O	500	19	41	JACKSONVILLE	FL	CANADA DRY BOTTLING CO. OF FLA.
CL	O	412	32	62	CHATTANOOGA	TN	FILTRATION SCIENCES INC
CL	A	400	30	32	HOLLYWOOD	FL	HEINICKE INSTRUMENTS CO
CL	O	370	34	17	ATLANTA	GA	REID-PROVIDENT LABORATORIES INC
CL	N	367	32	24	ORLANDO	FL	EDUCATIONAL COMPUTER CORP
CL	A	360	81	33	PUNTA GORDA	FL	PUNTA GORDA ISLES INC
CL	O	348	355	50	MIAMI	FL	POPULAR BANCSHARES CORP
CL	O	330	19	40	BIRMINGHAM	AL	DYATRON CORP.
CL	O	326	180	44	MONTGOMERY	AL	FEDERATED GUARANTY CORP.
CL	O	276	151	77	LONGWOOD	FL	AMERICAN PACIFIC CORP.
CL	O	267	157	37	MONTGOMERY	AL	FEDERATED GUARANITY LIFE INSURANCE
CL	O	219	114	389	MEMPHIS	TN	TBC CORP
CL	O	210	20	33	ST. AUGUSTINE	FL	TREE OF LIFE INC.
CL	A	205	186	35	MOBILE	AL	LAURENTIAN CAPITAL CORP.
CL	O	200	57	39	JACKSONVILLE	FL	GEORGE WASHINGTON CORP.
CL	O	194	10	14	HIALEAH	FL	EQUIPMENT COMPANY OF AMERICA
CL	X	170	58	61	MIAMI	FL	CARESSA INC
CL	O	162	23	47	JOHNSON CITY	TN	TENNESSEE-VIRGINIA ENERGY CORP.
CL	O	150	138	92	NASHVILLE	TN	COMDATA NETWORK INC.

Deloitte Haskins & Sells

Aud1	Trd	Emp	Ast	Sls	Cty	Sta	Name
DHS	N	14000	8917	4349	JUNO BEACH	FL	FPL GROUP INC.
DHS	N	9700	552	1062	CLEVELAND	TN	MAGIC CHEF INC
DHS	N	7000	11052	1097	MIAMI	FL	SOUTHEAST BANKING CORP
DHS	N	6600	614	142	BOCA RATON	FL	INTERNATIONAL CONTROLS CORP
DHS	N	6200	819	981	BIRMINGHAM	AL	VULCAN MATERIALS CO
DHS	O	6200	534	520	MIAMI	FL	WOMETCO ENTERPRISES INC
DHS	O	5200	8234	1036	PALM BEACH	FL	CITYFED FINANCIAL CORP.
DHS	N	4700	164	245	DECATUR	GA	HARLAND (JOHN H.) CO.
DHS	O	3900	149	180	FORT LAUDERDALE	FL	BURNUP & SIMS INC
DHS	L	3800	3248	1198	JACKSONVILLE	FL	GULF UNITED CORP.
DHS	N	3300	128	300	ATLANTA	GA	AMERICAN BUSINESS PRODUCTS INC
DHS	O	3300	788	1165	ATLANTA	GA	ATLANTA GAS LIGHT CO
DHS	O	3200	198	320	AUGUSTA	GA	LILY-TULIP INC.
DHS	O	2900	53	68	LEBANON	TN	CRACKER BARREL OLD CNTRY S
DHS	O	2600	1353	605	JACKSON	MS	MISSISSIPPI POWER & LIGHT CO
DHS	O	2000	82	295	MANGO	FL	SHOP & GO INC
DHS	A	1900	76	148	MIAMI LAKES	FL	LURIA (L) & SON INC.
DHS	O	1800	34	86	MORRISTOWN	TN	BERKLINE CORP
DHS	O	1600	4783	544	ST PETERSBURG	FL	FLORIDA FEDERAL SAVINGS & LOAN
DHS	O	1300	4711	531	MIAMI	FL	CENTRUST SAVINGS BANK
DHS	O	1200	2586	328	TAMPA	FL	FREEDOM SAVINGS & LOAN
DHS	O	946	877	75	MONTGOMERY	AL	COLONIAL BANCGROUP INC.
DHS	N	800	2775	358	MIAMI	FL	AMERICAN S&L ASSOC. OF FL
DHS	N	745	252	78	MIAMI	FL	DELTONA CORP
DHS	O	700	1927	911	CLEARWATER	FL	Pioneer Savings Bank
DHS	B	590	1852	214	MIAMI	FL	BISCAYNE FEDERAL SAVINGS & LOAN
DHS	X	580	126	46	MIAMI	FL	WOMETCO CABLE TV INC.
DHS	O	552	201	98	MEMPHIS	TN	CRUMP COMPANIES INC. (THE)
DHS	O	529	13	28	WEST PALM BEACH	FL	DYCOM INDUSTRIES INC.
DHS	O	479	2009	219	MIAMI	FL	CITIZENS SAVINGS FINANCIAL CRP
DHS	O	462	50	48	MOBILE	AL	QMS INC.
DHS	O	435	1223	143	BOYNTON BEACH	FL	SUNRISE S & L ASSO. OF FLORIDA
DHS	O	410	47	66	MELBOURNE	FL	DBA SYSTEMS INC
DHS	O	385	16	28	MAITLAND	FL	AUXTON COMPUTER ENTERPRISES INC
DHS	A	340	86	73	BOCA RATON	FL	LEVITT CORP.
DHS	O	330	651	70	OCALA	FL	MID-STATE FED. S & L ASSOC.
DHS	O	315	20	23	MELBOURNE	FL	SCIENTIFIC SYSTEMS SERVICES
DHS	O	313	543	60	MIAMI	FL	CAPITAL BANCORP
DHS	O	291	46	58	WEST PALM BEACH	FL	FLORIDA PUBLIC UTILITIES CO
DHS	O	269	913	98	Fort Lauderdale	FL	COMMONWEALTH SAVINGS & LOAN
DHS	O	255	60	18	ST. PETERSBURG	FL	LOAN AMERICA FINANCIAL CORP.
DHS	O	250	754	82	PENSACOLA	FL	FIRST MUTUAL SAVINGS ASSN. OF FLA.
DHS	O	239	44	58	MOBILE	AL	MOBILE GAS SERVICE CORP
DHS	O	217	15	16	ORLANDO	FL	CONTROL LASER CORP

Ernst & Whinney

Aud1	Trd	Emp	Ast	Sls	Cty		Sta	Name
EW	N	62000	6259	4152	NASHVILLE		TN	HOSPITAL CORP. OF AMERICA
EW	N	39000	6898	7904	ATLANTA		GA	COCA COLA CO.
EW	N	31000	1789	2281	MELBOURNE		FL	HARRIS CORP
EW	S	28000	4969	2860	JACKSONVILLE		FL	SEABOARD SYSTEM RAILROAD INC.
EW	N	22000	1394	1730	MIAMI		FL	KNIGHT-RIDDER NEWSPAPERS
EW	O	21000	316	547	NASHVILLE		TN	SHONEYS INC
EW	N	13000	977	2279	ATLANTA		GA	GENUINE PARTS CO
EW	N	11000	553	862	ATLANTA		GA	FUQUA INDUSTRIES INC
EW	O	10000	13591	1377	ATLANTA		GA	CITIZENS & SOUTHERN GEORGIA CORP
EW	N	9000	322	385	ALEXANDER CITY		AL	RUSSELL CORP.
EW	X	8000	468	2601	MEMPHIS		TN	MALONE & HYDE INC
EW	N	5600	99	112	BRENTWOOD		TN	WINNERS CORP
EW	O	5400	135	227	MACON		GA	BIBB CO
EW	O	5100	5981	682	JACKSONVILLE		FL	FLORIDA NATL BANKS OF FL
EW	O	5000	1136	427	JACKSONVILLE		FL	INDEPENDENT INSURANCE GROUP
EW	S	4600	7898	823	ATLANTA		GA	FIRST ATLANTA CORP.
EW	O	4400	511	526	HUNTSVILLE		AL	INTERGRAPH CORP.
EW	O	4300	262	538	HUNTSVILLE		AL	SCI SYSTEMS INC
EW	O	4300	5812	1688	CHATTANOOGA		TN	PROVIDENT LIFE & ACCIDENT INSUR.
EW	O	3800	86	253	CHATTANOOGA		TN	DIXIE YARNS INC
EW	O	3600	3684	380	MONTGOMERY		AL	FIRST ALABAMA BANCSHARES INC
EW	N	3600	5227	463	BIRMINGHAM		AL	AMSOUTH BANCORPORATION
EW	O	3100	77	132	THOMASTON		GA	THOMASTON MILLS INC.
EW	O	2900	4210	400	BIRMINGHAM		AL	SOUTHTRUST CORP.
EW	O	2700	58	170	HALEYVILLE		AL	TIDWELL INDUSTRIES INC
EW	N	2200	39	79	CHATTANOOGA		TN	WAYNE-GOSSARD CORP
EW	A	2000	41	183	PANAMA CITY		FL	SUNSHINE JR STORES INC
EW	O	1900	3116	313	NASHVILLE		TN	COMMERCE UNION CORP
EW	L	1800	59	103	ATLANTA		GA	BARWICK (E.T.) INDUSTRIES
EW	N	1800	212	288	TAMPA		FL	FLORIDA STEEL CORP
EW	O	1800	114	165	JACKSONVILLE		FL	CLOW CORP
EW	O	1800	89	130	ATLANTA		GA	GRAPHIC INDUSTRIES INC.
EW	O	1800	259	251	BIRMINGHAM		AL	ALABAMA BY-PRODUCTS CORP
EW	O	1800	144	196	ATLANTA		GA	HAVERTY FURNITURE CO. INC.
EW	O	1200	157	145	NASHVILLE		TN	INTERNATIONAL CLINICAL LABS.
EW	A	1100	46	145	BOCA RATON		FL	ZIMMER CORP
EW	O	1100	322	77	CORAL GABLES		FL	AVATAR HOLDINGS INC.
EW	O	1000	54	103	COLUMBUS		GA	BURNHAM SERVICE CORP.
EW	O	810	135	89	POMPANO BEACH		FL	COMPUTER PRODUCTS INC
EW	O	708	73	84	NORCROSS		GA	DIGITAL COMMUNICATIONS ASSOC
EW	X	700	97	156	CORAL GABLES		FL	COCA COLA BOTTLING CO. OF MIAMI
EW	L	600	563	41	KNOXVILLE		TN	UNITED AMER.BANK KNOXVILLE
EW	O	600	17	17	ATLANTA		GA	AMERIHEALTH INC.
EW	O	570	1056	106	MEMPHIS		TN	NATIONAL COMMERCE BANCORPORATION

Peat Marwick Mitchell

Aud1	Trd	Emp	Ast	Sls	Cty	Sta	Name
PMM	N	72000	1236	7774	JACKSONVILLE	FL	WINN DIXIE STORES INC
PMM	X	40000	738	3446	LAKELAND	FL	PUBLIX SUPER MARKETS INC.
PMM	N	31000	1089	2966	LARGO	FL	ECKERD (JACK) CORP
PMM	N	25000	3741	2905	MIAMI	FL	RYDER SYSTEM INC
PMM	O	11000	531	192	MONTGOMERY	AL	KINDER CARE LEARNING CENTERS INC
PMM	C	9000	437	1500	ATLANTA	GA	GOLD KIST INC
PMM	N	6600	3740	1362	BIRMINGHAM	AL	TORCHMARK CORP.
PMM	N	3900	594	135	MIAMI	FL	GENERAL DEVELOPMENT CORP
PMM	N	3600	647	2572	JACKSONVILLE	FL	CHARTER CO
PMM	O	3200	3723	374	JACKSONVILLE	FL	ATLANTIC BANCORPORATION
PMM	N	3140	198	388	BRENTWOOD	TN	MURRAY OHIO MANUFACTURING CO
PMM	O	3000	4789	454	NASHVILLE	TN	FIRST AMERICAN CORP. (TN)
PMM	O	2500	3240	335	BIRMINGHAM	AL	CENTRAL BANCSHARES OF THE SOUTH
PMM	N	2500	2271	955	COLUMBUS	GA	AMERICAN FAMILY CORP
PMM	O	2200	152	631	MOBILE	AL	DELCHAMPS INC.
PMM	O	2100	2864	281	JACKSON	MS	DEPOSIT GUARANTY CORP
PMM	O	1800	229	282	MIAMI	FL	JET FLORIDA SYSTEM INC.
PMM	O	1700	23	35	MACON	GA	RESTAURANT MANAGEMENT SERVICES INC
PMM	O	1600	1231	117	COLUMBUS	GA	CB&T BANCSHARES INC
PMM	O	1400	155	121	MARIETTA	GA	HEALTHDYNE INC.
PMM	N	1100	248	433	ATLANTA	GA	HOME DEPOT INC.
PMM	O	977	13	29	ATLANTA	GA	COURIER DISPATCH GROUP INC.
PMM	N	930	395	278	JACKSON	MS	FIRST MISSISSIPPI CORP.
PMM	X	900	45	35	SHELBYVILLE	TN	EMPIRE PENCIL CORP
PMM	O	900	70	156	BIRMINGHAM	AL	HOMECRAFTERS WAREHOUSE
PMM	O	851	262	27	JACKSONVILLE	FL	AMERICAN BANKS OF FLORIDA INC
PMM	O	850	19	41	CLEARWATER	FL	HEIST (C.H.) CORP.
PMM	O	840	103	184	CALHOUN	GA	HORIZON INDUSTRIES INC.
PMM	O	830	1	26	MIAMI	FL	CREATIVE RESTAURANT ENTERPRISES
PMM	O	825	48	25	MACON	GA	SECURITY LIFE INSURANCE CO. OF GA.
PMM	O	725	35	39	NASHVILLE	TN	SOUTHERN HOSPITALITY CORP.
PMM	N	688	334	231	MIAMI	FL	LENNAR CORP
PMM	O	596	2060	206	CLEARWATER	FL	FORTUNE FINANCIAL GROUP INC.
PMM	O	593	574	66	TUPELO	MS	BANCORP OF MISSISSIPPI
PMM	N	575	1233	133	NAPLES	FL	NAFCO FINANCIAL GROUP INC.
PMM	A	560	51	113	MIAMI LAKES	FL	IMPERIAL INDUSTRIES INC
PMM	O	555	1430	150	ST. PETERSBURG	FL	HOME FEDERAL BANK OF FLORIDA
PMM	O	550	25	29	ATLANTA	GA	BYERS COMMUNICATIONS SYSTEMS INC.
PMM	O	550	25	29	ATLANTA	GA	BYCOM SYSTEMS INC.
PMM	O	530	40	71	CALHOUN	GA	CARRIAGE INDUSTRIES INC.
PMM	O	462	658	74	AUGUSTA	GA	BANKERS FIRST CORPORATION
PMM	N	420	376	190	JACKSONVILLE	FL	AMERICAN HERITAGE LIFE INVEST CORP
PMM	O	416	33	33	NORCROSS	GA	ELECTROMAGNETIC SCIENCES INC
PMM	O	415	991	116	SAVANNAH	GA	GREAT SOUTHERN FEDERAL

Price Waterhouse

Aud1	Trd	Emp	Ast	Sls	Cty	Sta	Name
PW	N	18000	2806	2256	TAMPA	FL	WALTER (JIM) CORP.
PW	N	16000	285	538	NASHVILLE	TN	GENESCO INC
PW	N	13000	14829	1574	JACKSONVILLE	FL	BARNETT BANKS OF FLORIDA INC
PW	N	10000	337	626	THOMASVILLE	GA	FLOWERS INDUSTRIES INC
PW	O	8700	17319	1899	MARIETTA	GA	FIRST CITY BANCORP INC. (GA)
PW	O	7500	98	169	MEMPHIS	TN	SHONEY'S SOUTH INC
PW	A	7200	959	426	NORTH MIAMI	FL	RESORTS INTERNATIONAL INC
PW	A	5500	181	89	ATLANTA	GA	JOHNSTOWN AMERICAN COMPANIES
PW	O	3200	4026	405	TAMPA	FL	FIRST FLORIDA BANKS INC.
PW	O	2100	2788	271	ATLANTA	GA	BANK SOUTH CORP.
PW	O	2100	110	141	ATLANTA	GA	NATIONAL DATA CORP
PW	O	1900	182	152	ATLANTA	GA	MANAGEMENT SCIENCE AMERICA INC
PW	A	1800	277	288	ATLANTA	GA	TURNER BROADCASTING SYSTEM
PW	O	1600	2312	248	MEMPHIS	TN	UNION PLANTERS CORP
PW	N	1500	109	98	ST PETERSBURG	FL	MILTON ROY CO.
PW	O	1300	974	491	MIAMI	FL	AMERICAN BANKERS INS GRP INC (FLA)
PW	O	1300	307	629	SAVANNAH	GA	SAVANNAH FOODS & INDUSTRIES INC
PW	O	1200	42	265	SMYRNA	TN	CAPITOL AIR INC
PW	Z	1100	59	121	TAMPA	FL	CROWN INDUSTRIES INC
PW	N	1100	61	69	FORT LAUDERDALE	FL	MODULAR COMPUTER SYSTEMS INC
PW	O	1100	27	34	NORCROSS	GA	INMED CORP.
PW	B	1000	52	83	MIAMI	FL	AIRLIFT INTERNATIONAL INC
PW	A	1000	211	81	POMPANO BEACH	FL	FPA CORP
PW	O	780	64	83	JOHNSON CITY	TN	GENERAL SHALE PRODUCTS CORP
PW	A	700	63	80	LAKELAND	FL	SIKES CORP
PW	N	620	166	86	ST. PETERSBURG	FL	RJ FINANCIAL CORPORATION
PW	O	561	36	97	THOMASVILLE	GA	DAVIS WATER & WASTE INDUSTRIES
PW	N	470	44	71	TALLAHASSE	FL	MOBILE HOME INDUSTRIES INC.
PW	B	469	20	28	MILLEN	GA	RUSCO INDUSTRIES INC
PW	O	426	10	34	MIAMI	FL	NORTH AMERICAN BIOLOGICALS INC
PW	O	421	16	32	ATLANTA	GA	CABLE AMERICA INC.
PW	O	378	29	25	CLEARWATER	FL	CONCEPT INC
PW	Z	285	20	14	CYPRESS GARDENS	FL	FLORIDA CYPRESS GARDENS INC.
PW	O	275	1	1	TEMPLE TERRACE	FL	LEEDS SHOES INC
PW	B	250	19	14	DOTHAN	AL	COLEMAN AMERICAN COMPANIES INC
PW	O	232	66	14	ST. PETERSBURG	FL	CHEEZEM DEVELOPMENT CORP.
PW	O	205	18	13	ORLANDO	FL	MECHTRON INTERNATIONAL CORP
PW	O	200	1	32	TAMPA	FL	KEY ENERGY ENTERPRISES INC
PW	X	150	10	36	ATLANTA	GA	SPECIALIZED SERVICES INC.
PW	O	120	23	29	MIAMI	FL	AERO SYSTEMS INC
PW	O	98	17	28	MIAMI	FL	AMERICAN METALS SERVICE INC
PW	O	66	10	14	GAINESVILLE	FL	GAINESVILLE GAS CO.
PW	O	65	19	22	SARASOTA	FL	SNELLING & SNELLING INC
PW	O	60	1	1	PALM COAST	FL	CARDIAC CONTROL SYSTEMS INC.

Touche Ross

Aud1	Trd	Emp	Ast	Sls	Cty	Sta	Name
TR	O	24000	1459	2526	NASHVILLE	TN	SERVICE MERCHANDISE COMPANY INC
TR	O	15000	803	1424	MIAMI	FL	EVANS PRODUCTS CO
TR	N	12000	235	559	ATLANTA	GA	OXFORD INDUSTRIES INC
TR	N	9000	172	457	ATLANTA	GA	MUNFORD INC
TR	N	8300	1129	345	FORT LAUDERDALE	FL	REVLON GROUP INC.
TR	O	3500	5045	516	NASHVILLE	TN	THIRD NATIONAL CORP
TR	N	3200	207	463	NASHVILLE	TN	HEALTHAMERICA CORPORATION
TR	O	2600	425	116	ATLANTA	GA	DAYS INNS CORP.
TR	O	2100	235	155	BOCA RATON	FL	TELECOM PLUS INTERNATIONAL
TR	A	2000	55	99	SEMINOLE	FL	SUPERIOR SURGICAL MFG CO INC
TR	N	1700	213	203	MIAMI BEACH	FL	APL CORP.
TR	O	1500	3559	425	AUGUSTA	GA	FIRST RAILROAD & BANKING CO OF GA
TR	O	1400	2299	205	JACKSON	MS	FIRST CAPITAL CORP
TR	O	1100	75	26	MEMPHIS	TN	SEVEN OAKS INTERNATIONAL INC.
TR	O	958	89	110	ATLANTA	GA	AARON RENTS INC.
TR	O	890	44	116	JACKSON MISS.	MS	CAL MAINE FOODS INC
TR	X	825	42	45	KNOXVILLE	TN	STERCHI BROTHERS STORES INC
TR	O	800	70	72	NASHVILLE	TN	NELSON (THOMAS)INC.
TR	O	730	29	46	COMMERCE	GA	ROPER INDUSTRIES INC
TR	O	704	35	54	MEMPHIS	TN	PIPER INDUSTRIES INC.
TR	O	670	26	82	JACKSONVILLE	FL	LIL CHAMP FOOD STORES INC
TR	O	664	57	52	ATLANTA	GA	FIRST FINANCIAL MANAGEMENT CRP
TR	A	560	21	34	CALHOUN	GA	CROWN CRAFTS INC
TR	O	500	39	67	MIAMI	FL	BENIHANA NATIONAL CORP
TR	A	496	28	51	TAMARAC	FL	VISUAL GRAPHICS CORP
TR	O	450	1	25	CALHOUN	GA	ALDON INDUSTRIES INC
TR	O	400	496	45	MIAMI	FL	CITY NATIONAL BANK CORP.
TR	A	400	13	60	MIAMI	FL	SUN CITY INDUSTRIES INC
TR	O	397	1197	121	SARASOTA	FL	COAST FED. S & L ASSOC.
TR	O	384	18	67	BIRMINGHAM	AL	PASQUALE FOOD CO INC
TR	O	317	9	24	MARIETTA	GA	BANKER'S NOTE INC.
TR	O	308	13	17	ORLANDO	FL	REPCO INC
TR	O	300	569	63	GULFPORT	MS	HANCOCK BANK
TR	L	300	1	1	HIALEAH	FL	COSMETICALLY YOURS INC
TR	A	290	60	40	HIALEAH	FL	CITY GAS CO OF FLORIDA
TR	B	250	1	1	MARIETTA	GA	STEM INDUSTRIES INC.
TR	A	225	15	14	JACKSON	MS	SCHOOL PICTURES INC
TR	O	201	1	1	MEMPHIS	TN	CRAWFORD CORP.
TR	O	150	382	93	JACKSON	MS	LAMAR LIFE CORP
TR	O	140	1	17	MIAMI	FL	SPEC'S MUSIC INC.
TR	O	140	102	38	ST PETERSBURG	FL	JUSTICE INVESTMENT CORP.
TR	A	130	36	44	FORT LAUDERDALE	FL	ARMEL INC
TR	O	125	1	1	Nashville	TN	SUNGROUP INC
TR	O	109	126	13	VICKSBURG	MS	MERCHANTS CAPITAL CORP.

Offices By Firm - Central Region

CITY	ST	AA	AY	CL	DHS	EW	KMG	PMM	PW	TR
Akron	OH			1		1		1		1
Ann Arbor	MI				1					1
Battle Creek	MI								1	
Beachwood	OH								1	
Canton	OH			1		1	1			
Cincinnati	OH	1	1	1	1	1	1	1	1	1
Cleveland	OH	1	1	1	1	3	1	1	1	1
Columbus	OH	1	1	1	1	1	1	1	1	1
Dayton	OH	1		1	1	1			1	1
Detroit	MI	1	1	1	2	1	1	1	1	1
Dublin	OH								1	
Elkhart	IN				1					
Fort Wayne	IN				1	1				
Grand Rapids	MI	1		1	1	1				1
Indianapolis	IN	1	1	1	1	1	1	1	1	
Jackson	MI					1				
Kalamazoo	MI					1				
Lansing	MI					1	1			1
Lexington	KY			1	1	1				
Louisville	KY	1	1	1		1		1		1
Marquette	MI					1				
Saginaw	MI				1	1				
South Bend	IN			1		1		1	1	
Toledo	OH	1	2	1		1		1	1	1
Troy	MI		1							

CITY	ST	AA	AY	CL	DHS	EW	KMG	PMM	PW	TR
Youngstown	OH					1				
TOTALS										
		9	9	14	12	22	7	9	11	11

Market Share Leadership

Central Region

CITY or AREA	ST	Firm	Firm	Firm	Firm
Cincinnati	OH	AA	DHS		
Cleveland	OH	AA	EW	PMM	
Columbus	OH	AA	CL	DHS	
Dayton	OH	DHS	EW	TR	
Detroit	MI	AA	CL	TR	
Indianapolis	IN	AA	EW	PW	
Louisville	KY	CL	EW	TR	
Toledo	OH	AY	EW		

Personnel By Region
Central Region

Region	AA	AY	CL	DHS	EW	KMG	PMM	PW	TR
Central	1075	400	1100	625	1575	125	600	640	750

Major Clients By Firm
Central Region

Audl = Principal Accountants

Trd = Shows the where traded status of company shares
          A - American Stock Exchange
          N - New York Stock Exchange
          O - Over the Counter
          B - Company in some condition of bankruptcy
          C - Co-op or mutual
          L - Company in liquidation
          S - Subsidiary which reports separately
          U - Subsidiary whose auditor is different from parent
          X - Company which has gone private

Emp = Number of employees

Name = Company name

SIC = Four digit Standard Industrial Classification

Sta = State

Ast = Assets

Sls = Sales

Arthur Andersen

Aud1	Trd	Emp	Ast	Sls	Cty	Sta	Name
AA	N	29000	2366	3305	TOLEDO	OH	OWENS CORNING FIBERGLAS CORP
AA	N	28000	850	1920	CINCINNATI	OH	UNITED STATES SHOE CORP
AA	N	20000	1705	2146	COLUMBUS	IN	CUMMINS ENGINE COMPANY INC
AA	N	20000	1212	2387	COLUMBUS	OH	LIMITED INC
AA	O	16000	562	803	WILLOUGHBY	OH	FIGGIE INTERNATIONAL INC.
AA	O	13000	284	1362	MAPLE HEIGHTS	OH	FIRST NATIONAL SUPERMARKETS INC
AA	N	11000	8615	3298	JACKSON	MI	CONSUMERS POWER CO
AA	X	9500	300	617	CLEVELAND	OH	COLE NATIONAL CORP
AA	N	7500	7290	1755	AKRON	OH	OHIO EDISON CO
AA	N	7300	505	625	MUSKEGON	MI	SEALED POWER CORP
AA	N	5800	3833	1909	HAMMOND	IN	NORTHERN INDIANA PUBLIC SERVICE
AA	S	5200	897	400	FORT WAYNE	IN	GENERAL TELEPHONE CO OF INDIANA
AA	O	5000	201	320	JASPER	IN	KIMBALL INTERNATIONAL INC
AA	N	4900	115	233	BEACHWOOD	OH	FABRI-CENTERS OF AMERICA INC
AA	N	4800	98	226	JACKSON	MI	HAYES-ALBION CORP
AA	N	4600	2974	1397	CINCINNATI	OH	CINCINNATI GAS & ELECTRIC CO
AA	O	4600	273	529	INDIANAPOLIS	IN	STOKELY-VAN CAMP INC.
AA	O	4400	198	250	INDIANAPOLIS	IN	BASIC AMERICAN MEDICAL INC
AA	S	4400	1214	2026	DETROIT	MI	MICHIGAN CONSOLIDATED GAS CO.
AA	N	4400	168	377	CLEVELAND	OH	STANDARD PRODUCTS CO.
AA	O	4100	290	492	ZEELAND	MI	MILLER (HERMAN) INC.
AA	N	3900	2721	975	PLAINFIELD	IN	PUBLIC SERVICE CO OF INDIANA INC
AA	S	3800	857	367	MARION	OH	GENERAL TELEPHONE CO OF OHIO
AA	N	3700	1543	675	LOUISVILLE	KY	LOUISVILLE GAS & ELECTRIC CO
AA	N	3600	262	522	PONTIAC	MI	PERRY DRUG STORES INC
AA	X	3000	48	199	DETROIT	MI	CD ACQUISITION CORP.
AA	N	2900	2077	987	DAYTON	OH	DAYTON POWER & LIGHT CO.
AA	O	2800	24	126	SYRACUSE	IN	COMMODORE CORP
AA	N	2700	3030	309	MICHIGAN CITY	IN	HORIZON BANCORP (NJ)
AA	O	2700	130	241	JACKSON	MI	JACOBSON STORES INC
AA	S	2700	703	297	MUSKEGON	MI	GENERAL TELEPHONE CO OF MICHIGAN
AA	N	2600	3365	595	TOLEDO	OH	TOLEDO EDISON CO
AA	O	2200	178	186	TROY	MI	SCHERER (R.P.) CORP
AA	O	2000	3419	315	CINCINNATI	OH	FIRST NATIONAL CINCINNATI CORP
AA	N	2000	1309	538	LEXINGTON	KY	KENTUCKY UTILITIES CO
AA	A	1800	163	1408	DAYTON	OH	SUPER FOOD SERVICES INC
AA	O	1800	115	150	COLUMBUS	OH	ACCURAY CORP
AA	O	1500	50	73	CASS CITY	MI	WALBRO CORP
AA	N	1400	91	153	TROY	MI	KUHLMAN CORP.
AA	N	1200	98	128	CLEVELAND	OH	BANNER INDUSTRIES INC.
AA	O	1100	39	62	ANN ARBOR	MI	COMSHARE INC.
AA	O	1100	56	97	Walker	MI	ROSPATCH CORP
AA	N	1100	320	420	INDIANAPOLIS	IN	INDIANA ENERGY INC.
AA	O	994	40	75	LOUISVILLE	KY	DMI FURNITURE INC.

Arthur Young

Aud1	Trd	Emp	Ast	Sls	Cty	Sta	Name
AY	O	63000	4517	5087	LOUISVILLE	KY	BATUS INC.
AY	N	45000	3306	3674	TOLEDO	OH	OWENS ILLINOIS INC
AY	N	12000	494	918	TOLEDO	OH	SHELLER GLOBE CORP
AY	O	6700	8749	781	CLEVELAND	OH	SOCIETY CORP
AY	N	4900	295	523	FINDLAY	OH	COOPER TIRE & RUBBER CO
AY	O	3200	111	431	MAUMEE	OH	SEAWAY FOOD TOWN INC
AY	N	3100	90	135	YOUNGSTOWN	OH	GF CORP
AY	O	2800	148	162	LOUISVILLE	KY	CHI-CHI'S INC.
AY	S	2800	668	309	MANSFIELD	OH	UNITED TELEPHONE CO. OF OHIO
AY	N	2800	75	138	JACKSON	MI	SPARTON CORP
AY	O	2100	101	147	DAYTON	OH	DURIRON COMPANY INC
AY	O	2100	329	152	KANSAS CITY	MI	UNITED INTER-MOUNTAIN TELEPHON
AY	O	1800	92	108	CINCINNATI	OH	CINTAS CORP.
AY	O	1700	113	140	AMHERST	OH	NORDSON CORP
AY	O	1700	36	256	DEFIANCE	OH	DINNER BELL FOODS INC
AY	N	1500	443	773	KEEGO HARBOR	MI	PULTE HOME CORP
AY	S	1300	226	118	WARSAW	IN	UNITED TELEPHONE CO. INDIANA
AY	O	610	679	77	TOLEDO	OH	FIRST OHIO BANCSHARES INC.
AY	O	540	168	69	CLEVELAND	OH	MALRITE COMMUNICATIONS GROUP INC
AY	O	425	114	233	CLEVELAND	OH	PIONEER-STANDARD ELECTRONICS INC
AY	O	348	13	13	TOLEDO	OH	CRAFT HOUSE CORPORATION
AY	O	336	20	39	GIBSONBURG	OH	CHEMI-TROL CHEMICAL CO.
AY	O	317	38	50	LAPEER	MI	DURAKON INDUSTRIES INC.
AY	O	292	18	33	ANN ARBOR	MI	THETFORD CORP
AY	A	140	17	19	CINCINNATI	OH	LODGE & SHIPLEY CO
AY	L	90	1	1	CANTON	OH	METROPOLITAN INDUSTRIES INC
AY	O	80	1	1	SOUTHFIELD	MI	LEECO DIAGNOSTICS INC.
AY	O	49	20	1	CANTON	OH	RESOURCE EXPLORATION INC
AY	O	35	18	1	NORTH CANTON	OH	MONOGRAM OIL & GAS INC.
AY	O	32	23	22	HARTVILLE	OH	LOMAK PETROLEUM INC.
AY	O	29	1	1	NORTON	OH	OMNITRONICS RESEARCH CORP.
AY	O	10	18	29	TOLEDO	OH	APOLLO INDUSTRIES INC.
AY	O	5	1	1	CINCINNATI	OH	ALPHA SOLARCO INC.
AY	O	2	1	1	HILLIARD	OH	SCRIPTEL CORPORATION
AY	O	0	1	19	CINCINNATI	OH	FIBRE GLASS-EVERCOAT CO. INC.
AY	O	0	1	1	CINCINNATI	OH	SOLECTRIC CORPORATION
AY	L	0	1	11	HOLLAND	MI	SQUIRT-DETROIT BOTTLING

Coopers & Lybrand

Aud1	Trd	Emp	Ast	Sls	Cty	Sta	Name
CL	N	369000	31604	52774	DEARBORN	MI	FORD MOTOR CO
CL	N	165000	4178	17124	CINCINNATI	OH	KROGER CO
CL	N	57000	2528	3836	AKRON	OH	FIRESTONE TIRE & RUBBER CO OHIO
CL	N	47000	811	1100	DUBLIN	OH	WENDYS INTERNATIONAL INC
CL	N	43000	2832	2280	LOUISVILLE	KY	HUMANA INC
CL	S	30000	4076	2153	DETROIT	MI	MICHIGAN BELL TELEPHONE CO.
CL	N	23000	966	1460	CLEVELAND	OH	PARKER-HANNIFIN CORP
CL	N	20000	2377	2105	KALAMAZOO	MI	UPJOHN CO
CL	X	20000	506	1424	COLUMBUS	OH	SCOA INDUSTRIES INC.
CL	S	14900	3745	1670	CLEVELAND	OH	OHIO BELL TELEPHONE CO
CL	N	14000	1817	1154	TAYLOR	MI	MASCO CORP
CL	S	10000	1842	820	INDIANAPOLIS	IN	INDIANA BELL TELEPHONE CO. INC.
CL	N	7900	10823	1192	COLUMBUS	OH	BANC-ONE CORP.
CL	A	6600	935	928	LOUISVILLE	KY	BROWN FORMAN DISTILLERS CORP.
CL	S	6060	31313	3993	DEARBORN	MI	FORD MOTOR CREDIT CO.
CL	C	6000	3337	423	CINCINNATI	OH	WESTERN & SOUTHERN LIFE INSUR.
CL	O	5500	2113	1166	HAMILTON	OH	OHIO CASUALTY CORP
CL	N	5500	1596	672	HUDSON	OH	ALLTEL CORP.
CL	N	5100	937	467	CINCINNATI	OH	CINCINNATI BELL INC
CL	N	5000	134	169	DUBLIN	OH	RANCO INC
CL	O	4200	4142	302	LOUISVILLE	KY	FIRST KENTUCKY NATIONAL CORP
CL	A	4000	3810	1515	LOUISVILLE	KY	I.C.H. CORP.
CL	N	3700	143	259	CINCINNATI	OH	KDI CORP.
CL	A	3400	191	230	LOUISVILLE	KY	VERMONT AMERICAN CORP
CL	O	3300	89	179	BLUFFTON	IN	FRANKLIN ELECTRIC CO INC
CL	N	3200	145	328	ELKHART	IN	SKYLINE CORP
CL	O	3100	184	333	COLUMBUS	OH	CHEMLAWN CORP.
CL	O	3000	74	122	ELKHART	IN	NIBCO INC.
CL	O	2500	117	359	TAYLOR	MI	HIGHLAND SUPERSTORES
CL	Z	2400	4131	377	INDIANAPOLIS	IN	AMERICAN FLETCHER CORP
CL	O	2000	228	584	SCOTTSVILLE	KY	DOLLAR GENERAL CORP
CL	N	1900	117	147	FORT WAYNE	IN	TOKHEIM CORP
CL	O	1700	811	457	MAYFIELD VILLAGE	OH	PROGRESSIVE CORP - OHIO
CL	N	1700	91	123	INDIANPOLIS	IN	ANACOMP INC
CL	N	1600	203	401	TROY	MI	HANDLEMAN CO
CL	B	1500	95	127	KOKOMO	IN	CONTINENTAL STEEL CORP.
CL	N	1500	97	144	CADILLAC	MI	KYSOR INDUSTRIAL CORP
CL	O	1500	78	123	CLEVELAND	OH	UNITED STATES TRUCK LINES INC.
CL	O	1200	230	317	COLUMBUS	OH	SCHOTTENSTEIN STORES CORP.
CL	C	1000	2392	664	INDIANAPOLIS	IN	AMERICAN UNITED LIFE INSURANCE
CL	N	1000	84	79	SIDNEY	OH	MONARCH MACHINE TOOL CO
CL	O	1000	57	93	GOSHEN	IN	LIBERTY HOMES INC
CL	N	980	156	130	EVANSVILLE	IN	PYRO ENERGY CORP
CL	O	960	14	23	CINCINNATI	OH	MILLER SHOE INDUSTRIES INC.

Deloitte Haskins & Sells

Audt	Trd	Emp	Ast	Sls	Cty		Sta	Name
DHS	N	62000	9683	13552	CINCINNATI		OH	PROCTER & GAMBLE CO
DHS	N	53000	11830	11537	MIDLAND		MI	DOW CHEMICAL CO
DHS	N	31000	3293	3733	MIDDLETOWN		OH	ARMCO INC
DHS	N	23400	13621	4848	COLUMBUS		OH	AMERICAN ELECTRIC POWER CO INC
DHS	N	20000	255	490	DAYTON		OH	PONDEROSA INC.
DHS	N	19000	1030	1430	BEACHWOOD		OH	LEASEWAY TRANSPORTATION CORP
DHS	S	14000	75448	8742	DETROIT		MI	GENERAL MOTORS ACCEPTANCE CORP
DHS	O	11000	961	1177	ELKHART		IN	MILES LABORATORIES INC.
DHS	X	9000	262	419	CINCINNATI		OH	PALM BEACH INC
DHS	O	7000	219	352	DAYTON		OH	ELDER-BEERMAN STORES CORP
DHS	S	7000	3563	1507	S.W. CANTON		OH	OHIO POWER CO
DHS	O	6700	7252	827	BLOOMFIELD HILLS		MI	MICHIGAN NATIONAL CORP
DHS	O	6000	6062	608	COLUMBUS		OH	BANCOHIO CORP.
DHS	N	5800	221	462	DAYTON		OH	PHILIPS INDUSTRIES INC
DHS	O	5800	263	441	COLUMBUS		OH	LANCASTER COLONY CORP
DHS	O	5600	113	105	COLUMBUS		OH	RAX RESTAURANTS INC.
DHS	O	5300	1	1	COLUMBUS		OH	SCIOTO INVESTMENT CO.
DHS	N	5200	854	903	WICKLIFFE		OH	LUBRIZOL CORP
DHS	O	5000	1	1	INDIANAPOLIS		IN	CAPITAL INDUSTRIES INC.
DHS	N	3700	108	536	DETROIT		MI	ALLIED SUPERMARKETS INC.
DHS	O	3400	173	325	DAYTON		OH	REYNOLDS & REYNOLDS CO
DHS	N	3300	225	496	CLEVELAND		OH	BEARINGS INC
DHS	S	3200	3464	966	FORT WAYNE		IN	INDIANA & MICHIGAN ELECTRIC CO
DHS	O	2800	133	204	INDIANAPOLIS		IN	PT COMPONENTS INC.
DHS	S	2700	1897	733	COLUMBUS		OH	COLUMBUS & SOUTHERN OHIO ELECT.
DHS	O	2400	883	291	LEXINGTON		KY	KENTUCKY CENTRAL LIFE INSURANCE
DHS	O	2400	375	423	BLOOMFIELD HILLS		MI	CROSS & TRECKER CORP
DHS	S	2300	1536	471	INDIANAPOLIS		IN	INDIANAPOLIS POWER & LIGHT CO.
DHS	N	2300	1633	471	INDIANAPOLIS		IN	IPALCO ENTERPRISES INC.
DHS	O	2200	61	131	COLUMBUS		OH	KOBACKER STORES INC.
DHS	O	2000	2762	296	CINCINNATI		OH	FIFTH THIRD BANCORP
DHS	X	2000	78	185	COLUMBUS		OH	BEVERAGE MANAGEMENT INC
DHS	O	1900	34	65	WARREN		MI	ELIAS BROTHERS RESTAURANTS INC
DHS	O	1500	2576	264	INDIANAPOLIS		IN	MERCHANTS NATIONAL CORP
DHS	O	1400	1255	608	CINCINNATI		OH	CINCINNATI FINANCIAL CORP
DHS	A	1100	62	140	CINCINNATI		OH	CLOPAY CORP
DHS	O	1000	250	135	CINCINNATI		OH	SCRIPPS HOWARD BROADCASTING CO
DHS	O	880	70	111	COLUMBUS		OH	WILLIAMS (W.W.) CO.
DHS	O	870	17	71	Dayton		OH	SHOPSMITH INC.
DHS	O	850	37	47	DETROIT		MI	SHATTERPROOF GLASS CORP
DHS	S	830	571	260	ASHLAND		KY	KENTUCKY POWER CO
DHS	N	800	71	70	LAFAYETTE		IN	NATIONAL HOMES CORP
DHS	O	730	70	78	GREENVILLE		OH	AMERICAN AGGREGATES CORP
DHS	S	714	178	54	LEXINGTON		KY	KENTUCKY FINANCE CO INC

Ernst & Whinney

Aud1	Trd	Emp	Ast	Sls	Cty	Sta	Name
EW	N	42000	2814	3675	CLEVELAND	OH	EATON CORP
EW	N	42000	18330	13002	CLEVELAND	OH	STANDARD OIL COMPANY (OHIO)
EW	N	33000	3928	8182	ASHLAND	KY	ASHLAND OIL INC
EW	S	29000	4192	2215	CLEVELAND	OH	CHESAPEAKE AND OHIO RAILWAY CO
EW	N	28000	3954	3271	INDIANAPOLIS	IN	LILLY (ELI) & CO.
EW	N	28000	2260	3201	AKRON	OH	GOODRICH (B.F.) CO.
EW	N	26000	1337	1922	TOLEDO	OH	LIBBEY-OWENS FORD CO.
EW	N	24000	1760	3474	BENTON HARBOR	MI	WHIRLPOOL CORP
EW	O	21000	1000	1580	AKRON	OH	ROADWAY SERVICE INC.
EW	N	19000	1056	2195	CLEVELAND	OH	SHERWIN WILLIAMS CO
EW	O	19000	873	1012	CLEVELAND	OH	AMERICAN GREETINGS CORP
EW	N	18000	1375	1091	CANTON	OH	TIMKEN CO
EW	O	16000	335	683	NORTH CANTON	OH	HOOVER CO
EW	N	16000	1140	1946	CLEVELAND	OH	WHITE CONSOLIDATED INDUSTRIES
EW	N	15000	601	968	FREMONT	MI	GERBER PRODUCTS CO
EW	N	13000	13550	4907	FORT WAYNE	IN	LINCOLN NATIONAL CORP
EW	N	13000	682	895	DETROIT	MI	FEDERAL MOGUL CORP
EW	N	10000	483	905	DAYTON	OH	DAYCO CORP
EW	O	9700	129	228	COLUMBUS	OH	EVANS (BOB) FARMS INC
EW	N	9300	3735	6615	CLEVELAND	OH	TRW INCORPORATED
EW	N	9200	692	715	CLEVELAND	OH	MIDLAND-ROSS CORP.
EW	N	9000	229	389	ROCKFORD	MI	WOLVERINE WORLD WIDE INC
EW	N	9000	670	732	CINCINNATI	OH	CINCINNATI MILACRON INC
EW	O	9000	12505	1302	CLEVELAND	OH	NATIONAL CITY CORP
EW	N	8200	6588	2163	LOUISVILLE	KY	CAPITAL HOLDING CORP
EW	N	7000	166	555	MAPLE HEIGHTS	OH	COOK UNITED INC
EW	O	5800	6257	2376	CINCINNATI	OH	AMERICAN FINANCIAL CORP
EW	N	5700	560	344	CLEVELAND	OH	CLEVELAND CLIFFS IRON CO.
EW	O	5300	393	701	COLUMBUS	OH	WORTHINGTON INDUSTRIES INC
EW	O	5000	91	296	GRAND RAPIDS	MI	INTERSTATE MOTOR FREIGHT SYSTEM
EW	O	4500	7787	689	CLEVELAND	OH	AMERITRUST CORP
EW	O	4300	6240	634	COLUMBUS	OH	HUNTINGTON BANCSHARES INC
EW	N	4200	163	495	BEDFORD HEIGHTS	OH	FISHER FOODS INC.
EW	O	4100	73	69	KALAMAZOO	MI	CHECKER MOTORS CORP
EW	N	4100	1066	542	CLEVELAND	OH	NORTH AMERICAN COAL CORP
EW	O	3900	6980	636	DETROIT	MI	MANUFACTURERS NATIONAL CORP
EW	N	3600	533	265	CLEVELAND	OH	HANNA (M.A.) COMPANY
EW	A	3600	320	285	CLEVELAND	OH	FOREST CITY ENTERPRISES INC
EW	O	3600	53	72	INDIANAPOLIS	IN	CONSOLIDATED PRODUCTS INC.
EW	O	3600	143	255	CLEVELAND	OH	HIGBEE CO
EW	O	3300	42	64	INDIANAPOLIS	IN	STEAK'N'SHAKE INC
EW	N	3200	295	318	LOUISVILLE	KY	THOMAS INDUSTRIES INC
EW	N	3100	224	223	CLEVELAND	OH	ACME-CLEVELAND CORP
EW	O	3000	171	186	CLEVELAND	OH	PARK OHIO INDUSTRIES INC

KMG Main Hurdman

Aud1	Trd	Emp	Ast	Sls	Cty	Sta	Name
MH	N	5500	394	411	CANTON	OH	DIEBOLD INC
MH	A	4000	80	181	COLUMBUS	OH	CONSOLIDATED STORES CORP.
MH	L	160	24	14	LANSING	MI	GROSS TELECASTING INC
MH	O	55	5	1	CINCINNATI	OH	NATMAR INC.
MH	O	28	1	1	CANTON	OH	OLYMPIC SOLAR CORP
MH	B	21	13	18	CINCINNATI	OH	RIO VERDE ENERGY CORP.
MH	O	8	1	1	Erlanger	KY	ANGSTROM TECHNOLOGIES INC.
MH	O	0	71	1	GLADWIN	MI	MID MICHIGAN BANK CORP.
MH	O	0	12	21	CLEVELAND	OH	WRIGHT AIR LINES INC.

Peat Marwick Mitchell

Aud1	Trd	Emp	Ast	Sls	Cty	Sta	Name
PMM	N	25000	875	2396	TWINSBURY	OH	REVCO (D.S.) INC.
PMM	N	15000	799	1140	TROY	MI	EX-CELL-O CORP
PMM	N	13000	641	829	TOLEDO	OH	CHAMPION SPARK PLUG CO
PMM	O	9400	77	96	INDIANAPOLIS	IN	OVERLAND EXPRESS INC
PMM	N	8200	468	642	CINCINNATI	OH	EAGLE PICHER INDUSTRIES INC.
PMM	N	8000	393	651	CLEVELAND	OH	FERRO CORP.
PMM	O	6000	9770	1022	DETROIT	MI	COMERICA INC.
PMM	N	5400	483	671	WOOSTER	OH	RUBBERMAID INC
PMM	O	5200	254	177	INDIANAPOLIS	IN	FORUM GROUP INC.
PMM	N	4700	313	482	CINCINNATI	OH	CARLISLE CORP
PMM	O	4200	5326	513	KALAMAZOO	MI	FIRST OF AMERICA BANK CORP
PMM	S	4200	2997	699	EVANSVILLE	IN	CREDITHRIFT FINANCIAL INC
PMM	N	3400	269	434	CLEVELAND	OH	PREMIER INDUSTRIAL CORP
PMM	O	3300	92	267	FARMINGTON HILLS	MI	DOUGLAS & LOMASON CO.
PMM	S	3200	2478	619	EVANSVILLE	IN	CREDITHRIFT FINANCIAL CORP.
PMM	N	3100	129	264	MIAMISBURG	OH	HUFFY CORP.
PMM	N	2900	147	247	NILES	MI	NATIONAL-STANDARD CO
PMM	N	2300	763	375	CINCINNATI	OH	TAFT BROADCASTING CO
PMM	A	2300	53	96	PICKERINGTON	OH	BARRY (R.G.) CORP.
PMM	N	2200	149	314	CLEVELAND	OH	VAN DORN CO
PMM	O	1900	10196	1115	DETROIT	MI	FIRST FEDERAL OF MICHIGAN
PMM	O	1900	2404	217	AKRON	OH	FIRST BANCORPORATION OF OHIO
PMM	N	1700	3212	362	CLEVELAND	OH	TRANSOHIO FINANCIAL CORP
PMM	O	1500	2147	199	LOUISVILLE	KY	LIBERTY UNITED BANCORP.
PMM	O	1400	133	118	BROOKLYN HEIGHTS	OH	MISTER GASKET CO
PMM	O	1382	1	1	TRAVERSE CITY	MI	REEF ENERGY CORP
PMM	O	1200	28	66	RICHMOND	KY	BEGLEY CO
PMM	O	1100	1980	206	FLINT	MI	CITIZENS BANKING CORP.
PMM	A	900	35	54	PEPPER PIKE	OH	TRANZONIC COMPANIES
PMM	O	850	1	1	NAPPANEE	IN	MONARCH INDUSTRIES INC
PMM	O	700	607	310	SOUTHFIELD	MI	SRI CORP.
PMM	O	692	35	101	INDIANAPOLIS	IN	CIRCLE EXPRESS INC.
PMM	O	620	46	85	Chesterfield	MI	AMELCO CORP
PMM	O	582	44	49	NEW ALBANY	IN	ROBINSON NUGENT INC
PMM	O	554	19	34	LOUISVILLE	KY	FALLS CITY INDUSTRIES INC.
PMM	O	525	2405	263	ANN ARBOR	MI	GREAT LAKES FEDERAL S & L ASSOC.
PMM	O	500	28	66	LOUISVILLE	KY	LOUISVILLE BEDDING CO.
PMM	O	414	20	35	CLEVELAND	OH	BRODHEAD-GARRETT CO.
PMM	O	353	184	45	INDIANAPOLIS	IN	INDIANAPOLIS WATER CO
PMM	O	310	396	42	FORT WAYNE	IN	SUMMIT BANCORP.
PMM	O	272	866	100	INDIANAPOLIS	IN	FIRST INDIANA FEDERAL SAVINGS BANK
PMM	O	270	1675	540	LANSING	MI	JACKSON NATIONAL LIFE INSURANCE
PMM	O	263	17	23	WATERFORD	MI	TRANS-INDUSTRIES INC
PMM	O	250	1	12	JACKSON	MI	RYERSON & HAYNES INC

Price Waterhouse

Aud1	Trd	Emp	Ast	Sls	Cty	Sta	Name
PW	N	310000	9991	22420	TROY	MI	K MART CORP.
PW	N	134000	6954	9585	AKRON	OH	GOODYEAR TIRE & RUBBER CO
PW	N	62000	3940	2580	DAYTON	OH	NCR CORP
PW	N	61000	4556	5038	DETROIT	MI	BURROUGHS CORP
PW	N	38000	2424	3754	TOLEDO	OH	DANA CORP
PW	N	27000	2073	3021	AKRON	OH	GENCORP INC.
PW	N	17000	1726	2930	BATTLE CREEK	MI	KELLOGG CO
PW	N	11000	9492	2788	DETROIT	MI	DETROIT EDISON CO
PW	N	10800	506	720	LANCASTER	OH	ANCHOR HOCKING CORP
PW	N	10000	888	964	SOUTHBEND	IN	CLARK EQUIPMENT CO
PW	N	9000	642	1106	MUNCIE	IN	BALL CORP
PW	N	6800	213	262	ELKHART	IN	CTS CORP
PW	N	6800	539	508	BATESVILLE	IN	HILLENBRAND INDUSTRIES INC
PW	A	6800	150	225	CLEVELAND	OH	WORK WEAR CORP INC.
PW	N	6600	148	987	DETROIT	MI	BORMAN'S INC
PW	S	6200	1019	901	MIDLAND	MI	DOW CORNING CORPORATION
PW	N	5651	5651	1254	CLEVELAND	OH	CLEVELAND ELECTRIC ILLUMINATING
PW	N	5200	230	373	CINCINNATI	OH	CHEMED CORP.
PW	N	5200	467	379	MINNEAPOLIS	MI	MEDTRONIC INC
PW	O	4000	233	342	MONROE	MI	LA-Z-BOY CHAIR CO.
PW	O	3500	231	320	DELAWARE	OH	GREIF BROTHERS CORP
PW	O	3360	155	303	DAYTON	OH	DAYTON WALTHER
PW	A	3200	107	354	DRYDEN	MI	CHAMPION HOME BUILDERS CO
PW	O	3100	261	330	CINCINNATI	OH	GIBSON GREETINGS INC
PW	O	2200	57	173	INDIANAPOLIS	IN	DANNERS INC
PW	N	2100	110	193	CINCINNATI	OH	OMNICARE INC.
PW	O	2000	179	876	TROY	MI	KELLY SERVICES INC
PW	O	1700	49	86	LEXINGTON	KY	IRVIN INDUSTRIES INC
PW	A	1700	85	154	MENTOR	OH	RUSSELL BURDSALL & WARD INC
PW	C	1400	1370	325	CINCINNATI	OH	UNION CENTRAL LIFE INSURANCE
PW	A	1300	42	105	ELKHART	IN	RIBLET PRODUCTS CORP
PW	O	1200	74	82	VALPARAISO	IN	MC GILL MANUFACTURING CO. INC.
PW	O	1000	109	114	ST CLAIR	MI	DIAMOND CRYSTAL SALT CO
PW	B	1000	18	128	MUNCIE	IN	MARHOEFER PACKING CO. INC.
PW	O	1000	127	222	CINCINNATI	OH	HEEKIN CAN INCORPORATED
PW	O	910	38	71	TROY	MI	DAB INDUSTRIES INC
PW	O	900	65	112	EAST DETROIT	MI	REPUBLIC AUTOMOTIVE PARTS INC
PW	A	880	40	92	ELKHART	IN	EXCEL INDUSTRIES INC.
PW	O	800	50	76	STOW	OH	MORGAN ADHESIVES CO
PW	O	760	29	55	GROVEPORT	OH	UNITED MCGILL CORP
PW	O	655	44	55	AKRON	OH	TELXON CORPORATION
PW	O	645	34	36	CINCINNATI	OH	ROTO-ROOTER INC.
PW	O	642	46	57	IRON MOUNTAIN	MI	LAKE SHORE INC.
PW	O	580	36	39	INDIANAPOLIS	IN	AMERICAN MONITOR CORP.

Touche Ross

Aud1	Trd	Emp	Ast	Sls	Cty	Sta	Name
TR	N	128000	5354	9978	CINCINNATI	OH	FEDERATED DEPARTMENT STORES INC
TR	N	108000	12605	21256	HIGHLAND PARK	MI	CHRYSLER CORPORATION
TR	N	27000	1804	2564	DETROIT	MI	FRUEHAUF CORP.
TR	N	23000	2001	4040	SOUTHFIELD	MI	AMERICAN MOTORS CORP
TR	N	17000	2245	2740	DAYTON	OH	MEAD CORP
TR	N	8700	16676	1515	DETROIT	MI	NBD BANCORP INC.
TR	O	2900	210	828	COLUMBUS	OH	BIG BEAR INC.
TR	S	2600	2510	2387	DETROIT	MI	ANR PIPELINE CO.
TR	N	2100	120	178	AKRON	OH	MC NEIL CORP.
TR	N	1900	118	166	BLOOMFIELD HILLS	MI	CORE INDUSTRIES INC.
TR	S	1700	7149	793	TROY	MI	CHRYSLER FINANCIAL CORP
TR	O	1700	16	28	LOUISVILLE	KY	CHURCHILL DOWNS INC
TR	O	1300	166	272	COLUMBUS	OH	LIEBERT CORP.
TR	N	1200	85	48	DAYTON	OH	NORD RESOURCES CORP
TR	O	1100	23	26	GRAND RAPIDS	MI	HOLLY'S INC.
TR	O	1000	119	206	CLEVELAND	OH	MOR-FLO INDUSTRIES INC.
TR	O	800	174	118	SOLON	OH	AGENCY RENT-A-CAR INC
TR	O	790	37	200	LOUISVILLE	KY	CONNA CORP.
TR	O	680	52	68	DAYTON	OH	TECHNOLOGY INC.
TR	O	460	30	30	TROY	MI	ENERGY CONVERSION DEVICES INC.
TR	A	430	23	38	SOUTHFIELD	MI	HOWELL INDUSTRIES INC
TR	L	430	23	70	TOLEDO	OH	BAKER BROS INC
TR	O	376	18	26	DAYTON	OH	COMGEN TECHNOLOGY INC.
TR	O	375	18	31	LEMON TOWNSHIP	OH	CRYSTAL TISSUE CO
TR	O	281	739	50	BRIMINGHAM	MI	BLOOMFIELD SAVINGS
TR	O	250	29	35	TROY	MI	SANDY CORP.
TR	O	200	1	1	TOLEDO	OH	PET BAZAAR INC.
TR	O	175	1	1	CINCINNATI	OH	OHMART CORP.
TR	O	169	18	16	DEFIANCE	OH	DEFIANCE PRECISION PRODUCTS INC.
TR	O	162	1	1	LOUISVILLE	KY	FRESHER(THE) COOKER
TR	O	130	60	21	BEDFORD HEIGHTS	OH	TRANSCON BUILDERS INC
TR	A	124	10	20	DETROIT	MI	PARK CHEMICAL CO
TR		120	1	11	CINCINNATI	OH	ACCESS CORP
TR	O	114	111	35	GARY	IN	FIRST UNITED INC
TR	O	55	1	10	CHARLOTTE	MI	SPARTAN MOTORS INC
TR	N	54	113	22	CLEVELAND	OH	HALLWOOD GROUP INC.
TR	O	43	1	1	DAYTON	OH	QMAX TECHNOLOGY GROUP INC.
TR	O	26	1	1	TROY	MI	OVONIC DISPLAY SYSTEMS INC.
TR	O	21	1	1	DETROIT	MI	GENERAL METAL & ABRASIVES CO
TR	O	11	1	1	JACKSON	MI	ROBOTICS INTERNATIONAL CORP.
TR	O	0	1	1	ANN ARBOR	MI	CONTINENTAL CAPITAL EQUITIES INC.
TR	O	0	1	1	YOUNGSTOWN	OH	TREACHER'S (ARTHUR) INC.
TR	O	0	994	98	FLINT	MI	UNITED MICHIGAN CORP

Offices By Firm - Midwest Region

CITY	ST	AA	AY	CL	DHS	EW	KMG	PMM	PW	TR
Aurora	IL			1						
Bloomington	IL						1			
Bloomington	MN									1
Champaign	IL						1			
Chicago	IL	2	2	1	1	1	1	1	1	1
Davenport	IA				1			1		
Decatur	IL						1	1		
Des Moines	IA		1	1	1	1		1		
Duluth	MN						1			
Garden City	KS						1			
Kansas City	MO	1	1	1	1	1		1	1	1
Lincoln	NB			1				1		1
Madison	WI		1							
Mattoon	IL						1			
Milwaukee	WI	1	1	1	1	1		1	1	1
Minneapolis	MN	1	1	1	1	1	1	1	1	1
Monmouth	IL						1			
Oakbrook	IL							1	1	
Omaha	NB	1	1	1	1			1		1
Peoria	IL						1	1	1	
Rockford	IL			1				1		
Schaumburg	IL							1		1
Springfield	IL		1		1		1			
St. Charles	IL	1								
St. Louis	MO	1	1	1	1	1	1	2		1

CITY	ST	AA	AY	CL	DHS	EW	KMG	PMM	PW	TR
St. Paul	MN	1			1	1		1		1
Taylorville	IL						1			
Topeka	KS						1			1
Wichita	KS		1				1	1		
TOTALS		9	11	10	10	7	15	16	8	11

Market Share Leadership
Midwest Region

CITY or AREA	ST	Firm	Firm	Firm	Firm
Chicago	IL	AA	PMM		
Kansas City	MO	AA	AY	PMM	TR
Milwaukee	WI	AA	AY	TR	
Minneapolis	MN	AA	DHS	PMM	TR
Omaha	NB	AA	DHS	PMM	TR
St. Louis	MO	AA	PMM	PW	

Personnel By Region

Midwest Region

Region	AA	AY	CL	DHS	EW	KMG	PMM	PW	TR
Midwest	3600	900	975	650	1050	400	1650	900	950

Major Clients By Firm
Midwest Region

Audl = Principal Accountants

Trd = Shows the where traded status of company shares
      A - American Stock Exchange
      N - New York Stock Exchange
      O - Over the Counter
      B - Company in some condition of bankruptcy
      C - Co-op or mutual
      L - Company in liquidation
      S - Subsidiary which reports separately
      U - Subsidiary whose auditor is different from parent
      X - Company which has gone private

Emp = Number of employees

Name = Company name

SIC = Four digit Standard Industrial Classification

Sta = State

Ast = Assets

Sls = Sales

Arthur Andersen

Aud1	Trd	Emp	Ast	Sls	Cty	Sta	Name
AA	N	103000	4448	8164	ST LOUIS	MO	GENERAL DYNAMICS CORP
AA	N	93000	3216	8117	CHICAGO	IL	SARA LEE CORP.
AA	N	77000	3442	5080	ST LOUIS	MO	MAY DEPARTMENT STORES CO
AA	N	76000	7874	6383	ELK GROVE TOWNSHIP	IL	UAL INC
AA	N	76000	18149	9021	CHICAGO	IL	AMERICAN INFORMATION TECHNOLOGIES
AA	N	73000	5502	9942	NORTHBROOK	IL	DART & KRAFT INC.
AA	N	43000	11929	8686	PROSPECT HEIGHTS	IL	HOUSEHOLD INTERNATIONAL INC
AA	N	34000	3468	3360	ABBOTT PARK	IL	ABBOTT LABORATORIES
AA	N	33000	927	1624	GLENVIEW	IL	ZENITH ELECTRONICS CORP.
AA	N	32000	962	3162	DEERFIELD	IL	WALGREEN CO
AA	X	30000	1525	1432	CHICAGO	IL	NORTHWEST INDUSTRIES INC
AA	N	29000	1842	3520	CHICAGO	IL	QUAKER OATS CO
AA	N	25000	609	1302	CHICAGO	IL	CARSON PIRIE SCOTT & CO
AA	U	24000	5303	2688	CHICAGO	IL	ILLINOIS BELL TELEPHONE CO.
AA	N	22000	1732	2526	CHICAGO	IL	USG CORPORATION
AA	O	21000	748	1530	OVERLAND PARK	KS	YELLOW FREIGHT SYSTEM INC
AA	N	20000	2261	1625	OAK BROOK	IL	WASTE MANAGEMENT INC
AA	N	19000	16285	4964	CHICAGO	IL	COMMONWEALTH EDISON CO
AA	N	19000	1002	1539	SKOKIE	IL	BRUNSWICK CORP
AA	N	18000	1593	2038	CHICAGO	IL	DONNELLEY (R.R.)& SONS CO.
AA	N	16000	1614	2319	CHICAGO	IL	UNITED STATES GYPSUM CO
AA	N	14000	38893	4370	CHICAGO	IL	FIRST CHICAGO CORP
AA	N	14000	1537	1363	GREENBAY	WI	FORT HOWARD PAPER CO.
AA	N	13000	984	1104	BROOKFIELD	WI	REXNORD INC
AA	O	13000	1316	881	MINNEAPOLIS	MN	MINSTAR INC.
AA	N	12000	2521	1326	CHICAGO	IL	CENTEL CORP.
AA	C	12000	2751	469	OMAHA	NE	UNITED OF OMAHA LIFE INSUR. CO
AA	N	12000	1128	1571	OAK BROOK	IL	CBI INDUSTRIES INC.
AA	X	11000	1504	897	CHICAGO	IL	CHICAGO & NORTH WESTERN TRANS.
AA	N	11000	9893	10727	OMAHA	NE	INTERNORTH
AA	A	9500	330	612	CHICAGO	IL	AM INTERNATIONAL INC
AA	N	8800	721	880	WAUKEGAN	IL	OUTBOARD MARINE CORP
AA	N	8700	427	162	CHICAGO	IL	CHICAGO MILWAUKEE CORP
AA	N	8200	412	718	WAUWATOSA	WI	BRIGGS & STRATTON CORP.
AA	N	7800	277	613	OAK BROOK	IL	CECO INDUSTRIES INC.
AA	O	7400	133	1005	DOWNERS GROVE	IL	SERVICEMASTER INDUSTRIES INC
AA	N	7300	522	596	CHICAGO	IL	ILLINOIS TOOL WORKS INC
AA	N	7200	652	1169	LA CROSSE	WI	HEILEMAN (G.) BREWING CO. INC.
AA	O	6600	140	56	KANSAS CITY	MO	CENCOR INC
AA	O	6300	72	83	KANSAS CITY	MO	LA PETITE ACADEMY
AA	N	5700	331	844	JANESVILLE	WI	MANPOWER INC.
AA	N	5600	162	246	ST LOUIS	MO	ANGELICA CORP.
AA	N	5500	214	290	CHICAGO	IL	STEWART WARNER CORP
AA	N	5500	2037	2129	NAPERVILLE	IL	NICOR INC

Arthur Young

Aud1	Trd	Emp	Ast	Sls	Cty	Sta	Name
AY	N	145000	5043	3695	OAK BROOK	IL	MC DONALD'S CORP.
AY	N	72000	19291	7925	ST LOUIS	MO	SOUTHWESTERN BELL TELEPHONE CO.
AY	N	27000	5767	3198	KANSAS CITY	MO	UNITED TELECOMMUNICATIONS INC
AY	N	19000	1529	252	CHICAGO	IL	BALLY MANUFACTURING CORP
AY	X	18000	965	1623	CHICAGO	IL	MARMON GROUP INC.
AY	A	9900	486	932	MILWAUKEE	WI	SMITH (A.O.) CORP.
AY	N	8900	1957	1627	NORTHBROOK	IL	INTERNATIONAL MINERALS & CHEMICALS
AY	A	6200	308	2892	CHICAGO	IL	SWIFT INDEPENDENT CORP
AY	N	5600	352	620	CHICAGO	IL	WRIGLEY (WM. JR.) COMPANY
AY	O	4300	7055	615	ST LOUIS	MO	BOATMENS BANCSHARES INC
AY	S	3200	448	357	CHICAGO	IL	SIX FLAGS CORP.
AY	O	2400	1	11	OAKBROOK	IL	XCOR INTERNATIONAL INC
AY	O	2300	208	203	OMAHA	NE	FIRST DATA RESOURCES INC.
AY	O	2100	2701	272	KANSAS CITY	MO	CHARTERCORP
AY	N	1900	127	208	NORTH CHICAGO	IL	FANSTEEL INC
AY	N	1800	888	409	BISMARCK	ND	MDU RESOURCES GROUP INC.
AY	O	1800	64	118	CHICAGO	IL	SHELBY WILLIAMS INDUSTRIES INC.
AY	O	1700	2566	204	WICHITA	KS	FOURTH FINANCIAL CORP
AY	N	1700	133	99	SAINT PAUL	MN	BMC INDUSTRIES INC
AY	O	1615	54	247	DES MOINES	IA	CASEY'S GENERAL STORES INC.
AY	O	1600	73	127	MEQUON	WI	MEDALIST INDUSTRIES INC
AY	O	1500	140	312	OSHKOSH	WI	OSHKOSH TRUCK CORPORATION
AY	O	1300	2291	824	CEDAR RAPIDS	IA	LIFE INVESTORS INC
AY	N	1300	108	158	HESSTON	KS	HESSTON CORP
AY	O	1300	130	181	CHICAGO	IL	MIDWAY AIRLINES INC.
AY	O	1300	88	104	MINNEAPOLIS	MN	DATA CARD CORP.
AY	A	1051	34	58	MILWAUKEE	WI	BADGER METER INC
AY	O	1000	147	82	ROLLING MEADOWS	IL	GALLAGER(ARTHUR J.) & CO.
AY	O	908	173	90	MINNEAPOLIS	MN	NETWORK SYSTEMS CORP.
AY	O	900	18	35	KANSAS CITY	MO	PATTERSON (C.J.) CO.
AY	A	900	37	119	ST LOUIS	MO	BANK BUILDING & EQUIPMENT CORP.
AY	O	850	80	172	MINNEAPOLIS	MN	VAN DUSEN AIR INC.
AY	O	800	59	43	CHICAGO	IL	REGO GROUP INC
AY	N	790	29	41	MILWAUKEE	WI	WINTER (JACK) INC.
AY	A	700	34	84	CHICAGO	IL	GRI CORP
AY	N	618	271	127	JOPLIN	MO	EMPIRE DISTRICT ELECTRIC CO
AY	O	536	65	90	WICHITA	KS	RENT-A-CENTER INC
AY	O	510	11	23	BETTENDORF	IA	SIVYER STEEL CORP.
AY	O	500	33	46	WINFIELD	KS	GOTT CORP
AY	O	420	20	36	MILWAUKEE	WI	WAGNER (E.R.) MANUFACTURING CO
AY	O	330	17	47	WICHITA	KS	PAWNEE INDUSTRIES INCORPORATED
AY	O	300	70	159	MINNEAPOLIS	MN	INTERNATIONAL DAIRY QUEEN INC
AY	L	272	1	1	MT. PROSPECT	IL	DOC LIQUIDATION CORP.
AY	O	260	39	120	PARK RIDGE	IL	BRAND INSULATIONS INC

Coopers & Lybrand

Aud1	Trd	Emp	Ast	Sls	Cty	Sta	Name
CL	N	85000	6593	7846	ST PAUL	MN	MINNESOTA MINING & MANUFACTURING
CL	O	22000	354	84	WEBSTER GROVES	MO	RELIABLE LIFE INSURANCE COMPANY
CL	C	20000	13197	6684	BLOOMINGTON	IL	STATE FARM MUTUAL AUTO INS.
CL	S	17000	4800	2120	OMAHA	NE	NORTHWESTERN BELL TELEPHONE CO.
CL	B	10000	12	24	CHICAGO	IL	GOLDBLATT BROTHERS INC
CL	O	7300	434	727	ST PAUL	MN	ECONOMICS LABORATORY INC
CL	S	7000	1888	898	MILWAUKEE	WI	WISCONSIN BELL INC.
CL	O	5700	903	487	DEKALB	IL	DEKALB AGRESEARCH INC
CL	O	5000	39	135	MINNEAPOLIS	MN	REGIS CORP
CL	O	4300	2261	889	CHICAGO	IL	OLD REPUBLIC INTERNATIONAL CORP
CL	O	4100	1837	1111	MADISON	WI	AMERICAN FAMILY MUTUAL INSURANCE
CL	O	3500	351	512	MINNETONKA	MN	FINGERHUT COMPANIES INC.
CL	O	2800	222	312	RACINE	WI	MODINE MANUFACTURING CO
CL	O	2700	3093	1142	MINNEAPOLIS	MN	NORTHWESTERN NATIONAL LIFE INS.
CL	O	2500	26	56	MILWAUKEE	WI	SCHWERMAN TRUCKING CO
CL	N	2500	365	651	SKOKIE	IL	ANIXTER BROS INC
CL	N	2300	181	370	CHICAGO	IL	HELENE CURTIS INDUSTRIES INC
CL	X	2300	115	286	CHICAGO	IL	JUPITER INDUSTRIES INC
CL	O	2000	146	186	ROCKFORD	IL	WOODWARD GOVERNOR CO
CL	N	1900	60	88	Rolling Meadows	IL	RYMER CO
CL	O	1800	116	155	ROCKFORD	IL	CLARK (J.L.) MFG. CO.
CL	O	1800	145	97	CHICAGO	IL	UNION SPECIAL CORP
CL	N	1600	102	133	RACINE	WI	TWIN DISC INC
CL	O	1400	156	169	HINSDALE	IL	LAIDLAW INDUSTRIES INC.
CL	X	1400	50	56	AURORA	IL	LYON METAL PRODUCTS INC.
CL	B	1300	28	76	CHICAGO	IL	CONSOLIDATED PACKAGING CORP
CL	O	1200	48	61	OMAHA	NE	PACESETTER CORP.
CL	O	1200	81	109	ROCKFORD	IL	ELCO INDUSTRIES INC
CL	O	1100	80	102	AURORA	IL	BARBER GREENE CO
CL	O	1100	86	148	CHICAGO	IL	EVANS INC
CL	N	955	199	96	EAU CLAIRE	WI	NATIONAL PRESTO INDUSTRIES INC
CL	S	857	2051	903	INDEPENDENCE	KS	ARCO PIPE LINE CO
CL	N	840	74	60	NORTHFIELD	IL	ARTRA GROUP INC.
CL	A	765	24	42	SIOUX FALLS	SD	RAVEN INDUSTRIES INC
CL	A	680	44	70	CHICAGO	IL	CONTINENTAL MATERIALS CORP.
CL	O	580	17	19	NEENAH	WI	PLEXUS CORP.
CL	O	553	35	51	CHICAGO	IL	ENVIRODYNE INDUSTRIES INC
CL	O	540	29	35	LOVELAND	IA	HACH CO.
CL	O	500	1	22	CHICAGO	IL	WINDSOR INDUSTRIES INC.
CL	X	475	10	22	MINNEAPOLIS	MN	UNITED TRUCK LEASING
CL	O	437	33	54	SOUTH ST PAUL	MN	TWIN CITY BARGE INC.
CL	O	429	40	49	PESHTIGO	WI	BADGER PAPER MILLS INC
CL	O	358	1	1	BLOOMINGTON	MN	DISCUS CORPORATION
CL	O	350	26	42	CLAYTON	MO	SPARTECH CORP

Deloitte Haskins & Sells

Aud1	Trd	Emp	Ast	Sls	Cty	Sta	Name
DHS	N	94000	5034	6625	MINNEAPOLIS	MN	HONEYWELL INC
DHS	N	56000	8877	6747	ST LOUIS	MO	MONSANTO CO.
DHS	N	41000	5462	4061	MOLINE	IL	DEERE & CO
DHS	N	37000	3504	4073	NEENAH	WI	KIMBERLY-CLARK CORP.
DHS	N	17000	2107	3457	CHICAGO	IL	NAVISTAR INTERNATIONAL CORP.
DHS	N	13000	521	764	ST PAUL	MN	DELUXE CHECK PRINTERS INC
DHS	N	7600	1138	618	MINNEAPOLIS	MN	SOO LINE CORP.
DHS	N	7400	4048	1789	EAU CLAIRE	WI	NORTHERN STATES POWER CO
DHS	N	6600	1632	2937	DECATUR	IL	STALEY CONTINENTAL INC.
DHS	O	4800	306	534	ST PAUL	MN	PENTAIR INC
DHS	O	4000	244	145	MANITOWOC	WI	MANITOWOC COMPANY INC
DHS	S	3600	1138	618	MINNEAPOLIS	MN	SOO LINE RAILROAD CO
DHS	N	3200	46	49	DEKALB	IL	WURLITZER CO
DHS	N	2400	2348	411	WICHITA	KS	KANSAS GAS & ELECTRIC CO.
DHS	N	2200	891	257	MINNEAPOLIS	MN	INTER-REGIONAL FINANCIAL GROUP
DHS	N	2200	506	824	MINNEAPOLIS	MN	DIVERSIFIED ENERGIES INC
DHS	N	2000	381	674	ST LOUIS	MO	LACLEDE GAS CO
DHS	A	2000	122	195	ELK GROVE VILLAGE	IL	GALAXY CARPET MILLS INC
DHS	O	1900	68	125	DUBUQUE	IA	FLEXSTEEL INDUSTRIES INC
DHS	O	1600	189	149	MINNEAPOLIS	MN	CPT CORPORATION
DHS	O	1600	87	117	SAINT PAUL	MN	CONWED CORP
DHS	C	1300	234	524	MINNEAPOLIS	MN	MIDLAND COOPERATIVES
DHS	O	1200	72	221	OVERLAND	MO	HUTTIG SASH & DOOR CO
DHS	O	1185	77	61	WICHITA	KS	AIR MIDWEST INC
DHS	O	1100	1821	219	DES MOINES	IA	HAWKEYE BANCORPORATION
DHS	N	970	555	301	DUBUQUE	IA	INTERSTATE POWER CO
DHS	O	845	482	175	FERGUS FALLS	MN	OTTER TAIL POWER CO
DHS	O	720	116	93	MINNEAPOLIS	MN	LEE DATA CORP
DHS	O	500	10	26	WILMETTE	IL	HARVEST INDUSTRIES INC
DHS	O	495	42	49	LAKE BLUFF	IL	BUEHLER INTERNATIONAL INC.
DHS	O	315	22	39	WILMETTE	IL	CHATHAM CORP
DHS	O	225	1	1	SPRINGFIELD	IL	UNITED NATL. FINANCIAL
DHS	O	215	96	17	CHICAGO	IL	CONSOLIDATED WATER
DHS	O	160	1	1	MINNEAPOLIS	MN	POSSIS CORP
DHS	O	160	376	34	WATERLOO	IA	IOWA NATIONAL BANKSHARES CORP.
DHS	O	150	14	13	ST PAUL	MN	AERO SYSTEMS ENGINEERING INC
DHS	O	125	1	1	ALGONA	IA	UNIVERSAL MANUFACTURING CO
DHS	O	113	33	1	MINNETONKA	MN	MOLECULAR GENETICS INC.
DHS	O	110	15	28	MINNEAPOLIS	MN	HAWKINS CHEMICAL INC
DHS	O	97	1	1	CHICAGO	IL	INTERAND CORP
DHS	O	73	135	14	ROCK ISLAND	IL	FINANCIAL SERVICES CORP OF MIDWEST
DHS	O	58	1	1	MINNEAPOLIS	MN	SOLID CONTROLS INC.
DHS	O	42	16	1	Henry County	IL	IMARK INDUSTRIES INC.
DHS	O	26	1	1	Morton Grove	IL	R2 CORPORATION

Ernst & Whinney

Aud1	Trd	Emp	Ast	Sls	Cty	Sta	Name
EW	N	128000	4418	8793	MINNEAPOLIS	MN	DAYTON-HUDSON CORP
EW	N	97000	7268	11478	ST LOUIS	MO	MC DONNELL DOUGLAS CORP.
EW	N	28000	635	1400	ST LOUIS	MO	BROWN GROUP INC.
EW	N	20000	388	808	ST LOUIS	MO	EDISON BROTHERS STORES INC
EW	N	19000	1388	1420	ROLLING MEADOWS	IL	GOULD INC
EW	N	18000	1368	1958	CHICAGO	IL	MORTON-THIOKOL INC.
EW	N	16000	2320	2655	ST PAUL	MN	NWA INC.
EW	N	11000	669	760	Stoke	IL	BELL & HOWELL CO.
EW	N	9600	25484	2510	MINNEAPOLIS	MN	FIRST BANK SYSTEM INC
EW	N	9100	2967	4739	DECATUR	IL	ARCHER-DANIELS-MIDLAND CO.
EW	C	8800	14927	3032	DES MOINES	IA	BANKERS LIFE CO.
EW	N	8600	315	530	MINNEAPOLIS	MN	JOSTENS INC
EW	A	7000	561	1502	AUSTIN	MN	HORMEL (GEORGE A.) & CO.
EW	O	6200	341	630	ALTON	IL	JEFFERSON SMURFIT CORPORATION
EW	X	6200	216	366	KOHLER	WI	KOHLER CO
EW	N	5600	3474	762	EVANSTON	IL	WASHINGTON NATIONAL CORP
EW	O	5600	1655	447	DES MOINES	IA	EQUITABLE OF IOWA COMPANIES
EW	O	5400	237	473	MUSCATINE	IA	HON INDUSTRIES INC
EW	N	5000	2392	724	CHICAGO	IL	GATX CORP.
EW	N	5000	542	682	OAK BROOK	IL	NALCO CHEMICAL CO
EW	N	4900	365	684	NEWTON	IA	MAYTAG CO
EW	N	4800	314	443	WICHITA	KS	COLEMAN COMPANY INC
EW	O	4300	6763	648	ST LOUIS	MO	MERCANTILE BANCORPORATION INC
EW	N	3900	57	114	MINNEAPOLIS	MN	MUNSINGWEAR INC
EW	N	3200	175	278	OAK BROOK	IL	FEDERAL SIGNAL CORP
EW	N	2900	154	262	MINNEAPOLIS	MN	DONALDSON COMPANY INC
EW	A	2700	349	317	WICHITA	KS	GATES LEARJET CORP.
EW	O	2700	185	216	ORLAND PARK	IL	ANDREW CORP
EW	O	2500	42	63	CHICAGO	IL	OPELIKA MANUFACTURING CORP
EW	A	2200	165	350	MINNEAPOLIS	MN	VALSPAR CORP
EW	A	2100	96	141	Rolling Meadows	IL	KEARNEY NATIONAL INC
EW	O	1900	230	216	EDEN PRAIRIE	MN	NATIONAL COMPUTER SYSTEMS INC
EW	N	1900	250	339	MUSCATINE	IA	BANDAG INC
EW	O	1600	91	124	OVERLAND PARK	KS	PURITAN-BENNETT CORP
EW	N	1400	123	244	MINNETONKA	MN	TONKA CORP
EW	X	1200	38	64	ST LOUIS	MO	AFFILIATED HOSPITAL PRODUCTS INC
EW	O	1100	46	82	CHICAGO	IL	METHODE ELECTRONICS INC
EW	O	1100	63	49	CHICAGO	IL	SIMMONS AIRLINES
EW	O	950	21	53	NEWTON	IA	VERNON CO
EW	O	850	36	105	Milwaukee	WI	DRUG SYSTEMS INC.
EW	O	835	1130	126	ST LOUIS	MO	MARK TWAIN BANCSHARES INC
EW	A	800	10	28	CHICAGO	IL	TRIANGLE HOME PRODUCTS INC
EW	O	800	43	60	WILMETTE	IL	KEWAUNEE SCIENTIFIC EQUIPMENT
EW	N	775	68	85	SKOKIE	IL	SARGENT WELCH SCIENTIFIC CO.

KMG Main Hurdman

Aud1	Trd	Emp	Ast	Sls	Cty	Sta	Name
MH	O	3500	123	206	ST LOUIS	MO	HARVARD INDUSTRIES INC.
MH	N	1075	40	114	OAK BROOK	IL	MYERS (L.E.) GROUP
MH	O	620	20	43	BENSONVILLE	IL	BEELINE INC
MH	O	450	1	14	ARTHUR	IL	PROGRESS INDUSTRIES INC
MH	O	400	14	1	NAT'L.STOCK YARDS	IL	ST. LOUIS NATIONAL STOCK YARDS
MH	O	160	14	29	MINNEAPOLIS	MN	MULTAPLEX CORP.
MH	B	150	14	1	MINNEAPOLIS	MN	FLAME INDUSTRIES INC.
MH	O	64	96	1	MELROSE PARK	IL	MELROSE PARK NATIONAL BANK
MH	O	57	1	1	MINNEAPOLIS	MN	MODERN CONTROLS INC.
MH	X	50	1	1	CRYSTAL	MN	HABERCO INC.
MH	O	44	1	12	MONETT	MO	HENRY (JACK) & ASSOCIATES INC.
MH	O	40	1	1	JORDON	MN	THERADYNE CORP.
MH	O	32	1	1	DULUTH	MN	DULUTH GROWTH COMPANY
MH	O	31	1	1	WITCHITA	KS	GAME OPERATORS CORP
MH	O	22	5	5	WICHITA	KS	ALDEBARAN DRILLING CO. INC.
MH	O	10	1	1	EDEN PRAIRIE	MN	BIO MEDICUS INC
MH	A	9	65	64	OAK BROOK	IL	TELESPHERE INTERNATIONAL INC.
MH	O	8	1	1	SCHILLER PARK	IL	CURRENCY TECHNOLOGY CORP.
MH	O	8	1	1	NORTHBROOK	IL	BIO-LOGIC SYSTEMS CORP
MH	O	5	1	1	SCHILLER PARK	IL	BANKCOM CORP.
MH	O	0	322	31	WICHITA	KS	UNION BANCSHARES INC.

Peat Marwick Mitchell

Audt	Trd	Emp	Ast	Sls	Cty	Sta	Name
PMM	N	90000	4370	5443	SCHAUMBURG	IL	MOTOROLA INC
PMM	X	86000	10379	12595	CHICAGO	IL	BEATRICE FOODS CO.
PMM	N	86000	2823	3330	CHICAGO	IL	BORG WARNER CORP.
PMM	N	63000	2663	4285	MINNEAPOLIS	MN	GENERAL MILLS INC
PMM	N	62000	3257	4649	ST LOUIS	MO	EMERSON ELECTRIC CO
PMM	N	50000	1535	2626	ST LOUIS	MO	INTERCO INC
PMM	N	49000	3073	3680	MINNEAPOLIS	MN	CONTROL DATA CORP
PMM	N	43000	4818	5292	CHICAGO	IL	IC INDUSTRIES INC
PMM	N	28000	2691	3261	CHICAGO	IL	FMC CORP
PMM	N	16000	21419	2546	MINNEAPOLIS	MN	NORWEST CORP.
PMM	O	15000	9264	2882	LONG GROVE	IL	KEMPER CORP
PMM	N	13000	606	1388	KANSAS CITY	MO	PAYLESS CASHWAYS INC
PMM	N	12000	657	917	ST LOUIS	MO	CHROMALLOY AMERICAN CORP.
PMM	S	11000	1939	1014	CHICAGO	IL	ILLINOIS CENTRAL GULF RR CO.
PMM	O	9800	6898	2672	SAINT PAUL	MN	ST. PAUL COMPANIES INC.
PMM	O	9300	556	3081	HAZELWOOD	MO	WETTERAU INC
PMM	C	8000	1284	4371	KANSAS CITY	MO	FARMLAND INDUSTRIES INC
PMM	N	7800	505	1211	MINNEAPOLIS	MN	INTERNATIONAL MULTIFOODS CORP
PMM	O	7000	240	1327	ST LOUIS PARK	MN	NASH FINCH CO
PMM	N	6600	3196	1360	CHICAGO	IL	COMBINED INTERNATIONAL CORP
PMM	N	5400	6477	606	MILWAUKEE	WI	FIRST WISCONSIN CORP
PMM	O	5300	1896	606	CHICAGO	IL	UNICOA CORP
PMM	O	4400	254	458	ST PAUL	MN	FULLER (H.B.) CO.
PMM	O	4000	4924	493	KANSAS CITY	MO	COMMERCE BANCSHARES INC
PMM	O	3900	81	196	ST.LOUIS	MO	CPI CORP
PMM	O	3800	253	498	KANSAS CITY	MO	BUTLER MANUFACTURING CO
PMM	C	3700	3094	750	ST. PAUL	MN	MINNESOTA MUTUAL LIFE INSURANCE
PMM	O	3600	145	317	ABILENE	KS	DUCKWALL ALCO STORES INC
PMM	N	3500	190	369	MELROSE PARK	IL	ALBERTO-CULVER CO
PMM	N	3200	443	380	MINNEAPOLIS	MN	CRAY RESEARCH INC
PMM	N	3100	168	333	BROOKFIELD	WI	RTE CORP
PMM	O	3000	2756	324	MINNEAPOLIS	MN	NORTHWESTERN FINANCIAL CORP
PMM	N	3000	488	475	DES MOINES	IA	MEREDITH CORP
PMM	S	2300	4299	697	CHICAGO	IL	BORG WARNER ACCEPTANCE CORP.
PMM	O	2200	702	425	FORT SCOTT	KS	WESTERN CASUALTY & SURETY CO.
PMM	A	2100	87	72	ST LOUIS	MO	LA BARGE INC
PMM	N	2100	223	296	KANSAS CITY	MO	MARION LABORATORIES INC
PMM	C	2100	308	1009	OAK BROOK	IL	ACE HARDWARE CORP
PMM	O	2000	191	541	CHICAGO	IL	CENTRAL STEEL & WIRE CO
PMM	O	2000	41	69	KANSAS CITY	MO	UNITOG CO
PMM	N	1900	168	337	BLOOMINGTON	MN	TORO COMPANY
PMM	O	1800	141	313	VALLEY	NE	VALMONT INDUSTRIES INC
PMM	O	1700	2061	228	PEORIA	IL	MIDWEST FINANCIAL GROUP INC.
PMM	O	1700	102	250	MINNEAPOLIS	MN	APOGEE ENTERPRISES INC

Price Waterhouse

Aud1	Trd	Emp	Ast	Sls	Cty	Sta	Name
PW	N	70000	2637	5864	ST LOUIS	MO	RALSTON PURINA CO.
PW	N	62000	11808	6438	CHICAGO	IL	SANTA FE SOUTHERN PACIFIC
PW	N	61000	6839	2355	DEERFIELD	IL	BAXTER TRAVENOL LABORATORIES INC
PW	N	54000	6016	6725	PEORIA	IL	CATERPILLAR TRACTOR CO
PW	N	50000	25198	26922	CHICAGO	IL	AMOCO CORP.
PW	N	40000	5121	7000	ST LOUIS	MO	ANHEUSER-BUSCH COS. INC.
PW	S	29000	3783	2091	CHICAGO	IL	ATCHISON TOPEKA & SANTA FE RR CO
PW	N	25000	669	1110	CHICAGO	IL	HARTMARX CORP
PW	N	25000	1789	1787	MILWAUKEE	WI	JOHNSON CONTROLS INC
PW	N	24000	2632	3186	CHICAGO	IL	INLAND STEEL CO
PW	N	19000	2446	1938	CHICAGO	IL	TRIBUNE CO.
PW	N	16000	270	502	ST LOUIS	MO	KELLWOOD CO
PW	N	15000	675	886	MILWAUKEE	WI	ALLIS CHALMERS CORP
PW	O	14000	782	90	CHICAGO	IL	CHICAGO PACIFIC CORP.
PW	O	11000	670	1073	LA CROSSE	WI	TRANE CO
PW	N	9500	30528	2880	CHICAGO	IL	CONTINENTAL ILLINOIS CORP
PW	N	9400	1010	1229	CHICAGO	IL	STONE CONTAINER CORP
PW	N	9300	729	850	OAK BROOK	IL	INTERLAKE INC
PW	N	8800	550	701	CHICAGO	IL	AMSTED INDUSTRIES INC
PW	N	7700	441	787	MINNEAPOLIS	MN	BEMIS COMPANY INC.
PW	C	7600	17898	2417	MILWAUKEE	WI	NORTHWESTERN MUTUAL LIFE INSURANCE
PW	N	7300	6181	1592	ST LOUIS	MO	UNION ELECTRIC CO
PW	A	6900	419	541	NORTHBROOK	IL	PITTWAY CORP
PW	N	6200	2291	1441	MILWAUKEE	WI	WISCONSIN ELECTRIC POWER CO
PW	N	5000	1066	475	KANSAS CITY	MO	KANSAS CITY SOUTHERN INDUSTRIES
PW	N	5000	322	1034	FRANKLIN PARK	IL	DEAN FOODS CO
PW	O	4900	244	687	MILWAUKEE	WI	PABST BREWING CO
PW	X	4700	83	203	ELMHURST	IL	CHAMBERLAIN MANUFACTURING CORP
PW	N	4400	640	484	Brookfield	WI	HARNISCHFEGER CORP
PW	N	4400	4719	1167	DECATUR	IL	ILLINOIS POWER CO
PW	O	4300	369	1377	CHICAGO	IL	CFS CONTINENTAL INC.
PW	O	3500	223	248	RIVER GROVE	IL	WILSON SPORTING GOODS CO.
PW	O	3400	5172	512	ST LOUIS	MO	CENTERRE BANCORPATION
PW	X	3300	78	129	COLUMBUS	NE	DALE ELECTRONICS INC.
PW	X	3200	474	308	KANSAS CITY	MO	KANSAS CITY SOUTHERN RAILWAY CO
PW	O	2500	50	342	WATERLOO	IA	RATH PACKING CO
PW	O	2400	3720	356	MILWAUKEE	WI	MARINE (THE) CORP. (WI)
PW	O	2200	228	309	ST LOUIS	MO	PETROLITE CORP
PW	N	1900	1270	413	DULUTH	MN	MINNESOTA POWER & LIGHT CO.
PW	N	1700	164	192	CHICAGO	IL	PLAYBOY ENTERPRISES INC
PW	O	1600	78	265	OSHKOSH	WI	MORGAN PRODUCTS LTD.
PW	B	1300	1	21	CHICAGO	IL	AMFOOD INDUSTRIES INC
PW	O	1200	140	75	KANSAS CITY	MO	DST SYSTEMS INC
PW	N	1100	82	117	OAKBROOK	IL	PORTEC INC

Touche Ross

Aud1	Trd	Emp	Ast	Sls	Cty	Sta	Name
TR	N	466000	66417	40715	CHICAGO	IL	SEARS ROEBUCK & CO
TR	N	86000	2779	4671	MINNEAPOLIS	MN	PILLSBURY CO
TR	N	30000	1547	5498	OMAHA	NE	CONAGRA INC
TR	N	25000	1174	6588	EDEN PRAIRE	MN	SUPER VALU STORES INC
TR	N	22000	1103	1402	PALATINE	IL	SQUARE D CO
TR	N	12000	14116	4605	CHICAGO	IL	CNA FINANCIAL CORP
TR	O	8400	122	132	MILWAUKEE	WI	MARCUS CORP
TR	N	7000	2620	1004	EDEN PRAIRIE	MN	GELCO CORP
TR	O	6000	394	454	Riverwoods	IL	COMMERCE CLEARING HOUSE INC
TR	N	5000	918	404	ST LOUIS	MO	EDWARDS (A.G.) & SONS INC
TR	N	5000	285	567	KANKAKEE	IL	ROPER CORP
TR	O	4700	190	1119	MILWAUKEE	WI	FARM HOUSE FOODS CORP
TR	A	4200	381	481	ST LOUIS	MO	OZARK HOLDINGS
TR	N	3700	416	389	SOUTH MILWAUKEE	WI	BECOR WESTERN INC.
TR	O	3500	19	1	OMAHA	NE	PMD INVESTMENT CO.
TR	N	3300	292	492	MILWAUKEE	WI	UNIVERSAL FOODS CORP
TR	N	3139	292	367	ST PAUL	MN	AMERICAN HOIST & DERRICK CO
TR	O	3100	96	534	WAUKESHA	WI	GODFREY CO.
TR	N	2800	327	542	KANSAS CITY	MO	BLOCK (H & R) INC.
TR	O	2800	104	165	SOUTH BELOIT	IL	WARNER ELECTRIC BRAKE & CLUTCH
TR	N	2400	137	887	LANSING	IL	DIANA CORP.
TR	O	2400	75	101	OAK BROOK	IL	CHAMPION PARTS REBUILDERS INC
TR	N	2300	218	407	DES PLAINES	IL	DESOTO INC
TR	O	2000	3807	261	KANSAS CITY	MO	UNITED MISSOURI BANCSHARES INC
TR	O	2000	173	234	ST LOUIS	MO	LACLEDE STEEL CO.
TR	O	2000	140	208	MINNEAPOLIS	MN	GRACO INC
TR	O	1900	87	158	Milwaukee	WI	APPLIED POWER INC
TR	X	1800	74	97	KANSAS CITY	MO	RIVAL MFG. CO.
TR	O	1400	56	91	MILWAUKEE	WI	WEHR CORP
TR	N	1300	60	96	ST LOUIS	MO	VALLEY INDUSTRIES INC
TR	O	1200	83	102	MILWAUKEE	WI	BRADY (W.H.) CO.
TR	B	1200	23	67	ST. PAUL	MN	BRIGGS TRANSPORTATION CO
TR	O	1200	10	15	ST. LOUIS	MO	CURLEE CLOTHING CO.
TR	O	1200	281	132	MINNEAPOLIS	MN	PIPER JAFFRAY INC
TR	O	1100	30	86	ST. LOUIS	MO	MEDICARE-GLASER CORPORATION
TR	O	1000	1163	117	KOHLER	WI	FIRST INTERSTATE CORP. WISCONSIN
TR	N	842	86	140	CHICAGO	IL	ELGIN NATIONAL INDUSTRIES INC
TR	O	807	14	44	MINNEAPOLIS	MN	ANALYSTS INTERNATIONAL CORP.
TR	O	769	2626	303	OMAHA	NE	COMMERCIAL FEDERAL CORP.
TR	O	762	1	14	Shawnee Mission	KS	MID-AMERICAN LINES INC.
TR	O	700	68	60	MILWAUKEE	WI	AMERICAN MEDICAL SERVICES INC
TR	O	687	1	1	WAYZATA	MN	BUFFETS INC.
TR	O	625	1	21	KANSAS CITY	MO	AUTOMATIQUE INC
TR	N	580	546	159	MINNEAPOLIS	MN	GREEN TREE ACCEPTANCE INC

Offices By Firm - Southwest Region

CITY	ST	AA	AY	CL	DHS	EW	KMG	PMM	PW	TR
Abilene	TX		1							
Albuquerque	NM	1	1			1		1		1
Amarillo	TX		1					1		
Arlington	TX								1	
Austin	TX	1	1	1		1	1	1	1	1
Baton Rouge	LA				1	1				1
Boulder	CO				1					1
Colorado Springs	CO				1					
Corpus Cristi	TX					1		1		
Dallas	TX	1	1	2	1	3	1	2	2	1
Denver	CO	1	1	1	1	1	1	1	1	1
El Paso	TX			1				1		
Fayetteville	AR		1							
Fort Worth	TX	1	1	1	1	1	1	1	1	1
Houma	LA									1
Houston	TX	1	1	1	1	2	1	2	1	1
Irving	TX				1					
Lafayette	LA	1								
Laredo	TX					1				
Little Rock	AR		1		1	1		1	1	
Lubbock	TX						1	1		
Midland	TX			1			1	1	1	
New Orleans	LA	1	1	1	1	1	1	1	1	1
Odessa	TX						1	1		
Oklahoma City	OK	1	1	1	1	1	1	1	1	1

CITY	ST	AA	AY	CL	DHS	EW	KMG	PMM	PW	TR
Roswell	NM					1				
San Antonio	TX	1	1		1	1	1	1	1	1
Shreveport	LA						1			
Tulsa	OK	1	1	1	1		1	1	1	1
Waco	TX							1		
TOTALS		11	14	11	13	17	13	20	13	13

Market Share Leadership

Southwest Region

CITY or AREA	ST	Firm	Firm	Firm	Firm
Austin	TX	AA	CL	EW	PMM
Dallas/Fort Worth	TX	AA	AY	PMM	
Denver	CO	AA	PMM		
Houston	TX	AA	EW	PMM	
New Orleans	LA	AA	PMM	TR	
Oklahoma City	OK	AA	AY	PMM	PW
San Antonio	TX	EW	PMM		
Tulsa	OK	AA	AY	PMM	

Personnel By Region

Southwest Region

Region	AA	AY	CL	DHS	EW	KMG	PMM	PW	TR
Southwest	2525	1150	925	925	1125	375	1875	900	675

Major Clients By Firm

Southwest Region

Aud1 = Principal Accountants

Trd = Shows the where traded status of company shares
  - A - American Stock Exchange
  - N - New York Stock Exchange
  - O - Over the Counter
  - B - Company in some condition of bankruptcy
  - C - Co-op or mutual
  - L - Company in liquidation
  - S - Subsidiary which reports separately
  - U - Subsidiary whose auditor is different from parent
  - X - Company which has gone private

Emp = Number of employees

Name = Company name

SIC = Four digit Standard Industrial Classification

Sta = State

Ast = Assets

Sls = Sales

Arthur Andersen

Aud1	Trd	Emp	Ast	Sls	Cty	Sta	Name
AA	N	111000	20437	15400	HOUSTON	TX	TENNECO INC.
AA	N	66000	4662	4779	DALLAS	TX	HALLIBURTON CO
AA	N	46000	3225	4111	DALLAS	TX	DRESSER INDUSTRIES INC
AA	N	17000	1001	1145	HOUSTON	TX	BROWNING-FERRIS INDUSTRIES INC
AA	N	13000	955	1054	IRVING	TX	ZALE CORP
AA	A	13000	1080	1185	Houston	TX	CONTINENTAL AIRLINES CORP.
AA	N	13000	168	314	Addison	TX	TGI FRIDAY'S INC.
AA	S	12000	2490	1063	SAN ANGELO	TX	GENERAL TELEPHONE CO OF SOUTHWEST
AA	N	9900	22071	2179	DALLAS	TX	INTERFIRST CORP.
AA	N	9400	6817	2711	DALLAS	TX	CENTRAL & SOUTH WEST CORP.
AA	N	9000	3702	3345	OKLAHOMA CITY	OK	KERR MCGEE CORP
AA	N	8700	16819	1784	HOUSTON	TX	FIRST CITY BANCORPATION OF TEXAS
AA	N	8500	3300	2239	HOUSTON	TX	PENNZOIL CO
AA	O	8000	3738	789	GALVESTON	TX	AMERICAN NATIONAL INSURANCE
AA	N	7100	832	547	HOUSTON	TX	CAMERON IRON WORKS INC
AA	N	7000	193	322	EL PASO	TX	FARAH MANUFACTURING CO INC
AA	N	6000	991	945	DALLAS	TX	LAFARGE CORP.
AA	N	4600	1142	289	HOUSTON	TX	ZAPATA CORP
AA	N	4400	4241	3733	HOUSTON	TX	TRANSCO ENERGY CO
AA	N	4100	852	967	HOUSTON	TX	ENTEX INC
AA	N	4100	2276	1085	OKLAHOMA CITY	OK	OKLAHOMA GAS & ELECTRIC CO
AA	O	4000	154	240	DALLAS	TX	PEARLE HEALTH SERVICES INC.
AA	N	3600	847	922	HOUSTON	TX	US HOME CORP
AA	A	3500	2121	844	WOODLANDS	TX	MITCHELL ENERGY & DEVELOPMENT CORP
AA	N	3400	142	264	DALLAS	TX	TRIANGLE PACIFIC CORP
AA	N	3400	147	191	FORT WORTH	TX	PIER ONE INC.
AA	O	3300	4850	491	DENVER	CO	UNITED BANKS OF COLORADO INC
AA	O	2700	3792	312	NEW ORLEANS	LA	FIRST COMMERCE CORP.
AA	O	2600	292	242	LUFKIN	TX	LUFKIN INDUSTRIES INC
AA	A	2500	173	163	HOUSTON	TX	WEATHERFORD INTERNATIONAL INC
AA	S	2500	2723	925	CORPUS CHRISTI	TX	CENTRAL POWER & LIGHT CO.
AA	O	2450	396	288	Delaware	TX	DSC COMMUNICATIONS CORP.
AA	A	2400	160	175	HOUSTON	TX	CAMCO INC
AA	S	2400	1275	701	TULSA	OK	PUBLIC SERVICE CO. OF OKLAHOMA
AA	N	2300	1995	2662	SAN ANTONIO	TX	VALERO ENERGY CORP
AA	A	2100	948	251	DENVER	CO	PETRO-LEWIS CORP
AA	A	2100	210	44	DALLAS	TX	UNIVERSAL RESOURCES CORP
AA	O	2100	1866	754	SHREVEPORT	LA	SOUTHWESTERN ELECTRIC POWER CO
AA	N	1700	479	420	LAKEWOOD	CO	KN ENERGY INC.
AA	N	1600	358	169	DENVER	CO	UNITED CABLE TELEVISION CORP
AA	O	1600	41	110	DALLAS	TX	SOUND WAREHOUSE INCORPORATED
AA	O	1577	133	130	HOUSTON	TX	LIVINGWELL INC.
AA	N	1500	87	195	MIDLAND	TX	ELCOR CORP
AA	O	1500	194	110	LAFAYETTE	LA	OFFSHORE LOGISTICS INC

Arthur Young

Aud1	Trd	Emp	Ast	Sls	Cty	Sta	Name
AY	N	93000	3104	8581	BENTONVILLE	AR	WAL-MART STORES INC.
AY	N	78000	3076	4925	DALLAS	TX	TEXAS INSTRUMENTS INC
AY	N	50000	6425	6131	Dallas/FW. Airport	TX	AMR CORP
AY	N	38000	3636	3067	HOUSTON	TX	COOPER INDUSTRIES INC
AY	N	35000	4351	3257	NEW ORLEANS	LA	MC DERMOTT INTL. INC.
AY	N	25000	14045	15636	BARTLESVILLE	OK	PHILLIPS PETROLEUM CO
AY	O	17000	471	1136	SPRINGDALE	AR	TYSON FOODS INC
AY	N	8600	23206	2104	DALLAS	TX	REPUBLICBANK CORP.
AY	N	7500	474	912	DALLAS	TX	TYLER CORP
AY	N	7000	2995	1747	DENVER	CO	PUBLIC SERVICE CO. OF COLORADO
AY	N	6000	502	520	SAN ANTONIO	TX	DATAPOINT CORP.
AY	N	5900	126	196	SAN ANTONIO	TX	LUBY'S CAFETERIAS INC.
AY	N	5900	4337	3140	TULSA	OK	WILLIAMS COMPANIES
AY	N	5400	471	455	DALLAS	TX	TRINITY INDUSTRIES INC
AY	N	4800	864	560	FORT WORTH	TX	GEARHART INDUSTRIES INC.
AY	N	4600	1022	680	DALLAS	TX	SOUTHWEST AIRLINES CO
AY	O	4000	231	297	FORT WORTH	TX	JUSTIN INDUSTRIES INC
AY	A	3600	100	98	HOUSTON	TX	CRUTCHER RESOURCES CORP
AY	N	3600	400	234	HOUSTON	TX	SERVICE CORP. INTERNATIONAL
AY	O	3400	63	158	DENVER	CO	BAYLY CORP
AY	N	3300	237	217	BOULDER	CO	NBI INC.
AY	A	3000	239	61	DALLAS	TX	STERLING SOFTWARE INC.
AY	N	2400	244	206	METAIRIE	LA	NEWPARK RESOURCES INC
AY	O	1822	3803	349	OKLAHOMA CITY	OK	BANKS OF MID-AMERICA
AY	X	1800	319	717	AURORA	CO	FOXMEYER CORPORATION
AY	O	1700	204	277	DALLAS	TX	CRONUS INDUSTRIES INC.
AY	O	1600	21	36	FORT WORTH	TX	PANCHO'S MEXICAN BUFFET INC.
AY	N	1600	814	388	AMARILLO	TX	PIONEER CORP.
AY	N	1500	218	205	DALLAS	TX	UCCEL CORP.
AY	X	1400	329	139	DALLAS	TX	KAY (MARY) CORP.
AY	O	1369	72	99	CARROLLTON	TX	COMPUTER LANGUAGE RESEARCH INC
AY	O	1125	73	97	SAN ANTONIO	TX	CONROY INC
AY	S	1100	393	25	DALLAS	TX	MOBIL ALASKA PIPELINE
AY	S	1100	585	870	OKLAHOMA CITY	OK	NORTHWEST CENTRAL PIPELINE CO.
AY	O	1000	1267	126	LITTLE ROCK	AR	FIRST COMMERCIAL CORP.
AY	O	930	164	98	DALLAS	TX	COMMUNICATIONS INDUSTRIES INC
AY	O	845	90	287	AMARILLO	TX	ENERGAS CO.
AY	B	800	82	308	Irving	TX	COMMONWEALTH OIL REFINING CO INC
AY	N	770	613	169	DALLAS	TX	SUNSHINE MINING CO.
AY	A	750	103	76	OKLAHOMA CITY	OK	LSB INDUSTRIES INC
AY	O	740	41	76	IRVING	TX	MICHAELS STORES INC
AY	O	737	45	87	DALLAS	TX	FROZEN FOOD EXPRESS INDUSTRIES
AY	X	650	76	31	DENVER	CO	VAN SCHAACK & CO
AY	O	590	195	132	ALLEN	TX	INTECOM INC

Coopers & Lybrand

Aud1	Trd	Emp	Ast	Sls	Cty	Sta	Name
CL	N	70000	17975	7813	ENGLEWOOD	CO	U S WEST INC.
CL	S	32000	8469	3477	DENVER	CO	MOUNTAIN STATES TEL.& TEL.CO.
CL	O	23000	347	384	DENVER	CO	VICORP RESTAURANTS INC
CL	B	20000	2393	1880	DENVER	CO	MANVILLE CORP.
CL	N	5400	464	591	TULSA	OK	TELEX CORP
CL	N	5100	5556	1858	BEAUMONT	TX	GULF STATES UTILITIES CO
CL	N	2900	585	255	TULSA	OK	PARKER DRILLING CO.
CL	N	2800	1573	379	HOUSTON	TX	GLOBAL MARINE INC
CL	N	2800	51	37	HOUSTON	TX	TELECOM CORPORATION
CL	N	2700	63	58	Dallas	TX	LLC CORP.
CL	N	2100	109	198	DALLAS	TX	KEYSTONE CONSOLIDATED INDUSTRIES
CL	O	2100	60	185	ROGERS	AR	HUDSON FOODS INC.
CL	O	1900	150	389	FORREST CITY	AR	SANYO MANUFACTURING CORP.
CL	O	1500	82	114	LONGMONT	CO	MINISCRIBE CORPORATION
CL	N	1100	90	66	HOUSTON	TX	GALVESTON HOUSTON CO
CL	N	1000	780	315	PINEVILLE	LA	CENTRAL LOUISIANA ELECTRIC CO.
CL	O	1000	14	39	Irving	TX	CURTIS MATHES CORP
CL	N	890	872	234	TULSA	OK	READING & BATES CORP.
CL	O	615	54	82	FORT WORTH	TX	TEXSTYRENE CORP.
CL	O	610	53	42	DALLAS	TX	NETWORK SECURITY CORP.
CL	O	587	44	50	DALLAS	TX	COMMUNICATIONS CORP. OF AMERICA
CL	O	540	52	5	DENVER	CO	AUTO-TROL TECHNOLOGY CORP.
CL	N	510	104	117	HOUSTON	TX	PROLER INTERNATIONAL CORP
CL	O	441	84	44	TYLER	TX	TCA CABLE TV INC.
CL	O	400	19	1	DALLAS	TX	SHANLEY OIL CO.
CL	O	375	13	29	SAN ANTONIO	TX	SHOPPERS WORLD STORES INC
CL	O	354	14	33	DALLAS	TX	HALL-MARK ELECTRONICS CORP.
CL	O	343	41	26	DALLAS	TX	UTL CORP.
CL	O	312	27	41	DALLAS	TX	M/A/R/C INC.
CL	O	312	13	11	RICHARDSON	TX	ENVIRONMENTAL PROCESSING
CL	A	300	10	1	WOODLANDS	TX	USR INDUSTRIES INC.
CL	A	292	48	107	HOUSTON	TX	AMERICAN OIL & GAS CORP.
CL	A	290	153	28	DENVER	CO	CONSOLIDATED OIL & GAS INC
CL	O	270	288	35	TULSA	OK	UTICA BANKSHARES CORP
CL	O	260	130	61	ENGLEWOOD	CO	GUARANTY NATIONAL CORP
CL	O	250	1	11	TULSA	OK	CENTURY GEOPHYSICAL CORP
CL	B	220	20	1	OKLAHOMA CITY	OK	MIDWESTERN RESOURCES INC
CL	O	206	11	17	FORT WORTH	TX	FARED ROBOT SYSTEMS INC
CL	L	200	1	14	GRAND PRAIRIE	TX	AMTECH GROUP LTD
CL	O	200	44	50	LAFAYETTE	LA	TRANS LOUISIANA GAS CO. INC.
CL	O	173	13	1	DALLAS	TX	AMARCO RESOURCES CORP.
CL	A	170	141	69	DENVER	CO	WORLDWIDE ENERGY CORP.
CL	B	160	23	1	IRVING	TX	PIONEER TEXAS CORP
CL	O	159	16	34	DENVER	CO	MISTER STEAK INC

Deloitte Haskins & Sells

Aud1	Trd	Emp	Ast	Sls	Cty	Sta	Name
DHS	N	19000	3358	3391	DALLAS	TX	ENSERCH CORP
DHS	N	17000	10867	4170	DALLAS	TX	TEXAS UTILITIES CO
DHS	N	14000	13656	3238	NEW ORLEANS	LA	MIDDLE SOUTH UTILITIES INC
DHS	N	13000	1750	1261	HOUSTON	TX	HUGHES TOOL CO
DHS	S	12000	7829	3533	HOUSTON	TX	HOUSTON LIGHTING & POWER CO.
DHS	N	12000	8797	4062	HOUSTON	TX	HOUSTON INDUSTRIES INC
DHS	O	5600	161	272	NEW ORLEANS	LA	HOLMES (D.H.) CO LTD
DHS	N	5600	1611	1908	TULSA	OK	MAPCO INC
DHS	S	5300	3308	1365	LITTLE ROCK	AR	ARKANSAS POWER & LIGHT CO
DHS	N	4200	1011	404	DENVER	CO	IDEAL BASIC INDUSTRIES INC.
DHS	O	2900	347	421	NEW ORLEANS	LA	NEW ORLEANS PUBLIC SERVICE INC
DHS	O	2800	4094	1260	NEW ORLEANS	LA	LOUISIANA POWER & LIGHT CO
DHS	N	2400	122	166	TULSA	OK	FACET ENTERPRISES INC
DHS	O	2400	2552	278	BOULDER	CO	AFFILIATED BANKSHARES OF COL.
DHS	A	2300	65	66	HOUSTON	TX	MC FADDIN VENTURES INC.
DHS	A	2100	160	159	HOUSTON	TX	DIGICON INC
DHS	O	2000	224	253	PUEBLO	CO	CF&I STEEL CORP
DHS	O	1900	3029	371	DENVER	CO	WESTERN CAPITAL INVESTMENT CORP.
DHS	N	1600	947	198	HOUSTON	TX	ROWAN COMPANIES INC
DHS	N	1400	85	94	GARLAND	TX	VARO INC
DHS	O	1200	525	1381	DALLAS	TX	DORCHESTER GAS CORP
DHS	O	1100	1168	138	DENVER	CO	INTRAWEST FINANCIAL CORP
DHS	O	1100	1072	130	IRVING	TX	SOUTHLAND FINANCIAL CORP
DHS	N	930	156	290	COLORADO SPRINGS	CO	HOLLY SUGAR CORP
DHS	A	710	207	72	HOUSTON	TX	KIRBY EXPLORATION CO
DHS	A	610	708	130	BATON ROUGE	LA	UNITED COMPANIES FINANCIAL CORP
DHS	N	550	94	60	FORT WORTH	TX	PENGO INDUSTRIES INC.
DHS	O	544	79	260	SUGAR LAND	TX	IMPERIAL SUGAR CO.
DHS	O	523	974	275	DENVER	CO	HAMILTON OIL CORP.
DHS	O	450	103	105	BLYTHEVILLE	AR	ARKANSAS MISSOURI POWER CO
DHS	O	416	1588	183	TULSA	OK	SOONER FEDERAL S & L ASSO.
DHS	N	360	184	107	HOUSTON	TX	HOWELL CORP
DHS	O	275	26	11	IRVING	TX	SCOTT CABLE COMMUNICATIONS INC.
DHS	A	260	30	35	HOUSTON	TX	KLEER-VU INDUSTRIES INC.
DHS	O	206	20	35	SAN ANTONIO	TX	SATELCO INC.
DHS	N	165	339	99	DALLAS	TX	SABINE CORP
DHS	O	125	1	1	ALBUQUERQUE	NM	STARLINE INC.
DHS	O	120	27	1	DALLAS	TX	SYNTECH INTERNATIONAL INC.
DHS	O	119	27	15	HOUSTON	TX	GAMMA BIOLOGICALS INC
DHS	O	110	11	18	LITTLETON	CO	BINGO KING CO. INC.
DHS	O	83	1	10	BOULDER	CO	NOVAN ENERGY INC.
DHS	X	63	95	20	HOUSTON	TX	PRAIRIE PRODUCING CO.
DHS	N	60	270	53	HOUSTON	TX	WEINGARTEN REALTY INC.
DHS	O	50	82	21	DALLAS	TX	CHAPMAN ENERGY INC.

Ernst & Whinney

Aud1	Trd	Emp	Ast	Sls	Cty	Sta	Name
EW	N	57000	6307	8199	DALLAS	TX	LTV CORP.
EW	A	16000	862	1601	LITTLE ROCK	AR	DILLARD DEPARTMENT STORES INC.
EW	N	15000	20668	5677	HOUSTON	TX	AMERICAN GENERAL CORP
EW	O	13000	1051	1340	DALLAS	TX	NATIONAL GYPSUM CO
EW	N	13000	479	927	DALLAS	TX	E - SYSTEMS INC.
EW	N	9800	1469	1243	DIBOLL	TX	TEMPLE-INLAND INC.
EW	N	9700	407	563	AUSTIN	TX	TRACOR INC
EW	N	8900	278	582	FORT SMITH	AR	ARKANSAS BEST CORP
EW	O	8700	832	540	DALLAS	TX	REPUBLIC HEALTH CORPORATION
EW	N	8000	20076	1718	HOUSTON	TX	TEXAS COMMERCE BANCSHARES INC
EW	O	5600	78	187	BATON ROUGE	LA	PICCADILLY CAFETERIAS INC.
EW	N	5200	1067	834	HOUSTON	TX	BIG THREE INDUSTRIES INC.
EW	N	5000	255	397	DALLAS	TX	DALLAS CORP.
EW	N	5000	117	167	SAN ANTONIO	TX	FOX STANLEY PHOTO PRODUCTS INC
EW	N	4800	995	584	HOUSTON	TX	KANEB SERVICES INC
EW	A	4700	391	261	DALLAS	TX	AMERICAN HEALTHCARE MANAGEMENT INC
EW	O	4100	1	1	ALBUQUERQUE	NM	SHOP RITE FOODS INC
EW	N	3800	150	342	DALLAS	TX	REDMAN INDUSTRIES INC
EW	N	3700	6413	660	FORT WORTH	TX	TEXAS AMERICAN BANCSHARES INC.
EW	O	3600	213	1463	GREELEY	CO	MONFORT OF COLORADO INC
EW	O	3400	157	255	KERRVILLE	TX	LD BRINKMAN CORP
EW	N	3200	389	468	DALLAS	TX	GIFFORD HILL & COMPANY INC
EW	N	3100	1321	273	DALLAS	TX	LOMAS & NETTLETON FINANCIAL CORP
EW	O	3000	226	155	AUSTIN	TX	HEALTHCARE INTERNATIONAL
EW	N	3000	415	359	DALLAS	TX	TEXAS INDUSTRIES INC
EW	O	3000	2937	334	DENVER	CO	COLORADO NATIONAL BANKSHARES INC
EW	N	2500	137	175	FORT SMITH	AR	BALDOR ELECTRIC CO
EW	O	2400	197	257	HOUSTON	TX	STEWART & STEVENSON SERVICES INC
EW	O	2300	3472	352	SAN ANTONIO	TX	CULLEN FROST BANKERS INC
EW	N	2200	466	338	LITTLE ROCK	AR	FAIRFIELD COMMUNITIES INC
EW	N	1500	87	57	DALLAS	TX	WHITEHALL CORPORATION
EW	A	1478	2208	294	LITTLE ROCK	AR	WORTHEN BANKING CORP.
EW	O	1200	2864	242	NEW ORLEANS	LA	HIBERNIA CORP
EW	N	1100	73	108	RICHARDSON	TX	ELECTROSPACE SYSTEMS INC
EW	A	840	53	93	FORT SMITH	AR	MID-AMERICA INDUSTRIES INC
EW	O	810	93	265	DALLAS	TX	SPW CORP.
EW	O	720	311	721	DALLAS	TX	VOUGHT CORP
EW	O	717	43	86	HOUSTON	TX	SEISCOM DELTA INC
EW	N	650	218	197	HARVEY	LA	LOUISIANA GENERAL SERVICES
EW	O	599	21	27	DALLAS	TX	ANDERSON INDUSTRIES INC
EW	A	555	25	49	DALLAS	TX	ESI INDUSTRIES
EW	O	500	99	53	ALBUQUERQUE	NM	RANCHERS EXPLORATION & DVLP. CORP.
EW	O	500	26	26	LIBERTY	TX	ALLIANCE WELL SERVICE INC.
EW	A	497	21	35	DALLAS	TX	EXPLORATION SURVEYS INC.

KMG Main Hurdman

Aud1	Trd	Emp	Ast	Sls	Cty	Sta	Name
MH	N	6000	272	375	IRVING	TX	NCH CORP.
MH	O	4000	129	189	WACO	TX	CENTRAL FREIGHT LINES INC
MH	O	1200	377	120	WACO	TX	AMERICAN INCOME LIFE INSURANCE
MH	O	1000	1800	251	MIDLAND	TX	FIRST NATIONAL BANK OF MIDLAND
MH	O	300	12	14	GUYMON	OK	ADAMS HARD-FACING CO.
MH	O	210	20	18	MIDLAND	TX	BELL PETROLEUM SERVICES INC.
MH	O	202	12	19	El Paso	TX	AIR CARGO EQUIPMENT CORP.
MH	O	130	20	10	MIDLAND	TX	DAWSON GEOPHYSICAL CO.
MH	O	118	262	28	DENVER	CO	UNIWEST FINANCIAL CORP.
MH	O	66	37	13	HOUSTON	TX	TIME ENERGY SYSTEMS INC
MH	O	55	14	1	DALLAS	TX	ENERGY SOURCES INC
MH	O	42	4	2	MIDLAND	TX	MELTON DRILLING & EXPLORATION CO
MH	O	23	18	1	DENVER	CO	BELLWETHER EXPLORATION CO.
MH	O	23	1	1	DENVER	CO	RESOURCES EQUIPMENT CAPITAL CORP.
MH	O	22	1	1	DALLAS	TX	MAGNOLIA CHEMICAL CO INC
MH	O	21	1	1	DUNCANVILLE	TX	K MED CENTERS INC.
MH	O	18	1	1	ALICE	TX	WRIGHT BROTHERS ENERGY INC.
MH	O	18	1	1	ENGLEWOOD	CO	TERAYCO INTERNATIONAL LTD.
MH	O	10	1	1	MIDLAND	TX	ALTA ENERGY CORP.
MH	O	7	1	1	BOULDER	CO	XEDAR CORP
MH	L	6	1	1	DALLAS	TX	TRANSDATA CORP
MH	O	5	1	1	DENVER	CO	X O EXPLORATION INC
MH	O	5	1	1	DALLAS	TX	TEXAUST INC
MH	O	5	1	1	DALLAS	TX	NEWPORT PETROLEUMS INC.
MH	O	5	6	1	MIDLAND	TX	PARALLEL PETROLEUM CORP
MH	O	5	1	1	DENVER	CO	LOVE OIL COMPANY INC
MH	O	2	1	1	MIDLAND	TX	MEXCO ENERGY CORP
MH	O	2	1	1	DENVER	CO	INTERMOUNTAIN ENERGY INC.
MH	O	0	1	1	HOUSTON	TX	MIRA-PAK INC.
MH	O	0	31	1	HOUSTON	TX	ACAP CORP.

Peat Marwick Mitchell

Aud1	Trd	Emp	Ast	Sls	Cty	Sta	Name
PMM	N	16000	373	544	SAN ANTONIO	TX	CHURCH'S FRIED CHICKEN INC
PMM	N	14000	940	1825	HOUSTON	TX	ANDERSON CLAYTON & CO
PMM	N	14000	5392	5457	HOUSTON	TX	TEXAS EASTERN CORP
PMM	A	14000	1951	1944	HOUSTON	TX	TEXAS AIR CORP.
PMM	N	12000	22586	2205	DALLAS	TX	MCORP
PMM	O	11000	228	1172	DALLAS	TX	CULLUM COMPANIES INC.
PMM	N	7300	405	506	HOUSTON	TX	GORDON JEWELRY CORP
PMM	N	6100	2661	2198	EL DORADO	AR	MURPHY OIL CORP.
PMM	N	5900	2661	2198	EL DORADO	AR	MURPHY OIL CORP
PMM	N	5700	5026	2889	HOUSTON	TX	PANHANDLE EASTERN CORP.
PMM	S	5600	3696	3412	HOUSTON	TX	TEXAS EASTERN TRANSMISSION CORP.
PMM	O	4800	1751	577	Denver	CO	TELE COMMUNICATIONS INC
PMM	N	4300	541	160	SAN ANTONIO	TX	LA QUINTA MOTOR INNS INC.
PMM	N	4200	1425	648	NEW ORLEANS	LA	OCEAN DRILLING & EXPLORATION CO.
PMM	N	4000	628	319	NEW ORLEANS	LA	TIDEWATER INC.
PMM	O	3600	10246	1083	HOUSTON	TX	ALLIED BANCSHARES INC
PMM	A	3500	1817	2409	DALLAS	TX	AMERICAN PETROFINA INC
PMM	N	3400	3010	749	ALBUQUERQUE	NM	PUBLIC SERVICE CO OF NEW MEXICO
PMM	A	3300	114	199	DALLAS	TX	PIZZA INN INC
PMM	O	3200	42	33	RICHARDSON	TX	PEOPLES RESTAURANTS INC.
PMM	O	3100	4294	445	BATON ROUGE	LA	LOUISIANA BANCSHARES INC.
PMM	N	2900	149	301	HOUSTON	TX	CRS/SIRRINE INC.
PMM	N	2800	50	70	DALLAS	TX	ROYAL INTERNATIONAL OPTICAL CORP.
PMM	N	2700	722	385	DALLAS	TX	BELO (A.H.) CORP.
PMM	N	2600	1051	1049	TULSA	OK	ONEOK INC.
PMM	N	2600	722	768	DALLAS	TX	SOUTHERN UNION CO
PMM	O	2600	365	560	DALLAS	TX	DR PEPPER CO
PMM	N	2400	1575	830	AMARILLO	TX	SOUTHWESTERN PUBLIC SERVICE CO
PMM	N	2400	367	156	HOUSTON	TX	GULF RESOURCES & CHEMICAL CORP
PMM	O	2300	129	131	LOWELL	AR	HUNT (J.B.) TRANSPORT SERVICES INC
PMM	O	2000	2360	232	ALBUQUERQUE	NM	SUNWEST FINANCIAL SERVICES
PMM	O	1900	118	132	HOUSTON	TX	STEWART INFORMATION SERVICES
PMM	O	1900	2877	291	SAN ANTONIO	TX	NATIONAL BANCSHARES CORP. OF TX
PMM	O	1800	65	67	EL PASO	TX	LAMA (TONY) CO. INC.
PMM	O	1670	41	69	DALLAS	TX	CHILIS
PMM	A	1600	130	121	OKLAHOMA CITY	OK	CMI CORP
PMM	O	1600	3076	320	TULSA	OK	BANCOKLAHOMA CORP
PMM	A	1500	21	55	HARAHAN	LA	WIENER ENTERPRISES INC.
PMM	O	1500	99	72	TYLER	TX	DELTAUS CORP.
PMM	N	1500	64	108	ENNIS	TX	ENNIS BUSINESS FORMS INC
PMM	O	1500	39	54	TULSA	OK	A & M FOOD SERVICES INC.
PMM	O	1400	2132	289	OKLAHOMA CITY	OK	FIRST OKLAHOMA BANCORPORATION
PMM	O	1400	55	29	ALBUQUERQUE	NM	NUCLEAR PHARMACY INC.
PMM	O	1300	17	1	CLEBURNE	TX	SAMARNAN INVESTMENT CORP.

Price Waterhouse

Aud1	Trd	Emp	Ast	Sls	Cty	Sta	Name
PW	N	35000	1925	2841	FORT WORTH	TX	TANDY CORP
PW	N	12000	4618	4102	DALLAS	TX	DIAMOND SHAMROCK CORP.
PW	O	9000	1297	1281	GOLDEN	CO	COORS (ADOLPH) COMPANY
PW	N	8500	919	673	LOUISVILLE	CO	STORAGE TECHNOLOGY CORP.
PW	O	5600	243	1533	OKLAHOMA CITY	OK	WILSON FOODS CORP
PW	N	5300	1180	594	FORT WORTH	TX	WESTERN CO OF NORTH AMERICA
PW	O	4700	1137	706	ENGLEWOOD	CO	CYPRUS MINERALS COMPANY
PW	A	4500	1003	2372	DENVER	CO	TOTAL PETROLEUM (N. AMERICA) LTD
PW	O	4400	224	347	FT. WORTH	TX	COLOR TILE INC.
PW	N	1900	312	504	HOUSTON	TX	COMPAQ COMPUTER CORP.
PW	O	1900	85	96	LITTLE ROCK	AR	SYSTEMATICS INC.
PW	N	1700	140	138	HOUSTON	TX	DANIEL INDUSTRIES INC.
PW	N	1700	196	163	IRVING	TX	RECOGNITION EQUIPMENT INC
PW	N	1600	44	73	FORT WORTH	TX	TANDYCRAFTS INC
PW	A	1500	28	53	FORT WORTH	TX	TANDY BRANDS INC
PW	O	1100	52	57	FORT WORTH	TX	STRATOFLEX INC
PW	O	1000	202	72	TULSA	OK	NOBLE DRILLING CORP.
PW	A	930	69	60	FORT WORTH	TX	ICO INC.
PW	O	780	22	27	IRVING	TX	TOCOM INC
PW	S	752	1838	978	HOUSTON	TX	EXXON PIPELINE CO
PW	O	750	28	48	FORT WORTH	TX	BUFFTON CORP
PW	A	697	84	88	HOUSTON	TX	TECH-SYM CORP
PW	O	600	15	29	MIDLAND	TX	TACO VILLA INC.
PW	O	500	23	25	NEW ORLEANS	LA	TACA INTERNATIONAL AIRLINES
PW	O	411	390	38	COVINGTON	LA	FIRST NATIONAL CORP. (LA)
PW	N	390	710	441	DALLAS	TX	LEAR PETROLEUM CORP
PW	N	371	565	170	ARDMORE	OK	NOBLE AFFILIATES INC
PW	O	282	59	29	DENVER	CO	SCIENTIFIC SOFTWARE INTERCOMP.
PW	O	280	1	14	DALLAS	TX	RIVERSIDE PRESS INC
PW	O	277	19	21	HOUSTON	TX	WNS INC.
PW	O	277	19	21	HOUSTON	TX	WICKS'N'STICKS INC.
PW	O	270	76	25	FORT WORTH	TX	AMERICAN QUASAR PETROLEUM CO
PW	A	225	118	89	FORT WORTH	TX	WESTBRIDGE CAPITAL CORP.
PW	O	210	24	20	DALLAS	TX	USACAFES
PW	O	199	18	22	HOUSTON	TX	LANE TELECOMMUNICATIONS
PW	O	180	49	28	DALLAS	TX	HOGAN SYSTEMS INC
PW	O	110	10	1	GALVESTON	TX	HORNBECK OFFSHORE SERVICE INC.
PW	O	108	1	2	WHEATRIDGE	CO	MITRAL MEDICAL INTERNATIONAL INC.
PW	O	99	106	46	MIDLAND	TX	TIPPERARY CORP
PW	O	89	1	1	IRVING	TX	TELECI INC.
PW	O	77	26	7	HOUSTON	TX	PARTNERS OIL CO.
PW	O	76	44	11	OKLAHOMA CITY	OK	PLAINS RESOURCES INC.
PW	X	71	64	23	DALLAS	TX	BONANZA INTERNATIONAL INC
PW	A	63	149	26	HOUSTON	TX	CONQUEST EXPLORATION CO.

Touche Ross

Aud1	Trd	Emp	Ast	Sls	Cty	Sta	Name
TR	N	63000	3736	12719	DALLAS	TX	SOUTHLAND CORP
TR	N	16000	8294	7254	HOUSTON	TX	COASTAL CORP
TR	N	15000	1165	7095	OKLAHOMA CITY	OK	FLEMING COMPANIES INC
TR	N	8700	681	2628	HOUSTON	TX	SYSCO CORP
TR	N	6400	424	928	HOUSTON	TX	NATIONAL CONVENIENCE STORES INC
TR	O	6100	351	514	BATON ROUGE	LA	WILSON (H.J.) CO. INC.
TR	N	3600	1690	993	SHREVEPORT	LA	ARKLA INC.
TR	C	3500	375	2465	SAN ANTONIO	TX	ASSOCIATED MILK PRODUCERS
TR	N	3100	283	1019	DALLAS	TX	COMMERCIAL METALS CO
TR	N	2900	898	2293	SAN ANTONIO	TX	TESORO PETROLEUM CORP.
TR	O	2700	204	175	HARAHAN	LA	PETROLEUM HELICOPTERS INC
TR	N	2300	298	297	HOUSTON	TX	QUANEX CORP.
TR	N	2100	186	218	ANGLETON	TX	INTERMEDICS INC.
TR	N	1700	620	326	HOUSTON	TX	SOUTHDOWN INC
TR	O	1074	112	95	OKLAHOMA CITY	OK	KELLY JOHNSTON ENTERPRISES INC
TR	A	1000	30	68	IRVING	TX	GREINER ENGINEERING INC.
TR	A	1000	24	48	IRVING	TX	SYSTEMS PLANNING CORP.
TR	O	910	130	277	AURORA	CO	PACE MEMBERSHIP WAREHOUSE INC.
TR	A	850	41	154	TORRANCE	LA	WTC INTERNATIONAL
TR	A	600	37	50	HOUSTON	TX	TEAM INC.
TR	O	550	1	17	SAN ANTONIO	TX	SOMMERS DRUG STORES CO.
TR	N	514	608	382	DENVER	CO	M.D.C. Holdings Inc.
TR	A	500	40	26	TULSA	OK	KINARK CORP.
TR	O	440	31	22	NEW ORLEANS	LA	OFFSHORE NAVIGATION INC.
TR	O	430	54	66	HOUSTON	TX	POWELL INDUSTRIES INC.
TR	O	390	97	30	HOUSTON	TX	NICKLOS OIL & GAS CO.
TR	O	350	591	69	HOUSTON	TX	CHARTER BANCSHARES INC.
TR	O	301	859	72	AUSTIN	TX	FIRST FEDERAL S & L OF AUSTIN
TR	A	283	342	94	SHREVEPORT	LA	CRYSTAL OIL CO.
TR	O	240	18	1	FRANKLIN	LA	STERLING SUGARS INC
TR	O	230	1	14	DALLAS	TX	DIVERSIFIED HUMAN RESOURCES GROUP
TR	O	205	595	231	AUSTIN	TX	NATIONAL WESTERN LIFE INSURANCE CO
TR	O	186	227	24	DENVER	CO	COMMERCIAL BANCORPORATION OF COLO.
TR	O	175	411	50	TULSA	OK	FOURTH NATIONAL CORP.
TR	O	165	1	1	LAFAYETTE	CO	ASPEN RIBBONS INC
TR	O	160	32	11	MARKSVILLE	LA	GULFCO INVESTMENT INC
TR	O	160	19	10	HOUSTON	TX	GTS CORP.
TR	O	130	297	37	FORT COLLINS	CO	HOME FEDERAL S & L OF THE ROCKIES
TR	O	127	162	62	ENGLEWOOD	CO	WRITER (THE) CORP.
TR	O	121	1	16	DENVER	CO	SCOTTS LIQUID GOLD INC
TR	O	110	1	1	ARVADA	CO	TELEVISION TECHNOLOGY CORP.
TR	O	108	1	1	ENGLEWOOD	CO	ELECTROMEDICS INC
TR	O	91	22	1	BOULDER	CO	SYNERGEN INC.
TR	O	69	1	10	DALLAS	TX	TIME DC INC

Offices By Firm - Western Region

CITY	ST	AA	AY	CL	DHS	EW	KMG	PMM	PW	TR
Bakersfield	CA		1						1	
Beverly Hills	CA		1							
Century City	CA				1	1		1	1	
Costa Mesa	CA	1	1		1			1		
Fresno	CA		1			1	1		1	1
Hilo	HI				1					
Hollister	CA		1							
Honolulu	HI	1	1	1	1	1	1	1	1	1
Irvine	CA						1			
Las Vegas	NV	1			1	1				
Long Beach	CA					1		1		
Los Angeles	CA	1	1	1	1	1	1	1	1	1
Maui	HI				1	1				
Newport Beach	CA			1		1			1	1
Oakland	CA	1		1	1	1	1	1	1	1
Palo Alto	CA		1	1					1	
Phoenix	AZ	1	1	1	1	1	1	1	1	1
Reno	NV		1							
Riverside	CA					1			1	
Sacramento	CA		1	1	1	1	1	1	1	1
Salinas	CA				1					
Salt Lake City	UT	1	1	1	1	1	1	1	1	1
San Diego	CA	1	1	1	1	1	1	1	1	1
San Francisco	CA	1	1	1	1	1	1	1	1	1
San Jose	CA	1	1	1	1	1	1	1	1	1

CITY	ST	AA	AY	CL	DHS	EW	KMG	PMM	PW	TR
San Mateo	CA							1		
Scottsdale	AZ					1				
Tucson	AZ	1		1	1	1		1	1	
Walnut Creek	CA		1			1		2	1	
Woodland Hills	CA		1		1	1		1	1	1
		---	---	---	---	---	---	---	---	---
TOTALS		11	16	13	18	18	12	17	18	12
		===	===	===	===	===	===	===	===	===

Market Share Leadership

Western Region

CITY or AREA	ST	Firm	Firm	Firm	Firm
Honolulu	HI	CL	DHS	PMM	
Los Angeles/Century City	CA	AA	EW	PMM	PW
Oakland	CA	AA	PW		
Phoenix	AZ	AA	CL	PMM	TR
Sacramento	CA	CL	KMG	PMM	PW
Salt Lake City	UT	AA	DHS	PMM	
San Diego	CA	AY	DHS	PMM	PW
San Francisco	CA	AA	AY	CDHS	PMM
San Jose	CA	AA	AY	PMM	
Tucson	AZ	CL	DHS	PMM	

Personnel By Region

Western Region

Region	AA	AY	CL	DHS	EW	KMG	PMM	PW	TR
Western	2000	1150	1275	1300	1250	550	1475	1375	1000

Major Clients By Firm

Western Region

Audl = Principal Accountants

Trd = Shows the where traded status of company shares
       A - American Stock Exchange
       N - New York Stock Exchange
       O - Over the Counter
       B - Company in some condition of bankruptcy
       C - Co-op or mutual
       L - Company in liquidation
       S - Subsidiary which reports separately
       U - Subsidiary whose auditor is different from parent
       X - Company which has gone private

Emp = Number of employees

Name = Company name

SIC = Four digit Standard Industrial Classification

Sta = State

Ast = Assets

Sls = Sales

Arthur Andersen

Audi	Trd	Emp	Ast	Sis	Cty	Sta	Name
AA	A	50000	2648	4362	SANTA MONICA	CA	WICKES COMPANIES INC.
AA	N	47000	2766	3256	LOS ANGELES	CA	TELEDYNE INC
AA	N	42000	11586	14534	LOS ANGELES	CA	OCCIDENTAL PETROLEUM CORP
AA	N	42000	3433	2256	BEVERLY HILLS	CA	AMERICAN MEDICAL INTERNATIONAL
AA	N	35000	1026	1601	HONOLULU	HI	CASTLE & COOKE INC
AA	N	34000	1226	684	BEVERLY HILLS	CA	HILTON HOTELS CORP
AA	N	29000	19098	8431	SAN FRANCISCO	CA	PACIFIC GAS & ELECTRIC CO
AA	S	25000	5098	2444	Thousand Oaks	CA	GENERAL TELEPHONE CALIFORNIA
AA	N	22000	1134	1882	PALO ALTO	CA	CONSOLIDATED FREIGHTWAYS INC.
AA	N	17000	12593	5169	ROSEMEAD	CA	SOUTHERN CALIFORNIA EDISON CO
AA	N	15000	580	1682	PHOENIX	AZ	CIRCLE K CORP
AA	N	14000	582	1426	LOS ANGELES	CA	THRIFTY CORP.
AA	S	14000	796	1419	SANTA MONICA	CA	GAMBLE-SKOGMO INC.
AA	N	12000	19208	2758	SAN FRANCISCO	CA	CROCKER NATIONAL CORP
AA	N	11000	619	661	LOS ANGELES	CA	CAESARS WORLD INC
AA	N	10000	397	1277	RIVERSIDE	CA	FLEETWOOD ENTERPRISES INC
AA	A	8400	282	345	LAS VEGAS	NV	HORN & HARDART CO
AA	N	8000	553	353	LAS VEGAS	NV	MGM GRAND HOTELS INC
AA	N	7500	240	396	LOS ANGELES	CA	COLLINS FOODS INTERNATIONAL INC
AA	N	7200	817	697	NEWPORT BEACH	CA	SMITH INTERNATIONAL INC
AA	S	7200	1713	1887	SAN MATEO	CA	ALUMAX INC.
AA	A	7000	907	862	SUNNYVALE	CA	AMDAHL CORP
AA	N	6300	490	318	LAS VEGAS	NV	CIRCUS CIRCUS ENTERPRISES INC
AA	O	6200	99	126	FULLERTON	CA	NAUGLES INC.
AA	S	6100	980	905	LOS ANGELES	CA	FLYING TIGER LINE INC
AA	O	5500	552	624	CUPERTINO	CA	TANDEM COMPUTERS INC.
AA	O	5000	90	160	LOS ANGELES	CA	SIZZLER RESTAURANTS INTL. INC.
AA	O	4800	309	1	LOS ANGELES	CA	TRITON GROUP
AA	O	4300	167	269	CHATSWORTH	CA	TANDON CORP.
AA	S	4300	896	368	HONOLULU	HI	HAWAIIAN TELEPHONE CO
AA	O	4000	5401	551	SAN FRANCISCO	CA	CALIFORNIA FIRST BANK OF S.F.
AA	N	3900	124	121	GOLETA	CA	APPLIED MAGNETICS CORP
AA	A	3900	262	291	LOS ANGELES	CA	CAESARS NEW JERSEY INC.
AA	A	3500	225	853	LOS ANGELES	CA	RYKOFF-SEXTON INC.
AA	O	3400	271	289	CUPERTINO	CA	TYMSHARE INC
AA	N	3338	1060	1171	OAKLAND	CA	AMERICAN PRESIDENT COMPANIES LTD.
AA	N	3000	79	98	ENCINO	CA	TITAN CORP.
AA	S	2800	408	170	BAKERSFIELD	CA	CONTINENTAL TELEPHONE CO
AA	O	2700	169	288	SCOTTSDALE	AZ	KRUEGER (W.A.) CO.
AA	N	2700	172	235	SAN FRANCISCO	CA	HEXCEL CORP.
AA	N	2700	306	305	MONTEREY PARK	CA	AMERON INC
AA	O	2600	1427	655	CULVER CITY	CA	MGM/UA ENTERTAINMENT CO.
AA	O	2600	3939	371	PHOENIX	AZ	ARIZONA BANCWEST CORP
AA	X	2500	22	1	SAN LEANDRO	CA	BERKELEY BIO-MEDICAL CORP.

Arthur Young

Audt	Trd	Emp	Ast	Sls	Cty	Sta	Name
AY	N	105000	2020	1691	PASADENA	CA	BEVERLY ENTERPRISES
AY	N	88000	4184	9535	BURBANK	CA	LOCKHEED CORP.
AY	N	30000	2796	4168	IRVINE	CA	FLUOR CORP
AY	O	21000	2152	1365	SANTA CLARA	CA	INTEL CORP
AY	N	14000	765	624	SAN RAMON	CA	ADVANCED MEDICAL CONCEPTS
AY	S	9000	5694	1393	NEWPORT BEACH	CA	AVCO FINANCIAL SERVICES INC
AY	N	6800	956	1147	LOS ANGELES	CA	TIGER INTERNATIONAL INC.
AY	A	5300	334	354	WOODLAND HILLS	CA	DATAPRODUCTS CORP
AY	N	4900	786	635	SAN DIEGO	CA	PSA INC
AY	O	4800	371	364	Los Angeles	CA	SUMMIT HEALTH LTD.
AY	O	4800	936	1918	CUPERTINO	CA	APPLE COMPUTER INC.
AY	O	4700	110	714	COLTON	CA	STATER BROS. INC.
AY	N	2800	182	236	FULLERTON	CA	WYNNS INTERNATIONAL INC
AY	O	2700	150	191	WOODLAND HILLS	CA	INFORMATICS GENERAL CORP.
AY	O	2700	175	190	SANTA CLARA	CA	AVANTEK INC.
AY	N	2600	193	191	SAN JOSE	CA	SPECTRA -PHYSICS INC
AY	N	2600	8047	972	SAN DIEGO	CA	IMPERIAL CORP. OF AMERICA
AY	S	2400	181	172	SAN FRANCISCO	CA	WESTERN PACIFIC RAILROAD CO.
AY	O	2200	229	178	SANTA CLARA	CA	MONOLITHIC MEMORIES INC
AY	A	2100	510	546	FULLERTON	CA	WINN ENTERPRISES
AY	N	1800	5219	614	PHOENIX	AZ	MERABANK-FSB
AY	O	1400	180	156	MILPITAS	CA	DIASONICS INC
AY	O	1300	79	95	CHATSWORTH	CA	MICROPOLIS CORP
AY	O	1300	167	108	SAN DIEGO	CA	NUCORP ENERGY INC.
AY	O	1300	65	116	LAGUNA NIGEL	CA	FLUOROCARBON CO
AY	O	1200	84	115	MOUNTAIN VIEW	CA	SUN MICROSYSTEMS INC.
AY	N	1200	130	144	TORRANCE	CA	INTERNATIONAL TECHNOLOGY CORP.
AY	O	1200	66	105	SUNNYVALE	CA	CALIFORNIA MICROWAVE INC
AY	O	1000	61	85	SAN JOSE	CA	MAXTOR CORPORATION
AY	O	1000	742	207	SAN FRANCISCO	CA	ITEL CORP
AY	N	950	123	115	GARDENA	CA	TRICO INDUSTRIES INC
AY	O	923	174	123	Mountain View	CA	DAISY SYSTEMS CORP.
AY	O	898	106	105	SAN JOSE	CA	PRIAM CORP
AY	A	897	125	95	HONOLULU	HI	ALOHA INC.
AY	O	893	239	62	S. SAN FRANCISCO	CA	GENENTECH INC
AY	A	852	39	56	COSTA MESA	CA	MSI DATA CORP
AY	O	822	140	79	SAN JOSE	CA	VLSI TECHNOLOGY INC.
AY	O	811	70	53	SANTA CLARA	CA	UNGERMANN-BASS INC.
AY	O	780	36	46	PHOENIX	AZ	LAWHON (JOHN F) FURNITURE
AY	A	778	38	54	SANTA ANA	CA	EECO INC.
AY	O	672	120	56	MOUNTAIN VIEW	CA	EQUATORIAL COMMUNICATIONS CO.
AY	B	620	40	42	SANTA FE SPRINGS	CA	BERRY INDUSTRIES CORP.
AY	O	595	148	57	EMERYVILLE	CA	CETUS CORP.
AY	O	556	154	90	SANTA MONICA	CA	ELECTRO RENT CORP

Coopers & Lybrand

Aud1	Trd	Emp	Ast	Sls	Cty	Sta	Name
CL	N	74000	19538	8499	SAN FRANCISCO	CA	PACIFIC TELESIS
CL	N	31000	20279	21723	LOS ANGELES	CA	ATLANTIC RICHFIELD CO
CL	B	23000	221	293	CARPINTERRIA	CA	SAMBOS RESTAURANTS INC
CL	N	22000	1313	2405	SAN FRANCISCO	CA	AMFAC INC
CL	N	20000	10797	10738	LOS ANGELES	CA	UNOCAL CORP
CL	N	18000	1923	2714	SAN FRANCISCO	CA	GENSTAR CORP
CL	N	18000	2406	3062	SAN FRANCISCO	CA	CROWN ZELLERBACH CORP
CL	N	14000	745	973	PALO ALTO	CA	VARIAN ASSOCIATES INC.
CL	O	14000	2652	993	LOS ANGELES	CA	FARMERS GROUP INC
CL	N	13000	693	583	PHOENIX	AZ	RAMADA INNS INC
CL	O	7100	9931	1022	PHOENIX	AZ	VALLEY NATIONAL CORP
CL	N	5500	921	385	LAS VEGAS	NV	GOLDEN NUGGET INC
CL	N	5300	253	284	RANCHO BERNARDO	CA	OAK INDUSTRIES INC
CL	N	4300	303	316	PHOENIX	AZ	TALLEY INDUSTRIES INC
CL	O	3300	130	416	COMPTON	CA	ARDEN GROUP INC.
CL	N	2500	144	255	SAN FRANCISCO	CA	GRUBB & ELLIS CO.
CL	N	2400	193	177	CUPERTINO	CA	MEASUREX CORP
CL	O	2300	32	32	HONOLULU	HI	INTERISLAND RESORTS LTD.
CL	O	2100	3242	298	HONOLULU	HI	FIRST HAWAIIAN INC
CL	O	2000	86	57	SAN FERNANDO	CA	SFE TECHNOLOGIES
CL	O	2000	277	395	SAN JOSE	CA	CONVERGENT TECHNOLOGIES INC.
CL	N	1900	161	136	LOS ANGLES	CA	INTERNATIONAL RECTIFIER CORP
CL	O	1500	118	112	SUNNYVALE	CA	TRIAD SYSTEMS CORP
CL	N	1400	1029	374	RENO	NV	SIERRA PACIFIC RESOURCES
CL	N	1400	520	405	LOS ANGELES	CA	CALMAT CO.
CL	O	1300	423	928	SOUTH SAN FRANCISCO	CA	ATKINSON (GUY F.) CO.
CL	O	1200	51	116	SHERMAN OAKS	CA	OLSON INDUSTRIES
CL	O	1200	59	79	SAN FRANCISCO	CA	IMPELL CORP
CL	O	1200	96	194	TORRANCE	CA	FARMER BROTHERS CO
CL	A	1100	96	101	RENO	NV	LYNCH COMMUNICATION SYSTEMS INC.
CL	N	990	629	1513	SANTA MONICA	CA	TOSCO CORPORATION
CL	O	787	42	55	SAN DIEGO	CA	U.S. PRESS INC.
CL	A	674	59	35	SACRAMENTO	CA	SIERRA SPRING WATER COMPANY
CL	O	600	1	15	BURBANK	CA	TAX CORP. OF AMERICA
CL	O	588	23	40	SANTA ROSA	CA	NATIONAL CONTROLS INC.
CL	A	550	11	51	LONG BEACH	CA	KIT MANUFACTURING CO
CL	N	530	55	15	PHOENIX	AZ	CALLAHAN MINING CORP
CL	O	460	36	53	SAN JOSE	CA	CORVUS SYSTEMS INC.
CL	O	420	23	53	ANAHEIM	CA	GENERAL AUTOMATION INC
CL	O	342	55	33	LOS ANGELES	CA	LAACO INC.
CL	O	325	635	230	ENCINO	CA	ZENITH NATIONAL INSURANCE CORP
CL	O	320	32	63	SAN MATEO	CA	FRANKLIN RESOURCES INC
CL	O	300	11	25	GLENDALE	CA	WEATHERFORD (R.V.) CO.
CL	O	290	34	22	SANTA CLARA	CA	SIGMAFORM CORP

Deloitte Haskins & Sells

Aud1	Trd	Emp	Ast	Sis	Cty	Sta	Name
DHS	N	21000	2015	1904	ORANGE	CA	BAKER INTERNATIONAL CORP
DHS	N	14000	3261	2029	OAKLAND	CA	KAISER ALUMINUM & CHEMICAL
DHS	N	13000	4133	5063	LOS ANGELES	CA	PACIFIC LIGHTING CORP
DHS	S	13000	4133	5063	LOS ANGELES	CA	PACIFIC LIGHTING CORP.
DHS	N	12000	2176	6285	SAN FRANCISCO	CA	MC KESSON CORP.
DHS	N	11000	1226	949	PALO ALTO	CA	SYNTEX CORP
DHS	N	10000	411	1481	WALNUT CREEK	CA	LONGS DRUG STORES CORP.
DHS	N	10000	968	612	BEVERLY HILLS	CA	FIRST CITY INDUSTRIES INC.
DHS	S	9694	2390	4616	LOS ANGELES	CA	SOUTHERN CALIFORNIA GAS CO
DHS	N	9100	126	278	SHERMAN OAKS	CA	HOUSE OF FABRICS INC
DHS	N	8300	5325	1175	PHOENIX	AZ	AZP GROUP INC.
DHS	O	6800	407	408	SAN FRANCISCO	CA	UNITED ARTISTS COMMUNICATIONS
DHS	N	5600	778	1055	OAKLAND	CA	CLOROX CO.
DHS	O	5200	992	436	SAN FRANCISCO	CA	ST. LOUIS SOUTHWESTERN RAILWAY
DHS	O	5100	5294	577	SALT LAKE CITY	UT	FIRST SECURITY CORP (UT)
DHS	N	4900	3019	1042	SALT LAKE CITY	UT	UTAH POWER & LIGHT CO
DHS	N	4900	3086	1739	SAN DIEGO	CA	SAN DIEGO GAS & ELECTRIC CO
DHS	N	4000	128	324	ORANGE	CA	TRANSCON INC
DHS	O	3300	864	453	HONOLULU	HI	ALEXANDER & BALDWIN INC
DHS	N	3100	176	233	PALO ALTO	CA	WATKINS JOHNSON CO
DHS	A	3100	629	2435	Orange	CA	BERGEN BRUNSWIG CORP
DHS	O	2600	123	108	SANTA CLARA	CA	SILICONIX INC
DHS	A	2500	165	111	BEVERLY HILLS	CA	WRATHER CORP
DHS	C	2500	4617	1296	NEWPORT BEACH	CA	PACIFIC MUTUAL LIFE INSUR.
DHS	O	2300	114	160	SALT LAKE CITY	UT	ZIONS CO OPERATIVE MERCANTILE
DHS	N	2200	712	343	SAN FRANCISCO	CA	HOMESTAKE MINING CO
DHS	N	1700	1273	386	SAN FRANCISCO	CA	UNITED STATES LEASING INTL.
DHS	O	1700	234	206	LOS ANGELES	CA	QUOTRON SYSTEMS INC
DHS	O	1700	138	175	SAN FRANCISCO	CA	HARPER GROUP
DHS	N	1600	4807	491	PHOENIX	AZ	WESTERN SAVINGS & LOAN ASSOC.
DHS	O	1600	32	67	VAN NUYS	CA	OLGA CO
DHS	O	1523	131	132	PALO ALTO	CA	COHERENT INC.
DHS	B	1500	114	125	HONOLULU	HI	HAWAII CORPORATION
DHS	O	1500	4361	516	PHOENIX	AZ	FIRST FEDERAL S & L OF ARIZONA
DHS	A	1400	99	113	SHERMAN OAKS	CA	TRANSTECHNOLOGY CORP
DHS	O	1400	145	169	SAN DIEGO	CA	CIPHER DATA PRODUCTS INC.
DHS	N	1400	469	250	SAN FRANCISCO	CA	CP NATIONAL CORP.
DHS	A	1300	120	41	LOS ANGELES	CA	ANGELES CORPORATION
DHS	N	1200	93	117	BURBANK	CA	ZERO CORP.
DHS	O	1000	74	75	SAN DIEGO	CA	WAVETEK CORP.
DHS	N	1000	1604	447	TUCSON	AZ	TUCSON ELECTRIC POWER CO.
DHS	O	1000	25	16	TORRANCE	CA	CORDON INTERNATIONAL CORP
DHS	O	969	80	81	SAN JOSE	CA	FINNIGAN CORP
DHS	N	935	99	90	ANAHEIM	CA	PACIFIC SCIENTIFIC CO

Ernst & Whinney

Aud1	Trd	Emp	Ast	Sls	Cty	Sta	Name
EW	N	122000	3463	13890	SALT LAKE CITY	UT	AMERICAN STORES CO
EW	N	83000	118541	13880	SAN FRANCISCO	CA	BANKAMERICA CORP
EW	N	34000	48991	5235	LOS ANGELES	CA	FIRST INTERSTATE BANCORP.
EW	S	31000	1958	390	LOS ANGELES	CA	TRANSAMERICA FINANCIAL CORP
EW	N	30000	2701	2947	LOS ANGELES	CA	TIMES-MIRROR COMPANY
EW	N	17000	796	1130	LOS ANGELES	CA	WHITTAKER CORP
EW	N	16000	13751	5590	SAN FRANCISCO	CA	TRANSAMERICA CORP
EW	S	6100	2556	0	LOS ANGELES	CA	OCCIDENTAL OF CA LIFE INSURANCE
EW	S	5200	9560	850	LOS ANGELES	CA	UNION BANCORP INC.
EW	O	4600	381	1871	SAN DIEGO	CA	PRICE CO.
EW	O	4400	634	543	SAN FRANCISCO	CA	LIQUID AIR CORP OF NORTH AMERICA
EW	A	3600	203	332	SAN DIEGO	CA	CUBIC CORP
EW	N	2900	1005	644	SALT LAKE CITY	UT	QUESTAR CORP.
EW	O	2900	4439	460	HONOLULU	HI	BANCORP HAWAII INC.
EW	S	2800	9460	1076	SAN FRANCISCO	CA	FIRST NATIONWIDE FINANCIAL CORP
EW	N	2500	278	205	Santa Ana	CA	COMMUNITY PSYCHIATRIC CENTERS
EW	N	2400	9862	1028	BEVERLY HILLS	CA	GIBRALTAR FINANCIAL CORP.
EW	O	2300	979	512	LOS ANGELES	CA	MISSION INSURANCE GROUP INC.
EW	O	2200	187	190	SIMI VALLEY	CA	MICOM SYSTEMS INC.
EW	O	2100	275	215	SCOTTS VALLEY	CA	SEAGATE TECHNOLOGY
EW	N	2000	135	218	CITY OF COMMERCE	CA	ANTHONY INDUSTRIES INC
EW	O	1500	1484	597	LOS ANGELES	CA	FREMONT GENERAL CORP
EW	O	1500	101	95	TUCSON	AZ	BURR-BROWN CORP
EW	O	1200	105	317	HAWTHORNE	CA	MAXICARE HEALTH PLANS INC.
EW	N	1100	75	117	LOS ANGELES	CA	RB INDUSTRIES
EW	O	1100	32	79	LA JOLLA	CA	KRATOS INC
EW	B	978	88	76	PHOENIX	AZ	TEXSCAN CORP
EW	O	950	84	74	NEWPORT BEACH	CA	CAREMARK INC.
EW	O	946	78	69	GARDENA	CA	WESTERN WASTE INDUSTRIES
EW	O	890	131	234	CITY OF COMMERCE	CA	FEDERATED (THE) GROUP INC.
EW	O	700	34	127	ANAHEIM	CA	CLOTHESTIME (THE) INC.
EW	B	700	18	25	ANAHEIM	CA	ALTEC CORP
EW	A	651	24	56	CORONA	CA	SILVERCREST INDUSTRIES INC.
EW	O	650	19	34	SAN MATEO	CA	CALIFORNIA JOCKEY CLUB
EW	O	600	1	1	HUNTINGTON BEACH	CA	SONOMA INTERNATIONAL
EW	X	500	34	33	LOS ANGELES	CA	GREER HYDRAULICS OF CA INC
EW	O	460	66	50	NEWPORT BEACH	CA	HOME HEALTH CARE OF AMERICA
EW	A	449	33	31	ANAHEIM	CA	ODETICS INC.
EW	A	393	1	18	TUCSON	AZ	TEC INC
EW	N	387	76	61	ORANGE	CA	VARCO INTERNATIONAL INC
EW	O	310	34	47	SAN DIEGO	CA	MAXWELL LABORATORIES INC.
EW	O	288	48	34	FREMONT	CA	LAM RESEARCH CORP.
EW	O	282	28	39	CHANDLER	AZ	INTER-TEL INC.
EW	O	250	1	1	PASADENA	CA	SOUTHERN CROSS INDUSTRIES INC

KMG Main Hurdman

Aud1	Trd	Emp	Ast	Sls	Cty	Sta	Name
MH	N	62000	2842	2530	LOS ANGELES	CA	NATIONAL MEDICAL ENTERPRISES INC
MH	O	4100	81	96	SALT LAKE CITY	UT	JB'S RESTAURANTS
MH	O	3800	156	140	LAS VEGAS	NV	TRANS-STERLING INC.
MH	N	3100	316	320	IRVINE	CA	AFG INDUSTRIES INC.
MH	A	2560	64	137	LOS ANGELES	CA	VIRCO MANUFACTURING CORP
MH	O	2200	67	103	SANTA CLARA	CA	VIKING FREIGHT SYSTEM INC
MH	O	1700	3181	275	SALT LAKE CITY	UT	ZIONS UTAH BANCORPORATION
MH	O	972	50	124	SAN DIEGO	CA	COUSINS HOME FURNISHINGS INC.
MH	N	910	113	47	LAS VEGAS	NV	SHOWBOAT INC
MH	L	800	10	23	SALT LAKE CITY	UT	FASHION FABRICS INC
MH	O	456	527	54	HONOLULU	HI	CPB INC
MH	O	440	55	29	OREM	UT	WICAT SYSTEMS INC.
MH	O	330	47	42	ANAHEIM	CA	COMARCO INC
MH	A	277	301	17	Los Angeles	CA	FIRST CAPITAL HOLDINGS CORP.
MH	O	250	1	15	FULLERTON	CA	ROPAK CORPORATION
MH	O	225	1	1	LOS ANGELES	CA	DE ANZA LAND & LEISURE CORP.
MH	A	144	17	16	Walnut Creek	CA	PENTRON INDUSTRIES INC
MH	O	132	1	1	ANAHEIM	CA	ICEE-USA
MH	O	129	1	1	CHATSWORTH	CA	NETWORKS ELECTRONIC CORP
MH	O	123	1	1	CANOGA PARK	CA	PERTRON CONTROLS CORPORATION
MH	O	100	1	12	LOS ANGELES	CA	AMERICAN VANGUARD CORP
MH	A	89	201	15	San Mateo	CA	GEOTHERMAL RESOURCES INTL.
MH	O	88	1	12	COSTA MESA	CA	AIRTRICITY DEVELOPMENT CORPORATION
MH	O	84	10	14	SUNNYVALE	CA	WESTERN MICROWAVE INC.
MH	O	80	1	1	SANTA CLARA	CA	CITEL INC
MH	O	54	1	1	LOS ANGELES	CA	ARRAYS INC
MH	O	50	13	14	ANAHEIM	CA	WCS INTERNATIONAL
MH	O	45	1	1	MENLO PARK	CA	CARCO ELECTRONICS
MH	O	42	1	1	SACRAMENTO	CA	OCCUPATIONAL-URGENT CARE HEALTH
MH	O	32	1	1	SAN DIEGO	CA	SYSTEM ASSOCIATES OF CA
MH	O	31	1	1	CAMPBELL	CA	REDLAKE CORP
MH	O	30	1	1	FREMONT	CA	DESTINY SLENDER ME INTERNATIONAL
MH	O	24	1	1	RENO	NV	SPORT'S RESTAURANTS INC.
MH	O	20	1	1	LOS ANGELES	CA	QUICKPRINT OF AMERICA INC.
MH	O	20	7	3	LOS ANGELES	CA	OIL SECURITIES INC.
MH	O	11	1	1	HEALDSBURG	CA	VERSATRON CORPORATION
MH	O	10	1	1	SALT LAKE CITY	UT	NOVA PETROLEUM CORP
MH	O	10	1	1	RENO	NV	DRAGON MINING CORPORATION
MH	O	9	1	1	SANTA CLARA	CA	TRI-COMP SENSORS INC.
MH	O	8	1	1	LAS VEGAS	NV	VOLU-SOL MEDICAL INDUSTRIES INC.
MH	O	8	6	1	SANTA PAULA	CA	FALCON OIL & GAS CO. INC.
MH	O	7	1	1	SAN JOSE	CA	WIDERGREN COMMUNICATIONS INC
MH	O	6	1	1	SALT LAKE CITY	UT	AMERICAN GEOLOGICAL ENTERPRISES
MH	O	5	1	1	Hayward	CA	ADVANCED CELLULAR TECHNOLOGY INC.

Peat Marwick Mitchell

Audl	Trd	Emp	Ast	Sls	Cty	Sta	Name
PMM	N	167000	4841	19651	OAKLAND	CA	SAFEWAY STORES INC
PMM	N	37000	1411	1788	SANTA CLARA	CA	NATIONAL SEMICONDUCTOR CORP
PMM	N	31000	53503	5537	LOS ANGELES	CA	SECURITY PACIFIC CORP
PMM	N	26000	135	424	SAN FRANCISCO	CA	AMERICAN BUILDING MAINTENANCE
PMM	N	15000	29429	3362	SAN FRANCISCO	CA	WELLS FARGO & CO
PMM	O	13700	219	335	ANAHEIM	CA	KARCHER (CARL) ENTERPRISES INC
PMM	N	10000	952	1307	LOS ANGELES	CA	WESTERN AIR LINES INC.
PMM	N	7800	1124	950	SAN FRANCISCO	CA	POTLATCH CORP
PMM	N	7400	382	271	PHOENIX	AZ	WEBB (DEL E.) CORP.
PMM	X	7000	900	783	LOS ANGELES	CA	TWENTIETH CENTURY-FOX FILM CORP
PMM	N	6700	27229	3029	LOS ANGELES	CA	AHMANSON (H.F.) & CO.
PMM	N	5700	27375	3345	Irvine	CA	FINANCIAL CORP OF AMERICA
PMM	N	5700	19005	2276	LOS ANGELES	CA	CALFED INC.
PMM	O	4800	118	152	SUNNYVALE	CA	PIZZA TIME THEATRE INC.
PMM	N	4800	546	331	MENLO PARK	CA	COOPER VISION INC.
PMM	N	4300	13235	1389	GLENDALE	CA	GLENFED INC.
PMM	N	3900	10019	1119	SAN DIEGO	CA	HOME FEDERAL S & L (SAN DIEGO)
PMM	O	3700	521	259	MOUNTAIN VIEW	CA	XIDEX CORP
PMM	N	3500	197	315	TORRANCE	CA	STANDARD BRANDS PAINT CO
PMM	N	2700	585	53	LOS ANGELES	CA	STERLING BANCORP
PMM	N	2700	139	252	LOS ANGELES	CA	KERR GLASS MFG CORP
PMM	N	2400	302	353	OAKLAND	CA	WORLD AIRWAYS INC
PMM	N	2100	134	152	LOS ANGELES	CA	TRE CORP.
PMM	O	2000	216	159	NEWPORT BEACH	CA	COMPREHENSIVE CARE CORP
PMM	A	1900	169	177	IRVINE	CA	WESTERN DIGITAL CORP.
PMM	L	1900	320	156	PALO ALTO	CA	COOPER HOLDINGS INC.
PMM	O	1800	25	27	SPRINGVILLE	UT	VALTEK INC
PMM	O	1800	7470	725	LOS ANGELES	CA	COAST SAVINGS & LOAN ASSOCIATION
PMM	O	1700	43	48	SAN DIEGO	CA	NATIONAL MICRONETICS INC
PMM	N	1700	953	648	HONOLULU	HI	HAWAIIAN ELECTRIC INDUSTRIES
PMM	N	1600	89	88	SAN JOSE	CA	PLANTRONICS INC.
PMM	A	1400	285	451	LOS ANGELES	CA	DUCOMMUN INC
PMM	O	1300	1684	146	LOS ANGELES	CA	IMPERIAL BANCORP
PMM	N	1100	163	87	OAKLAND	CA	EQUITEC FINANCIAL GROUP INC.
PMM	O	1100	2572	276	SALT LAKE CITY	UT	AMERICAN S & L - SALT LAKE CITY
PMM	O	1000	50	68	TORRANCE	CA	SUNRISE MEDICAL INC.
PMM	A	1000	18	45	LOS ANGELES	CA	FREDERICKS OF HOLLYWOOD INC
PMM	O	1000	1309	195	Walnut Creek	CA	CENTRAL BANKING SYSTEM INC
PMM	A	990	151	94	HONOLULU	HI	HAL INC.
PMM	O	903	14	21	VENTURA	CA	AMERICAN RESTAURANTS CORPORATION
PMM	O	900	2906	321	SAN FRANCISCO	CA	FIDELITY FINANCIAL CORP
PMM	O	900	109	80	SALT LAKE CITY	UT	EVANS & SUTHERLAND COMPUTER CP
PMM	O	863	162	21	SAN DIEGO	CA	NORTHVIEW CORP.
PMM	O	860	25	42	SAN DIEGO	CA	WALKER SCOTT CORP

Price Waterhouse

Aud1	Trd	Emp	Ast	Sls	Cty	Sta	Name
PW	N	84000	5680	6505	PALO ALTO	CA	HEWLETT PACKARD CO
PW	N	68000	1932	9382	DUBLIN	CA	LUCKY STORES INC
PW	N	65000	23	1340	MENLO PARK	CA	SAGA CORP
PW	N	61000	38899	41742	SAN FRANCISCO	CA	CHEVRON CORP. (WAS STD. OIL CALIF)
PW	N	56000	2235	3978	LOS ANGELES	CA	CARTER HAWLEY HALE STORES INC
PW	N	30000	1490	2371	SANTA MONICA	CA	LEAR SIEGLER INC
PW	N	29000	2897	2015	BURBANK	CA	DISNEY (WALT) CO.
PW	N	17000	2254	2099	UNIVERSAL CITY	CA	MCA INC
PW	N	10000	249	319	IRVINE	CA	EL TORITO RESTAURANTS INC.
PW	N	9500	667	675	MENLO PARK	CA	RAYCHEM CORP
PW	N	8400	25471	3404	BEVERLY HILLS	CA	GREAT WESTERN FINANCIAL CORP
PW	N	5500	669	700	PHOENIX	AZ	SOUTHWEST FOREST INDUSTRIES INC
PW	O	5500	68	94	LARKSPUR	CA	VICTORIA STATION INC
PW	O	4900	216	268	SANTA ANA	CA	FIRST AMERICAN FINANCIAL CORP
PW	N	4500	725	1051	HAWTHORNE	CA	MATTEL INC
PW	N	4500	347	1093	SAN FRANCISCO	CA	DI GIORGIO CORP.
PW	N	3600	119	183	IRVINE	CA	NATIONAL EDUCATION CORP.
PW	O	3300	180	420	LA JOLLA	CA	SCIENCE APPLICATIONS INT'L CORP
PW	N	3200	2201	420	LOS ANGELES	CA	KAUFMAN & BROAD INC
PW	X	3000	68	378	PHOENIX	AZ	BAYLESS (A.J.) MARKETS INC
PW	O	2600	3867	427	SAN FRANCISCO	CA	BANCAL TRI STATE CORP
PW	O	2200	3016	299	LOS ANGELES	CA	LLOYDS BANK CALIFORNIA
PW	O	2100	81	62	San Diego	CA	COMPUTER & COMMUNICATIONS TECH
PW	O	2000	32	67	VAN NUYS	CA	HUNGRY TIGER INC
PW	N	2000	146	304	LOS ANGELES	CA	BELL INDUSTRIES INC.
PW	N	1900	93	151	MONTEREY PARK	CA	INTERNATIONAL ALUMINUM CORP
PW	Z	1900	2473	201	BEVERLY HILLS	CA	CITY NATIONAL CORP.
PW	O	1800	223	165	PHOENIX	AZ	INSPIRATION CONSOLIDATED COPPER CO
PW	N	1500	261	459	EMERYVILLE	CA	SHAKLEE CORP
PW	N	1500	220	291	LYNWOOD	CA	JORGENSEN STEEL
PW	O	1500	150	175	SANTA CLARA	CA	APPLIED MATERIALS INC
PW	A	1400	47	83	SYLMAR	CA	SIERRACIN CORP
PW	N	1400	62	166	TORRANCE	CA	LOGICON INC.
PW	A	1300	1653	228	CARMEL	CA	LANDMARK LAND COMPANY INC
PW	N	1300	83	103	CUCAMONGA	CA	DATA DESIGN LABORATORIES
PW	O	1100	372	140	MILPITAS	CA	LSI LOGIC CORP
PW	O	1000	398	32	SAN DIEGO	CA	SAN DIEGO FINANCIAL CORP.
PW	A	1000	58	105	PALO ALTO	CA	TAB PRODUCTS CO
PW	O	950	2200	203	PHOENIX	AZ	UNITED BANCORP OF ARIZONA
PW	O	840	87	109	CANOGA PARK	CA	REDKEN LABORATORIES INC
PW	O	822	88	122	CULVER CITY	CA	ASHTON-TATE
PW	O	800	195	53	SCOTTSDALE	AZ	LAND RESOURCES CORP
PW	O	800	37	23	SACRAMENTO	CA	AMERICAN RECREATION CENTERS INC.
PW	O	748	28	38	OAKLAND	CA	GARDENAMERICA CORP.

Touche Ross

Audl	Trd	Emp	Ast	Sls	Cty	Sta	Name
TR	N	58000	4646	4591	BEVERLY HILLS	CA	LITTON INDUSTRIES INC.
TR	N	47000	2333	5057	LOS ANGELES	CA	NORTHROP CORP
TR	N	37000	2931	2512	PHOENIX	AZ	GREYHOUND CORP
TR	N	14000	431	723	EL SEGUNDO	CA	COMPUTER SCIENCES CORP
TR	A	11100	263	239	Laguna Hills	CA	CARE ENTERPRISES
TR	N	11000	272	647	SAN BRUNO	CA	GAP INC. (THE)
TR	N	9400	615	933	PASADENA	CA	AVERY INTERNATIONAL CORP
TR	N	7600	438	607	CHULA VISTA	CA	ROHR INDUSTRIES INC.
TR	O	2740	247	367	NEWARK	CA	ROSS STORES
TR	N	2600	257	389	LOS ANGELES	CA	PEP BOYS MANNY MOE & JACK
TR	O	2600	28	52	PHOENIX	AZ	FAMOUS RESTAURANTS INC.
TR	N	2500	155	54	SANTA ANA	CA	GREATWEST HOSPITALS INC.
TR	N	2400	12130	1378	OAKLAND	CA	GOLDEN WEST FINANCIAL CORP
TR	O	2300	45	54	IRVINE	CA	RUSTY PELICAN RESTAURANTS INC.
TR	O	2184	87	71	PHOENIX	AZ	ADVANCED SEMICONDUCTOR MATERIALS
TR	O	2100	143	278	Carson	CA	PIC N SAVE CORP
TR	N	2100	8211	674	SAN DIEGO	CA	GREAT AMERICAN FIRST SAVINGS BANK
TR	O	2000	795	151	FONTANA	CA	KAISER STEEL CORP.
TR	O	1500	51	54	SAN MATEO	CA	CALNY INC.
TR	O	1500	175	240	LOS ANGELES	CA	EARLY CALIFORNIA INDUSTRIES INC
TR	N	1400	91	97	SAN MATEO	CA	URS CORP.
TR	O	1400	280	201	ENCINO	CA	NU-MED INC
TR	A	1400	88	168	OAKLAND	CA	GRAND AUTO INC
TR	O	1400	2860	340	FRESNO	CA	GUARANTEE FINANCIAL CORP OF CA.
TR	O	1400	292	300	OGDEN	UT	AMALGAMATED SUGAR CO
TR	C	1300	92	597	PHOENIX	AZ	ASSOCIATED GROCERS OF ARIZONA INC.
TR	O	1200	390	120	OAKLAND	CA	BUTTES GAS & OIL CO
TR	O	1100	1	18	SAN FRANCISCO	CA	TOPPS & TROWSERS
TR	N	1100	422	248	OAKLAND	CA	KAISER CEMENT CORP.
TR	N	1100	147	183	ORANGE	CA	HEALTHCARE USA
TR	O	1000	10	44	LOS ANGELES	CA	TRANSWORLD SERVICES INC
TR	A	1000	152	174	LOS ANGELES	CA	EVEREST & JENNINGS INTERNATIONAL
TR	O	906	109	59	SANTA ROSA	CA	OPTICAL COATING LABORATORY INC
TR	O	900	45	128	Fountain Valley	CA	NATIONAL LUMBER & SUPPLY INC.
TR	A	880	2155	237	HUNTINGTON BEACH	CA	MERCURY SAVINGS & LOAN ASSOC.
TR	L	800	723	229	LOS ANGELES	CA	BENEFICIAL STANDARD CORP
TR	O	792	35	26	RENO	NV	SANDS REGENT (THE)
TR	O	700	8741	2899	Los Angeles	CA	FIRST EXECUTIVE CORP.
TR	A	668	3140	354	GLENDALE	CA	CITADEL HOLDING CORP.
TR	Z	650	1	16	PHOENIX	AZ	PHOTOTRON CORP
TR	O	650	48	216	MENLO PARK	CA	ADIA SERVICES INC.
TR	N	644	3133	319	SANTA BARBARA	CA	FINANCIAL CORP OF SANTA BARBARA
TR	X	625	23	33	SALT LAKE CITY	UT	ALTA INDUSTRIES LTD
TR	O	600	11	27	ANAHEIM	CA	CERTRON CORP

Offices By Firm - Northwest Region

CITY	ST	AA	AY	CL	DHS	EW	KMG	PMM	PW	TR
Anchorage	AK		1	1	1			1	1	1
Beaverton	OR							1		
Bellevue	WA				1			1	1	1
Billings	MT							1		
Boise	ID	1		1						1
Coos Bay	OR						1			
Eugene	OR			1						
Fairbanks	AK						1			
Juneau	AK			1						
Portland	OR	1	1	1	1	1	1	1	1	1
Seattle	WA	1	1	1	1	1	1	1	1	1
Spokane	WA			1		1				
Tacoma	WA					1				
TOTALS		3	3	7	4	4	4	6	4	5

Market Share Leadership
Northwest Region

CITY or AREA	ST	Firm	Firm	Firm	Firm
Anchorage	AK	PMM	PW		
Portland	OR	AA	CL	DHS	PMM
Seattle/Tacoma	WA	AA	EW	TR	

Personnel By Region

Northwest Region

Region	AA	AY	CL	DHS	EW	KMG	PMM	PW	TR
Northwest	400	175	400	200	250	100	300	225	350

Major Clients By Firm
Northwest Region

Aud1 = Principal Accountants

Trd = Shows the where traded status of company shares
    A – American Stock Exchange
    N – New York Stock Exchange
    O – Over the Counter
    B – Company in some condition of bankruptcy
    C – Co-op or mutual
    L – Company in liquidation
    S – Subsidiary which reports separately
    U – Subsidiary whose auditor is different from parent
    X – Company which has gone private

Emp = Number of employees

Name = Company name

SIC = Four digit Standard Industrial Classification

Sta = State

Ast = Assets

Sls = Sales

Arthur Andersen

Aud1	Trd	Emp	Ast	Sls	Cty	Sta	Name
AA	N	35000	6005	5206	TACOMA	WA	WEYERHAEUSER CO
AA	S	24000	3830	1634	SEATTLE	WA	PACIFIC NORTHWEST BELL TELEPHONE
AA	N	23000	3268	3737	BOISE	ID	BOISE CASCADE CORP.
AA	N	12000	1397	1261	PORTLAND	OR	LOUISIANA-PACIFIC CORP.
AA	S	6700	1398	604	EVERETT	WA	GENERAL TELEPHONE NORTHWEST
AA	N	3200	303	952	SEATTLE	WA	UNIVAR CORP
AA	N	3100	2579	827	PORTLAND	OR	PORTLAND GENERAL ELECTRIC CO
AA	N	3050	537	433	SEATTLE	WA	ALASKA AIR GROUP INC.
AA	N	2200	212	325	PORTLAND	OR	POPE & TALBOT INC
AA	O	1600	124	143	MEDFORD	OR	MEDFORD CORP
AA	O	1400	103	133	BOISE	ID	TRUS JOIST CORP
AA	O	1400	141	192	PORTLAND	OR	PRECISION CASTPARTS CORP
AA	O	1100	426	411	SEATTLE	WA	WASHINGTON ENERGY CO.
AA	O	1100	69	84	PORTLAND	OR	ELECTRO SCIENTIFIC INDUSTRIES INC.
AA	O	460	523	56	CASPER	WY	AFFILIATED BANK CORP. WYO.
AA	O	275	22	11	EUGENE	OR	LIBERTY COMMUNICATIONS INC
AA	O	86	17	12	SALEM	OR	TWO (II) MORROW INC.
AA	O	86	94	11	SEATTLE	WA	FIRST NORTHWEST BANCORPORATION
AA	O	71	60	1	CORVALLIS	OR	CITIZENS BANK OF CORVALLIS
AA	O	29	19	12	BEAVERTON	OR	EDWARDS INDUSTRIES INC
AA	O	21	1	1	TILLAMOOK	OR	AEROLIFT INCORPORATED
AA	O	14	1	1	BELLEVUE	WA	NEVEX GOLD COMPANY INC
AA	O	4	60	142	AUBURN	WA	LEWIS (PALMER G.) CO. INC.
AA	O	0	84	10	ROSEBURG	OR	UNITED BANCORP
AA	O	0	1	1	Bellevue	WA	FRONTIER MINING & OIL CORP.

Arthur Young

Aud1	Trd	Emp	Ast	Sls	Cty	Sta	Name
AY	O	2000	42	101	SEATTLE	WA	COSTCO WHOLESALE CORP.
AY	O	1400	87	1	PORTLAND	OR	ORBANCO FINANCIAL SERVICES
AY	N	1300	223	333	KENT	WA	PAY N PAK STORES INC
AY	O	720	139	112	SEATTLE	WA	ACKERLEY COMMUNICATIONS INC.
AY	O	670	303	38	COOS BAY	OR	WESTERN BANK
AY	O	550	41	52	BEAVERTON	OR	VIEW-MASTER INT'L GROUP INC.
AY	O	198	166	19	SALEM	OR	COMMERCIAL BANCORP
AY	B	189	10	8	PORTLAND	OR	DANT & RUSSELL INC
AY	O	125	42	25	ANCHORAGE	AK	COOK INLET COMMUNICATIONS CORP.
AY	O	111	13	1	SEATTLE	WA	IMMUNEX CORPORATION
AY	O	75	17	16	FEDERAL WAY	WA	PACIFIC NUCLEAR SYSTEMS INC.
AY	O	75	1	1	KELLOGG	ID	CRESCENT SILVER MINES INC.
AY	O	68	11	23	GREAT FALLS	MT	GREAT FALLS GAS CO.
AY	O	48	1	1	WOODINVILLE	WA	PACER CORP.
AY	O	44	1	1	HILLSBORO	OR	FLIGHT DYNAMICS INC.
AY	O	23	1	1	BELLEVUE	WA	DATA LINE SYSTEMS INC.
AY	O	7	1	1	KIRKLAND	WA	NYPLAN INC.
AY	O	0	63	1	SPRINGFIELD	OR	VALLEY WEST BANCORP
AY	O	0	10	12	REDMOND	WA	INTEGRATED CIRCUITS INC

Coopers & Lybrand

Aud1	Trd	Emp	Ast	Sls	Cty	Sta	Name
CL	N	47000	12512	8651	SEATTLE	WA	BURLINGTON NORTHERN INC
CL	N	22000	936	2122	BOISE	ID	MORRISON KNUDSEN COMPANY INC
CL	O	2800	3459	358	BOISE	ID	MOORE FINANCIAL GROUP INC.
CL	O	2600	35	81	EUGENE	OR	INTERNATIONAL KING'S TABLE INC.
CL	N	2400	2318	714	BELLEVUE	WA	PUGET SOUND POWER & LIGHT CO
CL	X	1600	1	18	KIRKLAND	WA	CENTENNIAL VILLAS INC
CL	N	945	171	79	WALLACE	ID	HECLA MINING CO
CL	O	758	674	78	Portland	OR	PACWEST BANCORP
CL	O	747	133	76	BOISE	ID	MICRON TECHNOLOGY INC.
CL	O	600	95	33	SPOKANE	WA	AMERICAN SIGN & INDICATOR CORP
CL	O	500	21	26	BELLINGHAM	WA	UNIFLITE INC.
CL	O	170	9	33	BEAVERTON	OR	RESERS FINE FOODS INC
CL	O	115	80	19	SPOKANE	WA	PEGASUS GOLD INC.
CL	O	60	1	1	WILSONVILLE	OR	CARDIAC RESUSCITATOR CORP.
CL	O	59	40	1	BOZEMAN	MT	AMERICAN PLAN LIFE INSURANCE CO.
CL	O	54	1	1	MOUNTLAKE TERRACE	WA	STEPHENS ENGINEERING ASSOC. INC.
CL	O	22	1	1	THOMPSON FALLS	MT	UNITED STATES ANTIMONY CORP
CL	B	17	1	1	CORVALLIS	OR	FOAMAT FOODS CORP.
CL	O	12	1	1	SEATTLE	WA	IMRE CORPORATION
CL	O	9	14	1	BOISE	ID	FIRST IDAHO CORP.
CL	O	4	1	1	CODY	WY	APPLIED GENETICS INTL. (INC.
CL	O	3	1	1	SPOKANE	WA	GOLD COIN MINING INC.
CL	O	0	1	1	SPOKANE	WA	THUNDER MOUNTAIN GOLD INC.
CL	O	0	1	1	PORTLAND	OR	TENDER SENDER INC.
CL	O	0	1	1	PASCO	WA	NORTH AMERICAN SILVER CORP.
CL	O	0	31	78	EUGENE	OR	KINGS TABLE
CL	O	0	1	1	SPOKANE	WA	MITCHELL-LANE INC.
CL	O	0	1	1	COEUR D'ALENE	ID	CONSOLIDATED SILVER CORP
CL	O	0	58	48	BOISE	ID	CONTINENTAL LIFE & ACCIDENT CO

Deloitte Haskins & Sells

Aud1	Trd	Emp	Ast	Sls	Cty	Sta	Name
DHS	N	20000	1224	1438	BEAVERTON	OR	TEKTRONIX INC
DHS	O	11000	4764	2165	SEATTIE	WA	SAFECO CORP
DHS	N	10000	5122	1983	PORTLAND	OR	PACIFICORP
DHS	O	5600	8350	817	PORTLAND	OR	U.S. BANCORP
DHS	O	5500	8349	818	SEATTLE	WA	RAINIER BANCORPORATION
DHS	O	3400	1225	459	VANCOUVER	WA	PACIFIC TELECOM INC
DHS	O	2600	83	123	SPOKANE	WA	KEY TRONIC CORP.
DHS	N	2000	786	534	PORTLAND	OR	NERCO INC.
DHS	O	1600	1701	206	SPOKANE	WA	OLD NATIONAL BANCORPORATION
DHS	N	1600	1654	451	BOISE	ID	IDAHO POWER CO
DHS	N	1400	1383	459	SPOKANE	WA	WASHINGTON WATER POWER CO
DHS	O	1200	444	412	PORTLAND	OR	NORTHWEST NATURAL GAS CO
DHS	O	1100	114	116	SPOKANE	WA	ISC SYSTEMS CORP.
DHS	O	1100	72	112	MEDFORD	OR	BEAR CREEK CORP
DHS	O	710	693	77	SEATTLE	WA	SEATTLE TRUST & SAVINGS BANK
DHS	O	355	64	53	ALBANY	OR	OREGON METALLURGICAL CORP
DHS	O	270	38	40	LYNNWOOD	WA	INTERMEC CORP
DHS	S	210	280	50	PORTLAND	OR	NORTHWEST ACCEPTANCE CORP.
DHS	O	29	1	1	TUMWATER	WA	THERMAL SYSTEMS INC
DHS	O	20	21	12	CASPER	WY	AMERICAN NUCLEAR CORP
DHS	O	18	1	1	BELLEVUE	WA	CMC INTERNATIONAL INC
DHS	O	11	1	1	FAIRVIEW	OR	MULTNOMAH KENNEL CLUB
DHS	A	0	52	1	SEATTLE	WA	CLAREMONT CAPITAL CORP.

Ernst & Whinney

Aud1	Trd	Emp	Ast	Sls	Cty	Sta	Name
EW	O	8700	1057	1893	BELLEVUE	WA	PACCAR INC
EW	A	2700	164	217	EVERETT	WA	FLUKE (JOHN) MANUFACTURING CO.INC.
EW	O	2300	42	61	MOUNTLAKE TERRACE	WA	SEA GALLEY STORES INC.
EW	N	1800	278	102	TACOMA	WA	TACOMA BOATBUILDING CO
EW	O	1500	1491	179	TACOMA	WA	PUGET SOUND BANCORP
EW	O	934	1131	125	ANCHORAGE	AK	NATIONAL BANCORP OF ALASKA INC.
EW	O	501	126	146	BELLEVUE	WA	PENWEST LTD.
EW	O	133	101	12	BELLINGHAM	WA	BELLINGHAM NATIONAL BANK
EW	O	53	63	2	WALLACE	ID	COEUR D'ALENE MINES CORP.
EW	O	41	1	1	BELLEVUE	WA	TELECALC
EW	O	34	1	1	RIVERTON	WY	BUSINESS COMPUTER NETWORK INC.
EW	O	1	1	1	COEUR D'ALENE	ID	ROYAL APEX SILVER INC
EW	O	0	386	47	SPOKANE	WA	WTB FINANCIAL CORP
EW	O	0	1	10	PORTLAND	OR	INDUSTRIAL INVESTMENT CORP.
EW	O	0	518	50	Boise	ID	IB & T CORP.
EW	O	0	1	1	PORT TOWNSEND	WA	ALASKA POWER & TELEPHONE CO.

KMG Main Hurdman

Aud1	Trd	Emp	Ast	Sls	Cty	Sta	Name
MH	O	O	1	1	PORTLAND	OR	RAMAGON TOYS INC.

Peat Marwick Mitchell

Aud1	Trd	Emp	Ast	Sls	Cty	Sta	Name
PMM	O	8100	918	1152	PORTLAND	OR	WILLAMETTE INDUSTRIES INC
PMM	O	5000	135	783	KIRKLAND	WA	PACIFIC GAMBLE ROBINSON CO
PMM	O	4800	450	422	PORTLAND	OR	HYSTER CO
PMM	O	2700	75	183	PORTLAND	OR	SPROUSE REITZ CO INC
PMM	O	2000	249	164	EUGENE	OR	BOHEMIA INC
PMM	L	1600	102	170	SEATTLE	WA	NEW ENGLAND FISH COMPANY
PMM	O	1100	58	91	PORTLAND	OR	GRANTREE CORP
PMM	O	777	194	137	BEAVERTON	OR	MENTOR GRAPHICS CORP.
PMM	O	350	21	39	PORTLAND	OR	FABRIC WHOLESALERS INC
PMM	O	350	325	42	Anchorage	AK	ALASKA NATIONAL BANK OF THE NORTH
PMM	O	320	345	37	GREAT FALLS	MT	BANK OF MONTANA SYSTEM
PMM	O	301	22	66	SEATTLE	WA	EXPEDITORS INTL. OF WASHINGTON INC
PMM	O	254	834	92	ANCHORAGE	AK	ALASKA MUTUAL BANCORPORATION
PMM	O	240	29	9	BEND	OR	BROOKS RESOURCES CORP
PMM	O	147	11	13	POST FALLS	ID	TRANSTECTOR SYSTEMS INC.
PMM	O	135	454	54	SEATTLE	WA	SHORELINE SAVINGS ASSOCIATION
PMM	O	130	418	50	ANCHORAGE	AK	UNITED BANCORPORATION ALASKA
PMM	O	122	1	15	SEATTLE	WA	LINDAL CEDAR HOMES INC
PMM	O	122	1	1	BILLINGS	MT	BIG SKY TRANSPORTATION CO.
PMM	O	88	95	11	WENATCHEE	WA	CENTRAL BANCORPORATION INC
PMM	O	82	11	1	SHEPHERD	MT	UNITED TOTE INC.
PMM	O	80	133	21	KALISPELL	MT	FIRST FEDERAL SAVINGS BANK OF MT
PMM	O	56	27	13	PORTLAND	OR	INVESTORS INSURANCE CORP.
PMM	O	45	1	1	BELLEVUE	WA	SYLVAN LEARNING CORPORATION
PMM	O	27	16	1	HAMILTON	MT	RIBI IMMUNOCHEM RESEARCH INC
PMM	O	10	12	2	BILLINGS	MT	GENERAL HYDROCARBONS INC.
PMM	O	6	1	1	PORTLAND	OR	AMERICAN GUARANTY FINANCIAL CORP
PMM	O	0	39	1	SEATTLE	WA	GENETIC SYSTEMS CORP
PMM	O	0	1	1	CANYONVILLE	OR	GOLD GENIE WORLDWIDE INC.
PMM	O	0	1	1	SPOKANE	WA	GOLDEX INCORPORATED
PMM	L	0	49	1	PORTLAND	OR	COLUMBIA PACIFIC BANK & TRUST

Price Waterhouse

Audl	Trd	Emp	Ast	Sls	Cty	Sta	Name
PW	O	4100	504	946	BEAVERTON	OR	NIKE INC.
PW	N	3500	1743	425	BUTTE	MT	MONTANA POWER CO
PW	O	3200	488	459	LONGVIEW	WA	LONGVIEW FIBRE CO
PW	O	2400	42	71	BELLEVUE	WA	SKIPPER'S INC.
PW	O	1300	3360	332	TACOMA	WA	PACIFIC FIRST FINANCIAL CORP.
PW	O	1300	70	87	PORTLAND	OR	CASCADE CORP
PW	O	795	14	22	BELLEVUE	WA	FLAKEY JAKES INC.
PW	O	680	62	82	MCMINNVILLE	OR	CASCADE STEEL ROLLING MILLS INC
PW	O	430	520	65	ANCHORAGE	AK	ALASKA PACIFIC BANCORP.
PW	O	369	16	12	PORTLAND	OR	AMERICAN NETWORK INC.
PW	O	313	586	69	SEATTLE	WA	UNIVERSITY FEDERAL SAVINGS BANK
PW	O	284	45	21	PORTLAND	OR	STAR TECHNOLOGIES INC.
PW	O	267	72	53	VANCOUVER	WA	FALSTAFF BREWING CORP
PW	O	225	1	1	ALBANY	OR	REM METALS CORP
PW	O	214	578	68	BELLEVUE	WA	GREAT WESTERN FEDERAL SAVINGS
PW	O	207	14	12	KENT	WA	ADMAC INC.
PW	O	206	19	19	KENT	WA	FLOW SYSTEMS INC
PW	O	200	185	21	ANCHORAGE	AK	ALASKA BANCORPORATION
PW	O	160	150	21	ANCHORAGE	AK	ALASKA STATEBANK
PW	O	46	29	17	SANDY	OR	MELRIDGE INC.
PW	O	3	1	1	PORTLAND	OR	OFFICE SOLUTIONS INCORPORATED

Touche Ross

Aud1	Trd	Emp	Ast	Sls	Cty	Sta	Name
TR	N	104000	9246	13636	SEATTLE	WA	BOEING CO.
TR	N	36000	1125	5060	BOISE	ID	ALBERTSONS INC
TR	O	15000	763	1302	SEATTLE	WA	NORDSTROM INC
TR	N	3600	215	466	SEATTLE	WA	AIRBORNE FREIGHT CORP
TR	X	2900	104	155	BELLEVUE	WA	CRITON CORP.
TR	O	2000	353	128	BELLEVUE	WA	THOUSAND TRAILS INC.
TR	N	1600	163	127	PORTLAND	OR	FLOATING POINT SYSTEMS INC.
TR	X	1300	76	91	REDMOND	WA	ROCKCOR INC.
TR	O	1200	4238	4430	SEATTLE	WA	WASHINGTON MUTUAL SAVINGS BANK
TR	O	981	39	69	SEATTLE	WA	HORIZON AIR INDUSTRIES INC.
TR	A	658	840	87	CHEYENNE	WY	FIRST WYOMING BANCORPORATION
TR	O	635	55	33	Redmond	WA	ALL SEASONS RESORTS INC.
TR	O	592	75	56	REDMOND	WA	DATA I/O CORP.
TR	O	562	73	110	SEATTLE	WA	LYNDEN INC.
TR	O	510	13	55	SEATTLE	WA	NORTHERN AIR FREIGHT INC.
TR	N	430	156	219	SEATTLE	WA	CASCADE NATURAL GAS CORP
TR	O	425	25	52	BELLEVUE	WA	TIMBERLAND INDUSTRIES INC.
TR	O	384	119	133	PORTLAND	OR	FIRST FARWEST CORP
TR	O	250	13	22	SEATTLE	WA	TRAILER EQUIPMENT DISTRIBUTORS INC
TR	O	213	526	56	TACOMA	WA	UNITED BANK (TACOMA)
TR	O	188	358	43	WENATCHEE	WA	COLUMBIA FEDERAL SAVINGS BANK
TR	O	151	367	36	SEATTLE	WA	WESTSIDE BANCORP. INC.
TR	X	150	101	15	GREAT FALLS	MT	ALL STATES LEASING CO
TR	X	110	12	1	BOTHELL	WA	WESTERN MARINE ELECTRONICS CO.
TR	O	110	291	27	TACOMA	WA	UNITED MUTUAL SAVING BANK
TR	O	110	18	1	RIVERTON	WY	CRESTED CORP.
TR	O	91	1	1	REDMOND	WA	EMF CORP.
TR	O	90	1	1	RENTON	WA	WEB PRESS CORP
TR	O	57	118	1	BELLEVUE	WA	FIRST MUTUAL SAVINGS BANK
TR	O	48	1	1	SEATTLE	WA	MICROFAST SOFTWARE CORP.
TR	O	35	1	1	RIVERTON	WY	BRUNTON CO
TR	O	20	10	1	RIVERTON	WY	NUPEC RESOURCES INC.
TR	O	10	1	1	RENTON	WA	MICROPHONICS
TR	O	5	1	1	REDMOND	WA	SELF REGULATION SYSTEMS INC.
TR	O	4	1	4	HAILEY	ID	ATLANTIS MINING & MANUFACTURING
TR	O	0	1	1	SPOKANE	WA	WESTERN STRATEGIC MINERALS INC.
TR	O	0	1	12	RICHLAND	WA	SIGMA RESEARCH INC.
TR	O	0	1	1	RIVERTON	WY	RUBY MINING CO
TR	O	0	1	1	MACKAY	ID	DIVERSIFIED RESOURCES CORP.
TR	O	0	120	757	SEATTLE	WA	ASSOCIATED GROCERS INC.

Secondary Career Factors

Secondary Career Factors

Some of you may be wondering where our chapter is to address the old favorites like training, transferring, years to partner, opportunity for women, international assignments etc., etc. We have not forgotten these matters, but we impress upon you that these areas should not be of primary concern. We categorize these questions as secondary career factors not because they are unimportant, but because the firms for all practical purposes handle these areas in a similar manner. We again encourage you to develop questions which demonstrate creativity and are vital to your ultimate firm selection.

For your information and reference we have included the most commonly asked questions by recruits and what we have found to be the common Big Eight firm answer.

Are you recruiting for all the firms offices or just the local office?

The answer is nearly always 'yes'. In practice, however, the time and expense of arranging a visit to another office makes it far less likely that you would be invited to an office visit in another town.

Does your firm have special educational preferences for direct hire to tax or MCS?

Yes. While the firms will occasionally hire Bachelor degreed candidates directly into these disciplines, the vast majority of new hires have advanced degrees or special experience.

Does your firm encourage new employees to select an industry specialty soon after hire?

Yes (somewhat qualified). To the extent that specialization is possible it seems to be encouraged earlier and earlier. We suggest it may not be possible where the office staffing limitations have you working in a variety of industries.

Is it relatively easy to transfer among offices of the firm within the first three years of employment?

I believe too often the answer given to this question is a straight 'yes.' In reality transfers among offices, particularly at the lower staff levels, are based on needs. Other office opportunities are typically made known to the staff in all offices. You are given an opportunity to apply. Your performance is key to success. Do not assume that you can transfer to any location under your schedule.

Are international opportunities available to staff members within the first three years of employment?

Unless the circumstances are unusual, no. Considerable preparation must precede an international assignment. The cost of this preparation and the cost of the move usually dictates that the relocation involves a minimum duration of about 3 years. Partner level personnel are typically more prepared to make this type of commitment.

Which discipline within the firm is growing most rapidly?

MCS. On a percentage basis MCS is likely to be growing most rapidly for some time, since most firms (except Arthur Andersen) have less MCS revenue than any other area. During this past year MCS revenue grew on the average of 25% for the Big Eight firms. By contrast tax services averaged a 14% increase and auditing services grew 9%. Keep in mind that even at 9% the audit area for most firms continues to provide the majority of new revenue. (figures according to March, 1986 issue of Public Accounting Report)

Based on our geographic regions (see prior section for states included in regions) which are the fastest growing areas of the country for your firm?

Northeast (Boston area), Southeast (Florida area), and West (California area). While I never thought to consider geographic opportunities, many graduates are carefully reviewing where growth is likely to be in the future. The Boston area where a technology emphasis has the area booming looks very promising. With the tremendous influx of retirees to Florida, the state is estimated to soon be the sixth largest ahead of Illinois and Ohio. All the Big Eight firms are increasing their practices and opening new offices in this area. In the west many economists are predicting that California will soon, not only be the business center of the US, but the world. Most of the firms are experiencing significant growth on the entire west coast.

On the average how long does it take to become a partner with your firm?

10 to 12 years. Highly unusual to become a partner before thirty or before ten years of experience.

What percentage of people initially employed with your firm become partners?

About 5%.

What percentage of people initially hired are women?

50%. What percentage of partners are women?   Less than 5%.

Does your firm have a superior training program?

Yes.

Appendices

Offices By Firm - All States

Offices By Firm - All States

CITY	ST	AA	AY	CL	DHS	EW	KMG	PMM	PW	TR
Abilene	TX		1							
Akron	OH			1		1		1		1
Albany	NY		1	1		1		1		
Albuquerque	NM	1	1			1		1		1
Allentown	PA				1			1		
Amarillo	TX		1					1		
Anchorage	AK		1	1		1		1	1	1
Ann Arbor	MI				1					1
Arlington	TX								1	
Astoria	NY		1							
Atlanta	GA	1	2	1	2	2	1	2	2	1
Atlantic City	NJ		1							
Aurora	IL			1						
Austin	TX	1	1	1		1	1	1	1	1
Bakersfield	CA		1					1		
Baltimore	MD	1	1	1	1	1	1	1	1	1
Baton Rouge	LA				1	1				1
Battle Creek	MI							1		
Beachwood	OH							1		
Beaverton	OR						1			
Bellevue	WA				1			1	1	1
Bennington	VT						1			
Bethesda	MD								1	
Beverly Hills	CA		1							
Billings	MT						1			

CITY	ST	AA	AY	CL	DHS	EW	KMG	PMM	PW	TR
Birmingham	AL	1	1	1	1	1		1	1	1
Bloomington	IL						1			
Bloomington	MN									1
Boca Raton	FL			1		1				
Boise	ID	1		1						1
Boone	NC				1					
Boston	MA	1	1	1	1	1	1	1	1	2
Boulder	CO				1					1
Bridgeport	CT			1					1	
Buffalo	NY		1		1	1	1	1	1	1
Burlington	MA							1		
Canton	OH			1		1	1			
Century City	CA					1	1	1	1	
Champaign	IL						1			
Charleston	SC			1						
Charleston	WV					1	1			
Charlotte	NC	1	1	1	1	1	1	1	1	1
Chattanooga	TN	1			1	1	1			
Cherry Hill	NJ				1					
Chicago	IL	2	2	1	1	1	1	1	1	1
Cincinnati	OH	1	1	1	1	1	1	1	1	1
Clarksburg	WV						1			
Clearwater	FL						1			
Cleveland	OH	1	1	1	1	3	1	1	1	1
Colorado Springs	CO				1					

CITY	ST	AA	AY	CL	DHS	EW	KMG	PMM	PW	TR
Columbia	MD							1		
Columbia	SC	1	1	1	1	1			1	
Columbus	GA					1				
Columbus	OH	1	1	1	1	1	1	1	1	1
Coos Bay	OR						1			
Corpus Cristi	TX					1		1		
Costa Mesa	CA	1	1		1			1		
Dallas	TX	1	1	2	1	3	1	2	2	1
Danbury	CT						1			
Davenport	IA				1			1		
Dayton	OH	1		1	1	1			1	1
Daytona Beach	FL		1							
Decatur	IL						1	1		
Denver	CO	1	1	1	1	1	1	1	1	1
Des Moines	IA		1	1	1	1		1		
Detroit	MI	1	1	1	2	1	1	1	1	1
Dublin	OH							1		
Duluth	GA			1						
Duluth	MN						1			
Durham	NC									1
El Paso	TX			1				1		
Elkhart	IN			1						
Erie	PA					1				
Eugene	OR			1						
Fairbanks	AK						1			

CITY	ST	AA	AY	CL	DHS	EW	KMG	PMM	PW	TR
Fayetteville	AR		1							
Floral Park	NY			1						
Fort Lauderdale	FL	1	1	1	1	1	1	1	1	1
Fort Myers	FL			1						
Fort Wayne	IN			1		1				
Fort Worth	TX	1	1	1	1	1	1	1	1	1
Fresno	CA		1			1	1		1	1
Garden City	KS						1			
Garden City	NY						1			
Glastonbury	CT								1	
Grand Rapids	MI	1		1	1	1				1
Greeneville	TN						1			
Greensboro	NC	1			1		1			1
Greenville	SC		1		1	1	1	1		
Hackensack	NJ				1	1			1	
Hagerstown	MD						1			
Harrisburg	PA			1		1	1	1		
Hartford	CT	1	1	1	1	1		1	1	1
Hickory	NC				1					
Hilo	HI				1					
Hollister	CA			1						
Honolulu	HI	1	1	1	1	1	1	1	1	1
Houma	LA									1
Houston	TX	1	1	1	1	2	1	2	1	1
Indianapolis	IN	1	1	1	1	1	1	1	1	

CITY	ST	AA	AY	CL	DHS	EW	KMG	PMM	PW	TR
Irvine	CA						1			
Irving	TX				1					
Jackson	MS	1				1		1		1
Jackson	MI					1				
Jacksonville	FL	1	1	1	1	1		1	1	1
Jericho	NY			1				1	1	1
Johnson City	TN								1	
Juneau	AK			1						
Kalamazoo	MI				1					
Kansas City	MO	1	1	1	1	1		1	1	1
Knoxville	TN			1		1	1			
Lafayette	LA	1								
Lancaster	PA					1				
Lansing	MI					1	1		1	
Laredo	TX					1				
Las Vegas	NV	1			1	1				
Lawrenceville	NJ					1				
Lebanon	PA					1				
Lenoir	NC				1					
Lexington	KY			1	1	1				
Lincoln	NB			1				1	1	
Little Rock	AR		1		1	1		1	1	
Long Beach	CA					1		1		
Los Angeles	CA	1	1	1	1	1	1	1	1	1
Louisville	KY	1	1	1		1		1		1

CITY	ST	AA	AY	CL	DHS	EW	KMG	PMM	PW	TR
Lubbock	TX						1	1		
Lynchburg	VA			1						
Madison	WI		1							
Manchester	NH		1	1	1	1				
Marietta	GA									1
Marquette	MI					1				
Mattoon	IL						1			
Maui	HI				1	1				
Melbourne	FL				1					
Melville	NY	1		1		1				
Memphis	TN	1		1	1	1		1	1	1
Miami	FL	1	1	1	1	1	1	1	1	1
Midland	TX			1			1	1	1	
Milwaukee	WI	1	1	1	1	1		1	1	1
Minneapolis	MN	1	1	1	1	1	1	1	1	1
Mobile	AL				1	1				
Monmouth	IL						1			
Morgantown	NC					1				
Morristown	NJ					1			1	
Naples	FL			1						
Nashville	TN	1	1		1	1		1	1	2
New Haven	CT				1	1				
New Orleans	LA	1	1	1	1	1	1	1	1	1
New York	NY	1	2	1	2	1	1	1	3	2
Newark	NJ		1	1	1	1				1

CITY	ST	AA	AY	CL	DHS	EW	KMG	PMM	PW	TR
Newport Beach	CA			1		1			1	1
Newport News	VA			1						
Newton	MA								1	
Norfolk	VA		1	1		1		1	1	
Oakbrook	IL							1	1	
Oakland	CA	1		1	1	1	1	1	1	1
Odessa	TX						1	1		
Oklahoma City	OK	1	1	1	1	1	1	1	1	1
Omaha	NB	1	1	1	1			1		1
Orlando	FL	1	1	1	1	1	1	1	1	1
Palo Alto	CA		1	1					1	
Peoria	IL						1	1	1	
Philadelphia	PA	1	1	1	1	1	1	1	1	1
Phoenix	AZ	1	1	1	1	1	1	1	1	1
Pittsburgh	PA	1	1	1	1	1	1	1	1	1
Portland	ME		1	1		1		1		
Portland	OR	1	1	1	1	1	1	1	1	1
Princeton	NJ		1							
Providence	RI		1		1	1		1	1	
Punta Gorda	FL			1						
Raleigh	NC	1		1	1	1		1	1	1
Reading	PA					1				
Reno	NV		1							
Reston	VA		1							
Richmond	VA		1	1	1	1		1	1	1

CITY	ST	AA	AY	CL	DHS	EW	KMG	PMM	PW	TR
Riverside	CA					1			1	
Roanoke	VA				1			1		
Rochester	NY	1		1	1	1		1	1	1
Rockford	IL				1			1		
Roseland	NJ	1					1			
Roswell	NM					1				
Sacramento	CA		1	1	1	1	1	1	1	1
Saddlebrook	NJ		1							
Saginaw	MI				1	1				
Salinas	CA			1						
Salisbury	MD						1			
Salt Lake City	UT	1	1	1	1	1	1	1	1	1
San Antonio	TX	1	1		1	1	1	1	1	1
San Diego	CA	1	1	1	1	1	1	1	1	1
San Francisco	CA	1	1	1	1	1	1	1	1	1
San Jose	CA	1	1	1	1	1	1	1	1	1
San Mateo	CA							1		
Sanford	NC					1				
Sarasota	FL									1
Schaumburg	IL							1		1
Scottsdale	AZ					1				
Seattle	WA	1	1	1	1	1	1	1	1	1
Short Hills	NJ							1		
Shreveport	LA							1		
South Bend	IN				1	1		1	1	

CITY	ST	AA	AY	CL	DHS	EW	KMG	PMM	PW	TR
Southern Pines	NC				1					
Spartanburg	NC					1				
Spokane	WA			1	1					
Springfield	IL		1		1		1			
Springfield	MA			1			1			
St. Charles	IL	1								
St. Louis	MO	1	1	1	1	1	1	1	2	1
St. Paul	MN	1			1	1	1			1
St. Petersburg	FL		1		1	1	1		1	
Stamford	CT	1	1	1	1	1	1	1	1	1
State College	PA						1			
Syracuse	NY			1		1	1		1	
Tacoma	WA					1				
Tallahassee	FL		1							
Tampa	FL	1	1	1	1	1		1	1	1
Taylorville	IL						1			
Toledo	OH	1	2		1	1		1	1	1
Topeka	KS						1			1
Trenton	NJ					1	1	1		1
Troy	MI		1							
Tucson	AZ	1		1	1	1		1	1	
Tulsa	OK	1	1	1	1		1	1	1	1
Valley Forge	PA							1		
Vero Beach	FL							1		
Vienna	VA						1			

CITY	ST	AA	AY	CL	DHS	EW	KMG	PMM	PW	TR
Waco	TX						1			
Walnut Creek	CA		1			1		2	1	
Washington	DC	1	1	1	1	1	1	1	1	1
Waterbury	CT			1						
West Palm Beach	FL			1	1	1	1	1	1	
White Plains	NY						1	1		
Wichita	KS		1				1	1		
Wilmington	DE					1		1	1	
Winston-Salem	NC					1			1	1
Woodbury	NY				1					
Woodland Hills	CA		1			1	1	1	1	1
Worcester	MA		1				1			1
Youngstown	OH				1					
		69	94	96	106	119	86	113	96	87

Major Clients By Firm

Audl = Principal Accountants

Trd = Shows the where traded status of company shares
- A - American Stock Exchange
- N - New York Stock Exchange
- O - Over the Counter
- B - Company in some condition of bankruptcy
- C - Co-op or mutual
- L - Company in liquidation
- S - Subsidiary which reports separately
- U - Subsidiary whose auditor is different from parent
- X - Company which has gone private

Emp = Number of employees

Name = Company name

SIC = Four digit Standard Industrial Classification

Sta = State

Ast = Assets

Sls = Sales

Arthur Andersen

Audl	Trd	Emp	Name	SIC	Sta	Ast	Sls
AA	N	232000	ITT CORP.	3981	NY	14272	12715
AA	N	184000	GTE CORP.	4811	CT	26558	15732
AA	N	137000	MARRIOTT CORP	7011	MD	3664	4242
AA	X	112000	ARA SERVICES INC.	7392	PA	1693	2652
AA	N	111000	TENNECO INC.	3981	TX	20437	15400
AA	S	105000	INTERNATIONAL STANDARD ELECTRIC	3662	NY	4493	4647
AA	N	103000	GENERAL DYNAMICS CORP	3721	MO	4448	8164
AA	N	93000	SARA LEE CORP.	2099	IL	3216	8117
AA	N	77000	MAY DEPARTMENT STORES CO	5311	MO	3442	5080
AA	N	76000	UAL INC	4511	IL	7874	6383
AA	N	76000	AMERICAN INFORMATION TECHNOLOGIES	4811	IL	18149	9021
AA	N	73000	DART & KRAFT INC.	3981	IL	5502	9942
AA	N	66000	HALLIBURTON CO	1389	TX	4662	4779
AA	N	54000	TEXACO INC	2911	NY	37703	46297
AA	N	51000	CHAMPION INTERNATIONAL CORP	2435	CT	6098	5770
AA	A	50000	WICKES COMPANIES INC.	5211	CA	2648	4362
AA	N	50000	HOLIDAY CORP.	7011	TN	2448	1804
AA	N	47000	TELEDYNE INC	3981	CA	2766	3256
AA	N	47000	AMERICAN HOME PRODUCTS CORP	2834	NY	3395	4685
AA	N	46000	DRESSER INDUSTRIES INC	3981	TX	3225	4111
AA	N	43000	HOUSEHOLD INTERNATIONAL INC	6341	IL	11929	8686
AA	N	42000	OCCIDENTAL PETROLEUM CORP	1311	CA	11586	14534
AA	N	42000	AMERICAN MEDICAL INTERNATIONAL	8062	CA	3433	2256
AA	N	41000	COLGATE PALMOLIVE CO	2841	NY	2814	4524
AA	N	39000	DELTA AIR LINES INC	4511	GA	3627	4684
AA	N	38000	GEORGIA PACIFIC CORP	2436	GA	4866	6716
AA	O	37000	CADBURY SCHWEPPES PLC	2065	EN	2469	1655
AA	N	35000	WEYERHAEUSER CO	2421	WA	6005	5206
AA	N	35000	CASTLE & COOKE INC	0179	HI	1026	1601
AA	N	34000	HILTON HOTELS CORP	7011	CA	1226	684
AA	N	34000	ABBOTT LABORATORIES	2834	IL	3468	3360
AA	N	33000	ZENITH ELECTRONICS CORP.	3651	IL	927	1624
AA	N	33000	MERCK & CO INC	2833	NJ	4902	3548
AA	N	32000	WALGREEN CO	5912	IL	962	3162
AA	N	32000	INTERNATIONAL PAPER CO	2621	NY	6039	4502
AA	N	32000	KIDDE INC.	3981	NJ	1689	2164
AA	N	32000	GRUMMAN CORP	3721	NY	1586	3049
AA	N	31000	SOUTHERN CO	4911	GA	16531	6814
AA	X	30000	NORTHWEST INDUSTRIES INC	6711	IL	1525	1432
AA	N	29000	QUAKER OATS CO	2043	IL	1842	3520
AA	N	29000	OWENS CORNING FIBERGLAS CORP	3296	OH	2366	3305
AA	N	29000	PACIFIC GAS & ELECTRIC CO	4931	CA	19098	8431
AA	S	28800	ITT CONTINENTAL BAKING CO.	2051	NY	441	1472

AA	N	28000	UNITED STATES SHOE CORP	3144	OH	850	1920
AA	N	27000	FEDERAL EXPRESS CORP. (THE)	4712	TN	1900	2031
AA	N	26000	COMBUSTION ENGINEERING INC	3533	CT	2161	2408
AA	S	25000	GENERAL TELEPHONE CALIFORNIA	4811	CA	5098	2444
AA	N	25000	CARSON PIRIE SCOTT & CO	5311	IL	609	1302
AA	S	24000	PACIFIC NORTHWEST BELL TELEPHONE	4811	WA	3830	1634
AA	U	24000	ILLINOIS BELL TELEPHONE CO.	4811	IL	5303	2688
AA	N	23300	SCOTTYS INC	5211	FL	238	453
AA	N	23000	EG&G INC	3662	MA	430	1145
AA	N	23000	BOISE CASCADE CORP.	2421	ID	3268	3737
AA	N	23000	AMP INC.	3643	PA	1549	1636
AA	N	22000	USG CORPORATION	6711	IL	1732	2526
AA	N	22000	MERCANTILE STORES CO INC	5311	DE	1151	1880
AA	N	22000	CONTINENTAL TELECOM	4811	GA	5074	2557
AA	N	22000	CONSOLIDATED FREIGHTWAYS INC.	6711	CA	1134	1882
AA	O	21000	YELLOW FREIGHT SYSTEM INC	4213	KS	748	1530
AA	N	20000	WASTE MANAGEMENT INC	4953	IL	2261	1625
AA	N	20000	LIMITED INC	5621	OH	1212	2387
AA	N	20000	CUMMINS ENGINE COMPANY INC	3519	IN	1705	2146
AA	N	20000	COLT INDUSTRIES INC	3981	NY	1251	1579
AA	N	19000	WACKENHUT CORP	7393	FL	104	279
AA	N	19000	NATIONAL SERVICE INDUSTRIES INC	3646	GA	618	1191
AA	N	19000	COMMONWEALTH EDISON CO	4911	IL	16285	4964
AA	N	19000	BRUNSWICK CORP	3981	IL	1002	1539
AA	N	19000	AIR PRODUCTS & CHEMICALS INC	2813	PA	2593	1830
AA	N	18000	MANOR CARE INC	8051	MD	579	454
AA	N	18000	MARSH & MCLENNAN COMPANIES INC	6411	NY	1030	1368
AA	N	18000	DONNELLEY (R.R.)& SONS CO.	2751	IL	1593	2038
AA	N	17000	SOUTHERN CALIFORNIA EDISON CO	4911	CA	12593	5169
AA	N	17000	HUTTON (E.F.) GROUP INC	6341	NY	21749	3139
AA	A	17000	DWG CORP	5171	FL	918	1046
AA	N	17000	BROWNING-FERRIS INDUSTRIES INC	4953	TX	1001	1145
AA	N	16000	UNITED STATES GYPSUM CO	3275	IL	1614	2319
AA	N	16000	SUNTRUST BANKS INC.	6711	FL	19406	1819
AA	O	16000	FIGGIE INTERNATIONAL INC.	3981	OH	562	803
AA	N	15000	HERSHEY FOODS CORP	2066	PA	1197	2035
AA	S	15000	GEORGIA POWER CO	4911	GA	9031	3444
AA	N	15000	CIRCLE K CORP	5411	AZ	580	1682
AA	N	14000	THRIFTY CORP.	5912	CA	582	1426
AA	N	14000	GREAT NORTHERN NEKOOSA CORP	2611	CT	1968	1935
AA	S	14000	GAMBLE-SKOGMO INC.	2335	CA	796	1419
AA	N	14000	FORT HOWARD PAPER CO.	2621	WI	1537	1363
AA	N	14000	FIRST CHICAGO CORP	6711	IL	38893	4370
AA	N	13000	ZALE CORP	5944	TX	955	1054
AA	N	13000	TGI FRIDAY'S INC.	5812	TX	168	314
AA	N	13000	REXNORD INC	3568	WI	984	1104

Arthur Young

Audl	Trd	Emp	Name	SIC	Sta	Ast	Sls
AY	N	164000	MOBIL CORP.	2911	NY	41752	55960
AY	N	150000	PEPSICO INC	2086	NY	5861	8057
AY	N	145000	MC DONALD'S CORP.	5812	IL	5043	3695
AY	N	105000	BEVERLY ENTERPRISES	8062	CA	2020	1691
AY	N	93000	WAL-MART STORES INC.	5311	AR	3104	8581
AY	N	88000	LOCKHEED CORP.	3721	CA	4184	9535
AY	N	78000	TEXAS INSTRUMENTS INC	3674	TX	3076	4925
AY	N	76000	SPERRY CORP.	6153	NY	5773	5687
AY	N	72000	SOUTHWESTERN BELL TELEPHONE CO.	4811	MO	19291	7925
AY	N	68000	AMERICAN EXPRESS CO.	6341	NY	74777	11850
AY	O	63000	BATUS INC.	2111	KY	4517	5087
AY	N	56000	TEXTRON INC	3981	RI	4337	4991
AY	N	50000	AMR CORP	4511	TX	6425	6131
AY	N	45000	OWENS ILLINOIS INC	3221	OH	3306	3674
AY	N	41000	UNITED BRANDS CO	2011	NY	1012	3220
AY	N	41000	AMERICAN STANDARD INC	3743	NY	2270	2912
AY	N	38000	COOPER INDUSTRIES INC	3563	TX	3636	3067
AY	N	35000	MC DERMOTT INTL. INC.	1629	LA	4351	3257
AY	N	30000	FLUOR CORP	1629	CA	2796	4168
AY	N	27000	UNITED TELECOMMUNICATIONS INC	4811	MO	5767	3198
AY	N	26000	CHESEBROUGH PONDS INC	2844	CT	3008	2941
AY	N	25000	PHILLIPS PETROLEUM CO	1311	OK	14045	15636
AY	N	25000	PAN AM CORP.	4511	NY	2448	3484
AY	N	21000	WEST POINT PEPPERELL INC	2211	GA	783	1204
AY	O	21000	INTEL CORP	3674	CA	2152	1365
AY	N	19000	BALLY MANUFACTURING CORP	3999	IL	1529	252
AY	N	18000	NORTON CO	3291	MA	1002	1193
AY	X	18000	MARMON GROUP INC.	3351	IL	965	1623
AY	O	17000	TYSON FOODS INC	2016	AR	471	1136
AY	N	16000	PAINE WEBBER GROUP INC.	6341	NY	13589	1885
AY	N	16000	AMCA INTERNATIONAL LTD.	3441	NH	1387	1559
AY	N	14000	UNIVERSAL LEAF TOBACCO CO INC	5159	VA	488	1070
AY	N	14000	MC GRAW-HILL INC.	2721	NY	1274	1491
AY	N	14000	GENERAL INSTRUMENT CORP	3679	NY	829	994
AY	N	14000	ADVANCED MEDICAL CONCEPTS	5065	CA	765	624
AY	O	12000	STAUFFER CHEMICAL CO	2819	CT	2007	1526
AY	N	12000	SHELLER GLOBE CORP	3714	OH	494	918
AY	N	12000	FIREMAN'S FUND CORP.	6711	NJ	7986	3350
AY	N	11000	KOPPERS COMPANY INC.	2865	PA	1066	1400
AY	N	11000	INTERSTATE BAKERIES CORP.	2051	NY	177	704
AY	N	11000	COLLINS & AIKMAN CORP	2281	NY	530	1040
AY	N	10000	FIELDCREST MILLS INC	2211	NC	373	586
AY	A	9900	SMITH (A.O.) CORP.	3714	WI	486	932

AY	S	9000	AVCO FINANCIAL SERVICES INC	6145	CA	5694	1393
AY	N	8900	INTERNATIONAL MINERALS & CHEMICALS	2873	IL	1957	1627
AY	N	8600	REPUBLICBANK CORP.	6711	TX	23206	2104
AY	N	8600	OVERNITE TRANSPORTATION CO	4213	VA	301	470
AY	O	8300	PORTER (H.K.) COMPANY#INC.	3423	PA	124	139
AY	N	8000	WARNER COMMUNICATIONS INC	3981	NY	2286	2235
AY	N	8000	MACMILLAN INC	2731	NY	587	677
AY	N	8000	CAPITAL CITIES/ABC INC.	4833	NY	1885	1021
AY	N	8000	AMERADA HESS CORP	2911	NY	6219	7653
AY	O	7600	BANGOR PUNTA CORP	3981	CT	492	548
AY	N	7500	TYLER CORP	3321	TX	474	912
AY	N	7100	FEDDERS CORP	3585	NJ	85	104
AY	N	7000	PUBLIC SERVICE CO. OF COLORADO	4931	CO	2995	1747
AY	A	7000	MEDIA GENERAL INC	2711	VA	688	579
AY	N	6800	TIGER INTERNATIONAL INC.	4511	CA	956	1147
AY	N	6800	SONAT INC.	4923	AL	3570	2498
AY	O	6700	SOCIETY CORP	6711	OH	8749	781
AY	N	6600	AMETEK INC	3621	NY	401	503
AY	O	6500	CORESTATES FINANCIAL CORP	6711	PA	11080	1043
AY	N	6500	CHUBB CORP	6341	NJ	5763	2394
AY	A	6200	SWIFT INDEPENDENT CORP	2011	IL	308	2892
AY	N	6000	DATAPOINT CORP.	3573	TX	502	520
AY	N	5900	WILLIAMS COMPANIES	2874	OK	4337	3140
AY	N	5900	LUBY'S CAFETERIAS INC.	5812	TX	126	196
AY	N	5600	WRIGLEY (WM. JR.) COMPANY	2067	IL	352	620
AY	N	5400	TRINITY INDUSTRIES INC	3743	TX	471	455
AY	N	5300	TODD SHIPYARDS CORP	3731	NY	406	507
AY	A	5300	DATAPRODUCTS CORP	3573	CA	334	354
AY	O	5200	JONATHAN LOGAN INC	2335	NJ	221	383
AY	N	4900	PSA INC	4511	CA	786	635
AY	N	4900	COOPER TIRE & RUBBER CO	3011	OH	295	523
AY	O	4800	SUMMIT HEALTH LTD.	8062	CA	371	364
AY	N	4800	GEARHART INDUSTRIES INC.	3533	TX	864	560
AY	N	4800	ANALOG DEVICES INC	3662	MA	348	322
AY	O	4800	APPLE COMPUTER INC.	3573	CA	936	1918
AY	N	4800	BARNES GROUP INC.	3495	CT	254	432
AY	O	4700	STATER BROS. INC.	5411	CA	110	714
AY	A	4700	AVONDALE MILLS	2211	AL	176	238
AY	N	4600	SOUTHWEST AIRLINES CO	4511	TX	1022	680
AY	N	4500	COPPERWELD CORP	3312	PA	315	354
AY	S	4400	CAROLINA TELEPHONE & TELEGRAPH	4811	NC	836	439
AY	O	4300	BOATMENS BANCSHARES INC	6711	MO	7055	615
AY	O	4100	BRINTEC CORP.	3629	CT	162	300
AY	A	4000	KAY CORP	5149	VA	441	645
AY	O	4000	JUSTIN INDUSTRIES INC	3251	TX	231	297
AY	O	3900	INTERMET CORP.	3322	GA	132	265

Coopers & Lybrand

Audl	Trd	Emp	Name	SIC	Sta	Ast	Sls
CL	N	369000	FORD MOTOR CO	3711	MI	31604	52774
CL	N	338000	AMERICAN TELEPHONE & TELEGRAPH	4811	NJ	40463	34910
CL	S	338000	AT & T TECHNOLOGIES INC.	3661	NJ	40463	34910
CL	N	165000	KROGER CO	5411	OH	4178	17124
CL	N	114000	PHILIP MORRIS INC	2111	NY	17429	15964
CL	N	94000	BELLSOUTH	4811	GA	25008	10664
CL	N	92000	NYNEX CORP.	4811	NY	21000	10314
CL	N	87000	DIGITAL EQUIPMENT CORP	3573	MA	6369	6686
CL	N	85000	MINNESOTA MINING & MANUFACTURING	3981	MN	6593	7846
CL	N	79000	BELL ATLANTIC CORP.	4811	PA	19788	9084
CL	N	77000	AMERICAN BRANDS INC	2111	NY	4926	7308
CL	N	75000	JOHNSON & JOHNSON	3842	NJ	5095	6421
CL	N	74000	PACIFIC TELESIS	4811	CA	19538	8499
CL	N	73000	RAYTHEON CO	3662	MA	3441	6409
CL	N	70000	U S WEST INC.	4811	CO	17975	7813
CL	N	57000	FIRESTONE TIRE & RUBBER CO OHIO	3011	OH	2528	3836
CL	N	56000	DUN & BRADSTREET CORP.	7321	NY	2673	2772
CL	S	55000	NEW YORK TELEPHONE CO.	4811	NY	13664	7055
CL	N	53000	ZAYRE CORP	5311	MA	1582	4036
CL	S	53000	SOUTHERN BELL TEL. & TEL. CO.	4811	GA	13516	5784
CL	N	47000	WENDYS INTERNATIONAL INC	5812	OH	811	1100
CL	N	47000	BURLINGTON NORTHERN INC	4011	WA	12512	8651
CL	N	46000	OGDEN CORP	3981	NY	834	1026
CL	N	45000	HEINZ (H J) CO	2032	PA	2474	4048
CL	N	43000	HUMANA INC	8062	KY	2832	2280
CL	O	43000	GULF CORP	2911	PA	21284	28503
CL	N	40000	ALUMINUM COMPANY OF AMERICA	1051	PA	6354	5163
CL	C	39000	CONSOLIDATED RAIL CORP.	4011	PA	6568	3208
CL	N	38000	SUN COMPANY INC	2911	PA	12923	13769
CL	S	38000	SOUTH CENTRAL BELL TELEPHONE	4811	AL	10193	4014
CL	S	33000	BELL TELPHONE CO OF PA	4811	PA	5365	2444
CL	S	32000	MOUNTAIN STATES TEL.& TEL.CO.	4811	CO	8469	3477
CL	N	31000	TRAVELERS CORP	6341	CT	41642	14594
CL	N	31000	ATLANTIC RICHFIELD CO	2911	CA	20279	21723
CL	S	30000	MICHIGAN BELL TELEPHONE CO.	4811	MI	4076	2153
CL	S	29000	NEW ENGLAND TELEPHONE & TELEGRAPH	4811	MA	6595	3086
CL	N	28000	CBS INC.	4833	NY	3509	4677
CL	N	26000	HERCULES INC	2821	DE	2659	2587
CL	N	26000	AMERICAN CAN CO	3411	CT	3084	2855
CL	N	25000	AMERICAN INTERNATIONAL GROUP	6341	NY	15571	5782
CL	O	23000	VICORP RESTAURANTS INC	5812	CO	347	384
CL	B	23000	SAMBOS RESTAURANTS INC	5812	CA	221	293
CL	N	23000	PARKER-HANNIFIN CORP	3728	OH	966	1460

CL	O	22000	RELIABLE LIFE INSURANCE COMPANY	6311	MO	354	84
CL	S	22000	NEW JERSEY BELL TELEPHONE CO.	4811	NJ	5168	2504
CL	N	22000	MORRISON KNUDSEN COMPANY INC	1629	ID	936	2122
CL	N	22000	JAMES RIVER CORPORATION OF VA.	2621	VA	1741	2492
CL	N	22000	AMFAC INC	3981	CA	1313	2405
CL	N	20000	UNOCAL CORP	1311	CA	10797	10738
CL	N	20000	UPJOHN CO	2834	MI	2377	2105
CL	X	20000	SCOA INDUSTRIES INC.	5311	OH	506	1424
CL	C	20000	STATE FARM MUTUAL AUTO INS.	6331	IL	13197	6684
CL	B	20000	MANVILLE CORP.	3296	CO	2393	1880
CL	N	20000	BANK OF BOSTON CORP	6711	MA	28296	3436
CL	N	18000	GENSTAR CORP	3272	CA	1923	2714
CL	N	18000	CROWN ZELLERBACH CORP	2621	CA	2406	3062
CL	C	18000	AGWAY INC	3981	NY	1360	4067
CL	S	17000	NORTHWESTERN BELL TELEPHONE CO.	4811	NE	4800	2120
CL	O	16000	MORRISON INC	5812	FL	195	471
CL	S	16000	CHESAPEAKE & POTOMAC TEL CO (MD)	4811	MD	2747	1211
CL	N	15000	STONE & WEBSTER INC.	8911	NY	520	321
CL	O	15000	FOOD LION INC	5411	NC	440	1866
CL	N	15000	AMES DEPARTMENT STORES INC	5311	CT	683	1449
CL	S	14900	OHIO BELL TELEPHONE CO	4811	OH	3745	1670
CL	N	14000	VARIAN ASSOCIATES INC.	3673	CA	745	973
CL	N	14000	SOUTHERN NEW ENGLAND TELEPHONE	4811	CT	2424	1304
CL	N	14000	MASCO CORP	3432	MI	1817	1154
CL	N	14000	FOSTER WHEELER CORP	8911	NJ	1017	1228
CL	N	14000	GENERAL PUBLIC UTILITIES	4911	NJ	6176	2870
CL	O	14000	FARMERS GROUP INC	6411	CA	2652	993
CL	N	13000	RAMADA INNS INC	7011	AZ	693	583
CL	N	13000	DOMINION RESOURCES INC. (VA)	4911	VA	8481	2712
CL	O	12000	VIRGINIA ELECTRIC & POWER CO	4931	VA	7678	2612
CL	O	12000	SONOCO PRODUCTS CO	2631	SC	501	870
CL	N	12000	NL INDUSTRIES INC	1389	NY	1597	1423
CL	N	12000	HARSCO CORP	3321	PA	824	1261
CL	S	12000	CHESAPEAKE & POTOMAC TEL CO (VA)	4811	VA	2804	1260
CL	N	12000	AMAX INC	1061	CT	3561	1789
CL	N	11000	PHILADELPHIA ELECTRIC CO.	4931	PA	10165	3014
CL	N	11000	ETHYL CORP	2819	VA	1556	1548
CL	A	11000	BLOUNT INC	3498	AL	648	1166
CL	S	10000	INDIANA BELL TELEPHONE CO. INC.	4811	IN	1842	820
CL	B	10000	GOLDBLATT BROTHERS INC	5311	IL	12	24
CL	N	9100	USF & G CORP.	6711	MD	7674	3556
CL	N	9100	BALTIMORE GAS & ELECTRIC CO	4931	MD	4183	1755
CL	C	9000	NEW ENGLAND MUTUAL LIFE INSURANCE	6311	MA	10908	2300
CL	N	8200	ASARCO INC.	3331	NJ	1745	1167
CL	N	8000	STRIDE RITE CORP.	3149	MA	181	277
CL	C	8000	MASSACHUSETTS MUTUAL LIFE INS.	6311	MA	15579	2421

Deloitte Haskins & Sells

Audl	Trd	Emp	Name	SIC	Sta	Ast	Sls
DHS	N	811000	GENERAL MOTORS CORP	3711	NY	63832	96372
DHS	N	123000	ROCKWELL INTERNATIONAL CORP	3981	PA	7333	11338
DHS	N	94000	HONEYWELL INC	3981	MN	5034	6625
DHS	N	79000	TRANSWORLD CORP.	6711	NY	1329	2152
DHS	N	65000	GREAT ATLANTIC & PACIFIC TEA CO	5411	NJ	1608	6615
DHS	N	62000	PROCTER & GAMBLE CO	2841	OH	9683	13552
DHS	O	57000	RAPID AMERICAN CORP	5631	NY	2262	2183
DHS	N	56000	MONSANTO CO.	2819	MO	8877	6747
DHS	N	53000	DOW CHEMICAL CO	2869	MI	11830	11537
DHS	N	44000	UNION PACIFIC CORP	4011	NY	10710	7798
DHS	N	44000	MERRILL LYNCH & CO INC	6341	NY	48117	7117
DHS	X	43000	CONTINENTAL GROUP	3411	CT	3653	4942
DHS	N	41000	DEERE & CO	3523	IL	5462	4061
DHS	N	38000	PPG INDUSTRIES INC	3211	PA	4084	4346
DHS	C	38000	METROPOLITAN LIFE INSURANCE	6311	NY	76494	7316
DHS	N	37000	KIMBERLY-CLARK CORP.	2621	WI	3504	4073
DHS	S	32000	MC CRORY CORP.	5631	NY	1565	1038
DHS	N	31000	PENN CENTRAL CORP.	3674	CT	2874	2527
DHS	N	31000	ARMCO INC	3312	OH	3293	3733
DHS	C	30000	EQUITABLE LIFE ASSURANCE	6311	NY	47990	2595
DHS	N	30000	EMHART CORP	3981	CT	1523	1775
DHS	N	29000	TRANS WORLD AIRLINES INC.	4511	NY	2769	3725
DHS	X	27000	BLUE BELL INC.	2327	NC	709	1229
DHS	N	25000	SPRINGS INDUSTRIES INC	2211	SC	1013	1013
DHS	N	24000	SCHERING-PLOUGH CORP	2834	NJ	2773	1927
DHS	N	23400	AMERICAN ELECTRIC POWER CO INC	4911	OH	13621	4848
DHS	N	21000	BAKER INTERNATIONAL CORP	3533	CA	2015	1904
DHS	N	20000	UNIROYAL INC	3011	CT	1523	2115
DHS	N	20000	TEKTRONIX INC	3825	OR	1224	1438
DHS	N	20000	PONDEROSA INC.	5812	OH	255	490
DHS	N	20000	DUKE POWER CO	4911	NC	8024	2899
DHS	N	19000	LEASEWAY TRANSPORTATION CORP	4213	OH	1030	1430
DHS	N	19000	ENSERCH CORP	4923	TX	3358	3391
DHS	N	17000	TEXAS UTILITIES CO	4911	TX	10867	4170
DHS	N	17000	NAVISTAR INTERNATIONAL CORP.	3713	IL	2107	3457
DHS	N	17000	ALEXANDER & ALEXANDER SERVICES	6411	NY	2127	914
DHS	N	14000	PUBLIC SERVICE ELECTRIC & GAS CO	4931	NJ	10487	4409
DHS	N	14000	MIDDLE SOUTH UTILITIES INC	4911	LA	13656	3238
DHS	O	14000	MACK TRUCKS INC.	3711	PA	1062	2063
DHS	N	14000	KAISER ALUMINUM & CHEMICAL	3334	CA	3261	2029
DHS	S	14000	GENERAL MOTORS ACCEPTANCE CORP	6146	MI	75448	8742
DHS	N	14000	FPL GROUP INC.	8999	FL	8917	4349
DHS	S	13000	PACIFIC LIGHTING CORP.	492	CA	4133	5083

DHS	N	13000	PACIFIC LIGHTING CORP	4923	CA	4133	5083
DHS	N	13000	HUGHES TOOL CO	3533	TX	1750	1261
DHS	N	13000	DELUXE CHECK PRINTERS INC	2751	MN	521	764
DHS	N	12000	MC KESSON CORP.	5122	CA	2176	6285
DHS	N	12000	LOWE'S COMPANIES INC.	5031	NC	857	2073
DHS	N	12000	HOUSTON INDUSTRIES INC	4911	TX	8797	4062
DHS	S	12000	HOUSTON LIGHTING & POWER CO.	4931	TX	7829	3533
DHS	N	12000	FISCHBACH CORP.	1731	NY	533	1039
DHS	N	12000	CRANE CO	3312	NY	460	1099
DHS	N	11000	SYNTEX CORP	2834	CA	1226	949
DHS	O	11000	SAFECO CORP	6341	WA	4764	2165
DHS	O	11000	MILES LABORATORIES INC.	2834	IN	961	1177
DHS	N	10000	PACIFICORP	4911	OR	5122	1983
DHS	A	10000	NEW YORK TIMES CO.	2711	NY	1296	1394
DHS	N	10000	LONGS DRUG STORES CORP.	5912	CA	411	1481
DHS	N	10000	LOWENSTEIN (M.) CORP.	2221	NY	382	640
DHS	N	10000	FIRST CITY INDUSTRIES INC.	6552	CA	968	612
DHS	N	9700	MAGIC CHEF INC	3631	TN	552	1062
DHS	S	9694	SOUTHERN CALIFORNIA GAS CO	4924	CA	2390	4616
DHS	N	9300	CAROLINA POWER & LIGHT CO	4911	NC	6655	1935
DHS	N	9100	HOUSE OF FABRICS INC	5949	CA	126	278
DHS	X	9000	PALM BEACH INC	2311	OH	262	419
DHS	N	8400	PENNSYLVANIA POWER & LIGHT CO	4911	PA	6966	1977
DHS	N	8300	AZP GROUP INC.	4931	AZ	5325	1175
DHS	N	8200	BENEFICIAL CORP	6145	DE	8709	2059
DHS	N	7600	SOO LINE CORP.	4011	MN	1138	618
DHS	N	7600	ROBERTSON (H.H.) CO.	3444	PA	391	614
DHS	N	7400	NORTHERN STATES POWER CO	4931	WI	4048	1789
DHS	S	7100	PENNSYLVANIA CO	6711	CT	1252	1305
DHS	N	7000	SOUTHEAST BANKING CORP	6711	FL	11052	1097
DHS	S	7000	OHIO POWER CO	4911	OH	3563	1507
DHS	O	7000	ELDER-BEERMAN STORES CORP	5311	OH	219	352
DHS	O	6800	UNITED ARTISTS COMMUNICATIONS	7832	CA	407	408
DHS	O	6700	MICHIGAN NATIONAL CORP	6711	MI	7252	827
DHS	S	6700	APPALACHIAN POWER CO	4911	VA	2716	1323
DHS	N	6600	STALEY CONTINENTAL INC.	2046	IL	1632	2937
DHS	N	6600	INTERNATIONAL CONTROLS CORP	3728	FL	614	142
DHS	N	6200	VULCAN MATERIALS CO	1499	AL	819	981
DHS	O	6200	WOMETCO ENTERPRISES INC	2086	FL	534	520
DHS	O	6000	BANCOHIO CORP.	6711	OH	6062	608
DHS	N	5800	PHILIPS INDUSTRIES INC	3442	OH	221	462
DHS	O	5800	LANCASTER COLONY CORP	3229	OH	263	441
DHS	N	5700	STANDEX INTERNATIONAL CORP	3675	NH	219	379
DHS	N	5700	FEDERAL PAPER BOARD CO INC	2611	NJ	918	784
DHS	O	5600	U.S. BANCORP	6711	OR	8350	817
DHS	O	5600	RAX RESTAURANTS INC.	5812	OH	113	105

Ernst & Whinney

Audl	Trd	Emp	Name	SIC	Sta	Ast	Sls
EW	N	148000	REYNOLDS (R.J.) INDUSTRIES INC.	2111	NC	16930	16595
EW	N	128000	DAYTON-HUDSON CORP	5311	MN	4418	8793
EW	N	122000	AMERICAN STORES CO	5411	UT	3463	13890
EW	N	97000	MC DONNELL DOUGLAS CORP.	3721	MO	7268	11478
EW	N	83000	BANKAMERICA CORP	6711	CA	118541	13880
EW	N	67000	MARTIN MARIETTA CORP.	3334	MD	2258	4410
EW	N	62000	HOSPITAL CORP. OF AMERICA	8062	TN	6259	4152
EW	N	57000	LTV CORP.	3981	TX	6307	8199
EW	N	52000	CSX CORP.	4011	VA	11494	7320
EW	N	42000	STANDARD OIL COMPANY (OHIO)	1382	OH	18330	13002
EW	N	42000	EATON CORP	3714	OH	2814	3675
EW	N	39000	COCA COLA CO.	2086	GA	6898	7904
EW	N	34000	FIRST INTERSTATE BANCORP.	6711	CA	48991	5235
EW	N	33000	VF CORP	2328	PA	860	1481
EW	N	33000	ASHLAND OIL INC	2911	KY	3928	8182
EW	A	32000	WANG LABORATORIES INC	3573	MA	2376	2352
EW	S	31000	TRANSAMERICA FINANCIAL CORP	6145	CA	1958	390
EW	N	31000	HARRIS CORP	3573	FL	1789	2281
EW	N	30000	TIMES-MIRROR COMPANY	2711	CA	2701	2947
EW	S	29000	CHESAPEAKE AND OHIO RAILWAY CO	4011	OH	4192	2215
EW	S	28000	SEABOARD SYSTEM RAILROAD INC.	4011	FL	4969	2860
EW	N	28000	LILLY (ELI) & CO.	2834	IN	3954	3271
EW	N	28000	GOODRICH (B.F.) CO.	3011	OH	2260	3201
EW	N	28000	BROWN GROUP INC.	3144	MO	635	1400
EW	N	27000	STEVENS (J.P.) & CO.	2211	NY	1200	1858
EW	N	27000	REYNOLDS METALS CO	3334	VA	3647	3416
EW	N	26000	LIBBEY-OWENS FORD CO.	3211	OH	1337	1922
EW	N	24000	WHIRLPOOL CORP	3633	MI	1760	3474
EW	N	22000	KNIGHT-RIDDER NEWSPAPERS	2711	FL	1394	1730
EW	N	22000	BLACK & DECKER CORP.	3546	MD	1452	1732
EW	O	21000	SHONEYS INC	5812	TN	316	547
EW	O	21000	ROADWAY SERVICE INC.	4213	OH	1000	1580
EW	N	20000	EDISON BROTHERS STORES INC	5661	MO	388	808
EW	N	19000	TIME INC	2721	NY	3072	3404
EW	N	19000	SHERWIN WILLIAMS CO	2851	OH	1056	2195
EW	C	19000	HANCOCK (JOHN) MUTUAL LIFE INSUR.	6311	MA	26256	2351
EW	N	19000	GOULD INC	3573	IL	1388	1420
EW	O	19000	AMERICAN GREETINGS CORP	2771	OH	873	1012
EW	N	18000	TIMKEN CO	3562	OH	1375	1091
EW	N	18000	MORTON-THIOKOL INC.	3981	IL	1368	1958
EW	O	18000	JONES & LAUGHLIN STEEL CORP	3312	PA	3305	3267
EW	N	18000	ALCO STANDARD CORP	3981	PA	1288	3823
EW	N	17000	WHITTAKER CORP	3981	CA	796	1130

EW	H	17000	BECTON DICKINSON & CO.	3841	NJ	1241	1144
EW	N	16000	WHITE CONSOLIDATED INDUSTRIES	3981	OH	1140	1946
EW	N	16000	TRANSAMERICA CORP	6341	CA	13751	5590
EW	N	16000	PIEDMONT AVIATION INC	4511	NC	1487	1527
EW	N	16000	NWA INC.	4511	MN	2320	2655
EW	O	16000	HOOVER CO	3635	OH	335	683
EW	A	16000	DILLARD DEPARTMENT STORES INC.	5311	AR	862	1601
EW	O	15000	UNITED STATES INDUSTRIES INC	2522	CT	689	1076
EW	N	15000	STANLEY WORKS	3423	CT	778	1208
EW	N	15000	GERBER PRODUCTS CO	2032	MI	601	968
EW	N	15000	GULF & WESTERN INDUSTRIES INC.	3981	NY	4064	3844
EW	N	15000	AMERICAN GENERAL CORP	6341	TX	20668	5677
EW	O	13000	NATIONAL GYPSUM CO	3275	TX	1051	1340
EW	N	13000	LINCOLN NATIONAL CORP	6341	IN	13550	4907
EW	N	13000	GENUINE PARTS CO	5013	GA	977	2279
EW	N	13000	FEDERAL MOGUL CORP	3562	MI	682	895
EW	N	13000	E - SYSTEMS INC.	3662	TX	479	927
EW	N	12000	FAIRCHILD INDUSTRIES INC	3721	MD	702	856
EW	N	12000	FIRST WACHOVIA CORP.	6025	NC	17707	1753
EW	O	12000	BANK OF NEW ENGLAND CORP	6711	MA	17804	1710
EW	N	11000	FUQUA INDUSTRIES INC	3981	GA	553	862
EW	O	11000	BALTIMORE & OHIO RAILROAD CO	4011	MD	2107	1064
EW	N	11000	BELL & HOWELL CO.	3573	IL	669	760
EW	O	10807	PEOPLES BANCORPORATION (NC)	6711	NC	2380	255
EW	X	10000	SELIGMAN & LATZ INC	7231	NY	106	342
EW	N	10000	DAYCO CORP	3041	OH	483	905
EW	O	10000	CITIZENS & SOUTHERN GEORGIA CORP	6711	GA	13591	1377
EW	N	9800	TEMPLE-INLAND INC.	2492	TX	1469	1243
EW	N	9700	TRACOR INC	3662	TX	407	563
EW	O	9700	EVANS (BOB) FARMS INC	2011	OH	129	228
EW	N	9600	FIRST BANK SYSTEM INC	6711	MN	25484	2510
EW	N	9300	TRW INCORPORATED	3981	OH	3735	6615
EW	N	9200	MIDLAND-ROSS CORP.	3567	OH	692	715
EW	N	9100	ARCHER-DANIELS-MIDLAND CO.	3981	IL	2967	4739
EW	N	9000	WOLVERINE WORLD WIDE INC	3143	MI	229	389
EW	N	9000	RUSSELL CORP.	2253	AL	322	385
EW	O	9000	NATIONAL CITY CORP	6711	OH	12505	1302
EW	N	9000	CINCINNATI MILACRON INC	3541	OH	670	732
EW	N	8900	ARKANSAS BEST CORP	4212	AR	278	582
EW	C	8800	BANKERS LIFE CO.	6311	IA	14927	3032
EW	N	8700	SEA-LAND CORP.	4469	NJ	1966	1634
EW	O	8700	REPUBLIC HEALTH CORPORATION	8062	TX	832	540
EW	O	8700	PACCAR INC	3711	WA	1057	1893
EW	N	8600	JOSTENS INC	3911	MN	315	530
EW	O	8400	PNC FINANCIAL CORP.	6711	PA	18778	1790
EW	N	8300	DENNISON MANUFACTURING CO	2648	MA	463	662

KMG Main Hurdman

Audl	Trd	Emp	Name	SIC	Sta	Ast	Sls
MH	N	91000	UNION CARBIDE CORP	2869	CT	10581	9003
MH	N	62000	NATIONAL MEDICAL ENTERPRISES INC	8062	CA	2842	2530
MH	N	52000	NORTH AMERICAN PHILIPS CORP	3621	NY	2643	4395
MH	N	39000	PFIZER INC	2834	NY	4463	4025
MH	N	39000	CPC INTERNATIONAL INC	2046	NJ	3017	4210
MH	N	38000	AVON PRODUCTS INC	2844	NY	2289	2470
MH	N	17000	RITE AID CORP	5912	PA	756	1543
MH	N	13000	UNITED MERCHANTS & MFGRS INC.	2211	NY	729	795
MH	N	13000	DRAVO CORP	8911	PA	542	893
MH	O	12000	PEOPLES DRUG STORES INC	5912	VA	229	791
MH	N	12000	BROCKWAY INC.	3221	FL	493	1033
MH	N	6000	NCH CORP.	5161	TX	272	375
MH	N	5800	HECKS INC	5311	WV	303	523
MH	N	5700	HANDY & HARMAN	3356	NY	471	557
MH	N	5500	DIEBOLD INC	3499	OH	394	411
MH	N	5000	KOLLMORGEN CORP	3679	CT	236	311
MH	N	4400	LEHIGH VALLEY INDUSTRIES INC	3231	NY	112	50
MH	O	4100	JB'S RESTAURANTS	5812	UT	81	96
MH	O	4000	FAIR LANES INC	7933	MD	118	93
MH	O	4000	CENTRAL FREIGHT LINES INC	4213	TX	129	189
MH	A	4000	CONSOLIDATED STORES CORP.	5999	OH	80	181
MH	O	3800	TRANS-STERLING INC.	701	NV	156	140
MH	O	3500	HARVARD INDUSTRIES INC.	3489	MO	123	206
MH	O	3100	TSS-SEEDMAN'S INCORPORATED	5311	NY	49	163
MH	N	3100	AFG INDUSTRIES INC.	3211	CA	316	320
MH	A	2560	VIRCO MANUFACTURING CORP	2531	CA	64	137
MH	N	2500	STANDARD MOTOR PRODUCTS INC	3694	NY	175	243
MH	A	2400	NATIONAL PATENT DEVELOPMENT CORP	3842	NY	215	118
MH	O	2300	NPS TECHNOLOGIES GROUP INC	4911	NJ	53	164
MH	O	2200	VIKING FREIGHT SYSTEM INC	4212	CA	67	103
MH	O	2000	CHEMICAL LEAMAN CORP	4213	PA	98	163
MH	A	1850	TIE COMMUNICATIONS INC.	3661	CT	455	501
MH	O	1800	FMS MANAGEMENT SYSTEMS INC	5812	FL	15	18
MH	O	1700	ZIONS UTAH BANCORPORATION	6711	UT	3181	275
MH	S	1700	GRUMMAN AMERICAN AVIATION CORP	3721	NY	103	170
MH	A	1700	DURO - TEST CORP.	3646	NJ	46	68
MH	N	1500	WILLCOX & GIBBS INC	3636	NY	100	208
MH	O	1500	DAUPHIN DEPOSIT CORP.	6711	PA	2598	251
MH	A	1500	ALPHA INDUSTRIES INC	3674	MA	81	69
MH	A	1300	TRANS LUX CORP	7394	CT	51	31
MH	B	1300	FRIER INDUSTRIES INC	3143	NJ	15	26
MH	O	1200	VALLEY FAIR CORP	5311	NJ	15	34
MH	A	1200	INTERNATIONAL HYDRON CORP.	3832	NY	52	49

MH	O	1200	AMERICAN INCOME LIFE INSURANCE	6311	TX	377	120
MH	A	1100	SOLITRON DEVICES INC	3679	FL	65	46
MH	O	1100	AMERICAN SAVINGS BANK-FSB	6033	NY	3614	367
MH	N	1075	MYERS (L.E.) GROUP	1623	IL	40	114
MH	O	1000	FIRST NATIONAL BANK OF MIDLAND	6025	TX	1800	251
MH	O	1000	BLASIUS INDUSTRIES INC	3069	NJ	21	41
MH	B	980	TOBIN PACKING CO INC	2011	NY	19	93
MH	O	972	COUSINS HOME FURNISHINGS INC.	5712	CA	50	124
MH	O	961	CRAZY EDDIE	5732	NY	66	136
MH	N	910	SHOWBOAT INC	7999	NV	113	47
MH	N	900	CLAIRE'S STORES INC	5699	FL	26	56
MH	A	900	CABLEVISION SYSTEMS CORP.	4833	NY	309	32
MH	X	880	GULFSTREAM LAND & DEVELOPMENT CO	6552	FL	184	141
MH	O	840	ROGERS CABLESYSTEMS OF AMERICA INC	3662	DE	291	94
MH	L	800	FASHION FABRICS INC	599	UT	10	23
MH	O	798	PETROLEUM HEAT AND POWER CO. INC.	5074	CT	75	160
MH	O	758	ARNOLD INDUSTRIES INC.	3873	PA	77	54
MH	O	710	MEENAN OIL CO INC	5983	NY	58	244
MH	O	620	BEELINE INC	5137	IL	20	43
MH	A	610	TECHNODYNE INC.	3621	NY	32	35
MH	C	600	HARLEYSVILLE MUTUAL INSURANCE	6331	PA	538	297
MH	O	580	UNION ELECTRIC STEEL CORP	3325	PA	54	43
MH	S	562	CAROLINA COACH CO.	4131	NC	12	18
MH	A	550	PORTA SYSTEMS CORP	3613	NY	48	41
MH	O	540	CHOMERICS INC	3643	MA	34	46
MH	O	524	HOOPER HOLMES INC.	8091	NJ	13	55
MH	O	490	MOXIE INDUSTRIES INC	2834	GA	28	53
MH	O	475	NICO INC.	7399	NY	53	154
MH	A	475	ELECTRO AUDIO DYNAMICS INC	3651	NY	33	33
MH	O	470	TOP BRASS ENTERPRISES INC	5732	NY	49	48
MH	O	456	CPB INC	6711	HI	527	54
MH	O	450	PROGRESS INDUSTRIES INC	3443	IL	1	14
MH	O	440	WICAT SYSTEMS INC.	3573	UT	55	29
MH	O	402	ACTMEDIA INCORPORATED	7311	CT	45	44
MH	O	400	ST. LOUIS NATIONAL STOCK YARDS	0799	IL	14	1
MH	O	400	COMMUNITY BANCSHARES CORP	6711	NJ	405	44
MH	O	390	E & B MARINE INC	5961	NJ	27	56
MH	O	390	ANDERSEN GROUP	3679	CT	37	43
MH	O	373	RONSON CORP	2899	NJ	19	32
MH	O	370	SUPER RITE FOODS INC.	5141	PA	99	376
MH	O	330	REFAC TECHNOLOGY DEVELOPMENT CORP.	7392	NY	13	10
MH	O	330	COMARCO INC	3573	CA	47	42
MH	O	325	HERSHEY CREAMERY	2024	PA	17	34
MH	O	325	CHECKPOINT SYSTEMS INC.	3662	NJ	24	27
MH	O	320	PENN FUEL GAS	4924	PA	48	77
MH	O	310	DELTA DATA SYSTEMS CORP	3573	PA	24	31

Peat Marwick Mitchell

PMM	N	304000	GENERAL ELECTRIC CO	3612	CT	26432	28285
PMM	N	179000	PENNEY (J.C.) COMPANY INC	5311	NY	10522	13747
PMM	N	167000	SAFEWAY STORES INC	5411	CA	4841	19651
PMM	N	102000	XEROX CORP	3861	CT	9817	8948
PMM	N	90000	MOTOROLA INC	3662	IL	4370	5443
PMM	N	86000	BORG WARNER CORP.	3981	IL	2823	3330
PMM	X	86000	BEATRICE FOODS CO.	2026	IL	10379	12595
PMM	N	81000	CITICORP	6711	NY	173597	22504
PMM	N	76000	MELVILLE CORP	5661	NY	1807	4775
PMM	N	72000	WINN DIXIE STORES INC	5411	FL	1236	7774
PMM	N	63000	GENERAL MILLS INC	2043	MN	2663	4285
PMM	L	63000	CITY INVESTING CO. LIQ. TRUST	6341	NY	2678	169
PMM	N	62000	EMERSON ELECTRIC CO	3621	MO	3257	4649
PMM	N	50000	INTERCO INC	2337	MO	1535	2626
PMM	N	49000	CONTROL DATA CORP	3573	MN	3073	3680
PMM	N	48000	SINGER CO	3636	CT	1392	2416
PMM	N	45000	BURLINGTON INDUSTRIES INC	2221	NC	2139	2802
PMM	N	44000	STOP & SHOP COMPANIES INC	5411	MA	1112	3689
PMM	N	43000	IC INDUSTRIES INC	3981	IL	4818	5292
PMM	N	41000	AETNA LIFE & CASUALTY CO	6341	CT	58294	18612
PMM	X	40000	PUBLIX SUPER MARKETS INC.	5411	FL	738	3446
PMM	N	40000	NORFOLK SOUTHERN CORP.	4011	VA	9769	3825
PMM	N	37000	NATIONAL S"MICONDUCTOR CORP	3674	CA	1411	1788
PMM	N	37000	AMERICAN CYANAMID CO	2821	NJ	3405	3536
PMM	N	33000	ALLEGHENY INTERNATIONAL INC	3634	PA	1507	2057
PMM	N	32000	SMITHKLINE BECKMAN CORP	2834	PA	3733	3257
PMM	N	32000	MANUFACTURERS HANOVER CORP	6711	NY	75224	8385
PMM	N	31000	SECURITY PACIFIC CORP	6711	CA	53503	5537
PMM	N	31000	GILLETTE CO	3421	MA	2425	2400
PMM	N	31000	ECKERD (JACK) CORP	5912	FL	1089	2966
PMM	O	30000	CANON INC.	3832	JP	5005	4779
PMM	N	29000	HONDA MOTOR CO LTD	3751	JP	4648	8152
PMM	N	28000	FMC CORP	3981	IL	2691	3261
PMM	N	26000	AMERICAN BUILDING MAINTENANCE	7349	CA	135	424
PMM	N	25000	REVCO (D.S.) INC.	5912	OH	875	2396
PMM	N	25000	RYDER SYSTEM INC	7513	FL	3741	2905
PMM	N	24000	SQUIBB CORP	2834	NJ	2453	2042
PMM	N	23000	IU INTERNATIONAL CORP.	3981	DE	1	1878
PMM	N	23000	GENERAL SIGNAL CORP	3662	CT	1483	1801
PMM	N	21000	ARMSTRONG WORLD INDUSTRIES	3996	PA	1093	1679
PMM	N	20000	PUROLATOR COURIER INC.	4712	NJ	444	800
PMM	N	20000	CELANESE CORP	2824	NY	2809	3046
PMM	B	18000	KDT INDUSTRIES INC.	5311	MA	77	281

PMM	N	18000	BEST PRODUCTS CO INC	5311	VA	1332	2235
PMM	S	17000	SOUTHERN RAILWAY CO.	4011	VA	4682	1795
PMM	N	17000	CONTINENTAL CORP	6341	NY	11495	5092
PMM	O	17000	ALLEGHENY BEVERAGE CORP	2086	MD	612	958
PMM	N	16000	OLIN CORP	3981	CT	1598	1751
PMM	N	16000	NORWEST CORP.	6711	MN	21419	2546
PMM	N	16000	MELLON BANK CORP.	6711	PA	33406	3222
PMM	N	16000	DOVER CORP	3534	NY	1017	1440
PMM	N	16000	CHURCH'S FRIED CHICKEN INC	5812	TX	373	544
PMM	N	15000	WELLS FARGO & CO	6711	CA	29429	3362
PMM	O	15000	KEMPER CORP	6341	IL	9264	2882
PMM	N	15000	EX-CELL-O CORP	3621	MI	799	1140
PMM	A	14000	TEXAS AIR CORP.	4511	TX	1951	1944
PMM	N	14000	TEXAS EASTERN CORP	4922	TX	5392	5457
PMM	N	14000	USAIR GROUP INC.	4511	VA	1951	1765
PMM	N	14000	PITTSTON CO	5171	CT	925	1251
PMM	O	14000	ROSES STORES INC	5331	NC	313	1009
PMM	N	14000	ANDERSON CLAYTON & CO	2074	TX	940	1825
PMM	O	13700	KARCHER (CARL) ENTERPRISES INC	5812	CA	219	335
PMM	N	13000	POLAROID CORP	3861	MA	1385	1295
PMM	N	13000	PAYLESS CASHWAYS INC	5211	MO	606	1388
PMM	N	13000	MOHASCO CORP	2271	NY	399	760
PMM	N	13000	CHAMPION SPARK PLUG CO	3694	OH	641	829
PMM	Z	13000	AMERICAN BROADCASTING COMPANIES	4833	NY	2335	0
PMM	N	12000	WEIS MARKETS INC	5411	PA	428	1017
PMM	N	12000	ROHM & HAAS CO	2869	PA	1734	2051
PMM	N	12000	MCORP	6711	TX	22586	2205
PMM	O	12000	FIRST UNION CORP	6711	NC	16567	1688
PMM	N	12000	CHROMALLOY AMERICAN CORP.	3981	MO	657	917
PMM	O	11000	KINDER CARE LEARNING CENTERS INC	8351	AL	531	192
PMM	S	11000	ILLINOIS CENTRAL GULF RR CO.	4011	IL	1939	1014
PMM	O	11000	CULLUM COMPANIES INC.	5411	TX	228	1172
PMM	N	10000	WESTERN AIR LINES INC.	4511	CA	952	1307
PMM	O	9800	ST. PAUL COMPANIES INC.	6341	MN	6898	2672
PMM	N	9600	IRVING BANK CORP.	6711	NY	21651	2028
PMM	O	9400	OVERLAND EXPRESS INC	4213	IN	77	96
PMM	S	9400	COMMERCIAL CREDIT CO.	6153	MD	7373	1320
PMM	O	9300	WETTERAU INC	5141	MO	556	3081
PMM	C	9000	GOLD KIST INC	2017	GA	437	1500
PMM	N	8200	EAGLE PICHER INDUSTRIES INC.	2641	OH	468	642
PMM	O	8100	WILLAMETTE INDUSTRIES INC	2611	OR	918	1152
PMM	N	8000	FERRO CORP.	2899	OH	393	651
PMM	C	8000	FARMLAND INDUSTRIES INC	5172	MO	1284	4371
PMM	N	7800	POTLATCH CORP	2421	CA	1124	950
PMM	N	7800	INTERNATIONAL MULTIFOODS CORP	c462	MN	505	1211
PMM	O	7500	PEOPLE EXPRESS AIRLINES INC.	4511	NJ	1066	978

Price Waterhouse

Audl	Trd	Emp	Name	SIC	Sta	Ast	Sls
PW	N	406000	INTERNATIONAL BUSINESS MACHINES	3573	NY	52634	50056
PW	N	310000	K MART CORP.	5311	MI	9991	22420
PW	N	185000	UNITED TECHNOLOGIES CORP	3724	CT	10528	15749
PW	N	146000	DU PONT (E.I.) DE NEMOURS & CO.	3981	DE	25140	29483
PW	N	146000	EXXON CORP	2911	NY	69160	91620
PW	N	144000	ALLIED-SIGNAL INC.	1311	NJ	13271	9115
PW	N	134000	GOODYEAR TIRE & RUBBER CO	3011	OH	6954	9585
PW	N	129000	EASTMAN KODAK CO	3861	NY	12143	10631
PW	N	126000	WESTINGHOUSE ELECTRIC CORP	3621	PA	9682	10700
PW	N	118000	WOOLWORTH (F W) CO	5331	NY	2535	5958
PW	N	117000	GRACE (W.R.) & CO.	3981	NY	5421	7260
PW	O	105000	TOSHIBA CORPORATION	3679		11847	12539
PW	N	84000	HEWLETT PACKARD CO	3825	CA	5680	6505
PW	N	80000	UNITED STATES STEEL CORP	3312	PA	18446	18429
PW	N	80000	SCHLUMBERGER LTD	1389	NY	11282	6119
PW	N	70000	RALSTON PURINA CO.	2048	MO	2637	5864
PW	N	68000	LUCKY STORES INC	5411	CA	1932	9382
PW	N	65000	SAGA CORP	5812	CA	23	1340
PW	N	62000	SANTA FE SOUTHERN PACIFIC	4011	IL	11808	6438
PW	N	62000	NCR CORP	3574	OH	3940	2580
PW	N	62000	ALCAN ALUMINIUM LTD	3355		6861	5718
PW	N	61000	BURROUGHS CORP	3573	MI	4556	5038
PW	N	61000	CHEVRON CORP. (WAS STD. OIL CALIF)	2911	CA	38899	41742
PW	N	61000	BAXTER TRAVENOL LABORATORIES INC	2834	IL	6839	2355
PW	N	56000	CARTER HAWLEY HALE STORES INC	5311	CA	2235	3978
PW	N	54000	CATERPILLAR TRACTOR CO	3531	IL	6016	6725
PW	N	50000	AMOCO CORP.	1311	IL	25198	26922
PW	N	49000	CIGNA CORP.	6341	PA	45000	16197
PW	N	45000	CHASE MANHATTAN CORP	6711	NY	87685	9733
PW	N	45000	CAMPBELL SOUP CO	2032	NJ	2438	3989
PW	N	45000	BETHLEHEM STEEL CORP	3312	PA	4743	5118
PW	N	40000	WARNER-LAMBERT CO	2834	NJ	2358	3200
PW	N	40000	EASTERN AIR LINES INC	4511	NY	3870	4815
PW	N	40000	ANHEUSER-BUSCH COS. INC.	2082	MO	5121	7000
PW	N	38000	DANA CORP	3714	OH	2424	3754
PW	N	36000	BRISTOL MYERS CO	2844	NY	3721	4444
PW	N	35000	TANDY CORP	5732	TX	1925	2841
PW	N	34000	INGERSOLL-RAND CO.	3563	NJ	2243	2637
PW	N	33000	BORDEN INC	2026	NY	2932	4716
PW	O	31000	GRAND UNION CO	5411	NJ	585	2529
PW	N	30000	LEAR SIEGLER INC	3662	CA	1490	2371
PW	N	30000	GANNETT CO INC	2711	NY	2313	2209
PW	N	29000	PITNEY BOWES INC	3579	CT	1763	1832

PW	N	29000	DISNEY (WALT) CO.	7996	CA	2897	2015
PW	S	29000	ATCHISON TOPEKA & SANTA FE RR CO	4011	IL	3783	2091
PW	N	27000	GENCORP INC.	3981	OH	2073	3021
PW	N	26000	CORNING GLASS WORKS	3229	NY	2032	1691
PW	N	25000	JOHNSON CONTROLS INC	3822	WI	1789	1787
PW	N	25000	HARTMARX CORP	2311	IL	669	1110
PW	N	24000	INLAND STEEL CO	3312	IL	2632	3186
PW	N	22000	SCOTT PAPER CO.	2621	PA	3517	3050
PW	N	22000	CONSOLIDATED EDISON CO OF N.Y.	4931	NY	8945	5498
PW	N	21000	STERLING DRUG INC	2834	NY	1618	1848
PW	S	21000	CAVENHAM (USA) INC	5411	CT	624	2529
PW	N	20000	CHEMICAL NEW YORK CORP	6711	NY	56990	5651
PW	N	19000	TRIBUNE CO.	2711	IL	2446	1938
PW	C	19000	NEW YORK LIFE INSURANCE	6311	NY	27978	3830
PW	N	18000	WALTER (JIM) CORP.	3981	FL	2806	2256
PW	N	18000	UNION CAMP CORP	2611	NJ	2661	1866
PW	N	17000	MCA INC	7814	CA	2254	2099
PW	N	17000	KELLOGG CO	2043	MI	1726	2930
PW	N	17000	DATA GENERAL CORP	3573	MA	1262	1239
PW	N	16000	PERKIN ELMER CORP	3832	CT	1135	1305
PW	N	16000	KELLWOOD CO	2335	MO	270	502
PW	N	16000	GENESCO INC	3143	TN	285	538
PW	N	15000	WESTVACO CORP	2621	NY	1923	1722
PW	N	15000	ALLIS CHALMERS CORP	3511	WI	675	886
PW	N	14000	WESTERN UNION CORP	4821	NJ	2259	1134
PW	O	14000	CHICAGO PACIFIC CORP.	3639	IL	782	90
PW	N	13000	MORGAN (J.P.) & CO. INC.	6711	NY	69375	6575
PW	N	13000	CROWN CORK & SEAL CO INC	3411	PA	866	1487
PW	N	13000	BARNETT BANKS OF FLORIDA INC	6711	FL	14829	1574
PW	N	12200	INTERPUBLIC GROUP OF COMPANIES	7311	NY	802	691
PW	C	12000	MCI COMMUNICATIONS CORP	4899	DC	4510	2542
PW	N	12000	MARINE MIDLAND BANKS INC	6711	NY	23386	2495
PW	N	12000	M/A-COM INC	3662	MA	871	848
PW	N	12000	HAMMERMILL PAPER CO	2621	PA	1278	1877
PW	N	12000	DIAMOND SHAMROCK CORP.	2911	TX	4618	4102
PW	S	12000	CONNECTICUT GENERAL LIFE	6311	CT	22246	3922
PW	N	11000	WARNACO INC	2321	CT	307	591
PW	O	11000	TRANE CO	3585	WI	670	1073
PW	N	11000	SANDERS ASSOCIATES INC	3662	NH	618	886
PW	N	11000	NATIONAL DISTILLERS & CHEMICAL	2821	NY	2020	2289
PW	N	11000	NIAGARA MOHAWK POWER CORP	4911	NY	7014	2695
PW	N	11000	GENERAL HOST CORP	5411	CT	546	564
PW	N	11000	DETROIT EDISON CO	4911	MI	9492	2788
PW	N	11000	BANKERS TRUST NEW YORK CORP	6711	NY	50581	4699
PW	N	10800	ANCHOR HOCKING CORP	3229	OH	506	720
PW	N	10000	FLOWERS INDUSTRIES INC	2051	GA	337	626

Touche Ross

Audl	Trd	Emp	Name	SIC	Sta	Ast	Sls
TR	N	466000	SEARS ROEBUCK & CO	5311	IL	66417	40715
TR	X	152000	UNITED PARCEL SERVICE	4212	CT	4162	7687
TR	N	128000	FEDERATED DEPARTMENT STORES INC	5311	OH	5354	9978
TR	N	108000	CHRYSLER CORPORATION	3711	MI	12605	21256
TR	N	104000	BOEING CO.	3721	WA	9246	13636
TR	N	97000	RCA CORP	3651	NY	87000	8972
TR	N	86000	PILLSBURY CO	2041	MN	2779	4671
TR	N	64000	ALLIED STORES CORP	5311	NY	2772	4135
TR	N	64000	ASSOCIATED DRY GOODS CORP	5311	NY	2289	4385
TR	N	63000	SOUTHLAND CORP	5411	TX	3736	12719
TR	C	61000	PRUDENTIAL INS. CO. OF AMERICA	6311	NJ	91139	14332
TR	N	58000	LITTON INDUSTRIES INC.	3481	CA	4646	4591
TR	N	55000	MACY (R.H.) & CO. INC.	5311	NY	2357	4368
TR	N	49000	SUPERMARKETS GENERAL CORP	5411	NJ	1104	5123
TR	N	47000	NORTHROP CORP	3721	CA	2333	5057
TR	N	37000	GREYHOUND CORP	3981	AZ	2931	2512
TR	N	36000	ALBERTSONS INC	5411	ID	1125	5060
TR	N	30000	CONAGRA INC	2041	NE	1547	5498
TR	N	27000	FRUEHAUF CORP.	3715	MI	1804	2564
TR	N	25000	SUPER VALU STORES INC	5141	MN	1174	6588
TR	O	24000	SERVICE MERCHANDISE COMPANY INC	5311	TN	1459	2526
TR	N	23000	AMERICAN MOTORS CORP	3711	MI	2001	4040
TR	N	22000	SQUARE D CO	3613	IL	1103	1402
TR	N	22000	LOEWS CORP	6341	NY	16120	6700
TR	O	18000	KUBOTA LTD.	3569		2856	2647
TR	N	18000	AUTOMATIC DATA PROCESSING INC.	7374	NJ	1018	1030
TR	N	17000	MEAD CORP	2621	OH	2245	2740
TR	N	16000	COASTAL CORP	4923	TX	8294	7254
TR	O	15000	NORDSTROM INC	5621	WA	763	1302
TR	N	15000	FLEMING COMPANIES INC	5141	OK	1165	7095
TR	O	15000	EVANS PRODUCTS CO	5211	FL	803	1424
TR	N	14000	COMPUTER SCIENCES CORP	7372	CA	431	723
TR	N	13000	GENERAL CINEMA CORP	2086	MA	945	967
TR	N	12000	TRIANGLE INDUSTRIES INC	3357	NJ	1478	1693
TR	N	12000	OXFORD INDUSTRIES INC	2321	GA	235	559
TR	S	12000	LERNER STORES CORP.	5631	NY	267	700
TR	N	12000	CNA FINANCIAL CORP	6341	IL	14116	4605
TR	A	11100	CARE ENTERPRISES	8051	CA	263	239
TR	N	11000	GAP INC. (THE)	5611	CA	272	647
TR	N	11000	ALEXANDERS INC	5311	NY	178	520
TR	N	10000	ERBAMONT N.V.	2834	CT	960	772
TR	O	9800	RELIANCE GROUP HOLDINGS INC.	6331	NY	5057	2517
TR	N	9400	AVERY INTERNATIONAL CORP	2641	CA	615	933

TR	N	9100	SEA CONTAINERS LTD.	3799		1265	573
TR	N	9000	MUNFORD INC	5411	GA	172	457
TR	O	8800	WOODWARD & LOTHROP INC	5311	DC	302	404
TR	N	8800	FOXBORO CO	3823	MA	495	572
TR	N	8700	SYSCO CORP	5149	TX	681	2628
TR	N	8700	NBD BANCORP INC.	6711	MI	16676	1515
TR	O	8400	MARCUS CORP	5812	WI	122	132
TR	N	8300	REVLON GROUP INC.	5411	FL	1129	345
TR	N	8100	BLAIR (JOHN) & CO.	2752	NY	554	982
TR	S	7700	RELIANCE FINANCIAL SERVICES CORP.	6399	NY	3436	2064
TR	N	7600	ROHR INDUSTRIES INC.	3728	CA	438	607
TR	N	7500	BANK OF NEW YORK COMPANY INC	6711	NY	18486	1594
TR	N	7000	HALL (FRANK B.) & CO. INC.	6411	NY	1219	417
TR	N	7000	GELCO CORP	6341	MN	2620	1004
TR	N	6800	MARCADE GROUP INC.	2331	NJ	27	69
TR	N	6400	NATIONAL CONVENIENCE STORES INC	5411	TX	424	928
TR	O	6100	WILSON (H.J.) CO. INC.	5399	LA	351	514
TR	N	6100	MANHATTAN INDUSTRIES INC	2321	NY	214	472
TR	O	6000	COMMERCE CLEARING HOUSE INC	2741	IL	394	454
TR	O	5300	BERKSHIRE HATHAWAY INC.	3981	MA	3181	832
TR	N	5000	ROPER CORP	3631	IL	285	567
TR	N	5000	EDWARDS (A.G.) & SONS INC	6211	MO	918	404
TR	A	4900	SERVISCO	7218	NJ	67	117
TR	A	4900	PROFESSIONAL CARE INC.	8051	NY	34	56
TR	O	4700	FARM HOUSE FOODS CORP	5141	WI	190	1119
TR	A	4200	SHOPWELL INC	5411	NY	109	557
TR	A	4200	OZARK HOLDINGS	4511	MO	381	481
TR	N	3900	NUCOR CORP	3441	NC	560	758
TR	N	3828	BURNDY CORP	3679	CT	215	219
TR	N	3700	BECOR WESTERN INC.	3532	WI	416	389
TR	O	3600	PIERCE (S.S.) CO. INC.	2037	NY	201	435
TR	N	3600	INTEGRATED RESOURCES INC	7392	NY	1283	440
TR	N	3600	ARKLA INC.	4923	LA	1690	993
TR	N	3600	AIRBORNE FREIGHT CORP	4712	WA	215	466
TR	O	3500	THIRD NATIONAL CORP	6711	TN	5045	516
TR	O	3500	PMD INVESTMENT CO.	533	NE	19	1
TR	C	3500	ASSOCIATED MILK PRODUCERS	5143	TX	375	2465
TR	O	3400	NATIONAL (THE) GUARDIAN CORP.		CT	118	64
TR	O	3400	HECHINGER CO	5251	MD	353	489
TR	N	3300	UNIVERSAL FOODS CORP	2022	WI	292	492
TR	O	3300	COMSTOCK GROUP INC.	1731	CT	141	469
TR	O	3280	SAATCHI & SAATCHI COMPANY PLC	7311	EN	28	21
TR	N	3200	HEALTHAMERICA CORPORATION	8324	TN	207	463
TR	X	3200	KANE MILLER CORP	6711	NY	163	768
TR	N	3139	AMERICAN HOIST & DERRICK CO	3536	MN	292	367
TR	O	3100	GODFREY CO.	5141	WI	96	534

The US Top Twenty

The US Top Twenty

Not long after publication we expect to be asked why we have included only the Big Eight firms in our analysis. Certainly other national, regional, and even local firms are major recruiters of university accounting graduates and MBAs. It may not seem entirely fair. In answering this question we would like to begin by presenting the vital statistics for just the 20 largest US firms based on domestic revenues.

We believe this is important information because it not only clearly demonstrates the tremendous variations in size between the first and second tier firms, but also the significant variations among the Big Eight.

Firm	$ US Revenue	# US Offices	# Prof. Staff
Arthur Andersen	$1,182	69	14,400
Peat Marwick	1,004	113	10,700
Ernst & Whinney	809	119	9,400
Coopers & Lybrand	779	96	9,500
Price Waterhouse	645	96	8,000
Arthur Young	545	94	6,400
Deloitte Haskins	528	106	6,900
Touche Ross	513	87	6,200
Laventhol & Horwath	240	50	3,200
KMG Main Hurdman	234	86	3,000
Grant Thornton	175	80	3,000
McGladrey Hendrickson	117	73	1,800
Pannell Kerr Forster	84	45	1,000
Seidman & Seidman	83	41	1,000
Kenneth Leventhal	74	13	550
Oppenheim Appel Dixon	54	12	600
Moss Adams	21	15	275

Firm	$ US Revenue	# US Offices	# Prof. Staff
Cherry Bekaert & Holland	20	24	280
Clifton Gunderson	19	25	300
Richard Eisner	14	1	150

(revenues in millions)

As you can see, the variation in size between even the 7th and 11th largest firms is dramatic. Likely to be dramatic, too, will be the differences in office environment, size of clients, mix of clients, firm structure, professional education offered, specialized industry training, transfer opportunities, income possibilities, etc. We are not judging either environment, just attempting to demonstrate that they are very different.

It is also our experience that students considering employment with the Big Eight are generally not considering smaller national and/or a local firm at the same time. In our opinion it was only logical that this career guide be prepared to correspond to the primary career choice being made.

Another factor we considered was that some of the recruiting efforts for the smaller firms are very different from those of the Big Eight. Though considerable hiring does, of course, occur at the entry level, many of these firms look for Big Eight trained professionals to complement their staffs. This common opportunity to move to the smaller firm later in one's career is just one more reason that we decided to focus solely on the Big Eight for university graduates.

(The statistical information above is based on 1985 results. These figures are from either the November, 1985 issue of the International Accounting Bulletin/Lafferty Publications, or the March, 1986 issue of Public Accounting Report/Professional Publications.)